Paths

I Have

Walked

Jo Ann Fuson Staples

 FriesenPress

One Printers Way
Altona, MB R0G 0B0
Canada

www.friesenpress.com

ISBN
978-1-03-917443-6 (Hardcover)
978-1-03-917442-9 (Paperback)
978-1-03-917444-3 (eBook)

1. BIOGRAPHY & AUTOBIOGRAPHY, PERSONAL MEMOIRS

Distributed to the trade by The Ingram Book Company

My memoir is dedicated to Eva Cheryl Lewis Taylor, my best friend forever (BFF) for fifty-seven years. Eva walked out of my life on July 23, 2020, after contracting COVID-19. She would often say, "No matter what we're doing, there's always lots of laughter and happiness." We traveled some paths together! Eva, my BFF, did you really know how much I loved you?

My BFF, Eva Taylor, having a wonderful day at Kentucky's Berea College's handicraft center,
One of our many shared beautiful moments.

"A pilgrim's reward is the memory of having been there."

Words carved on a rock outside Victoria Falls, Zimbabwe

Issac and Mary Liz North, my grandparents. Hard working substance farmers.

Character
Information Sheet

Robert Gambrel – He appears in the early part of the book, in Pineville, Kentucky, and he married my mother and then later in Newport, Kentucky in the first part of the book killed my mother. He disappears in the book after the trial. I also referred to him as "Old Bob" and Bob, but there are no other "Bob's" until after the trial.

Robert Rackstraw – This the man I dated and lived with after I moved to California, which takes place after the trial. There is no connection or overlap between Bob Rackstraw and the other "Bob." This should not be confusing as Rackstraw is referred to as Robert or Bob, and he is also identified as the suspect in the D.B. Cooper skyjacking case. There should be no confusion as this part of the manuscript makes no reference to the Bob who killed my mother.

George Brooks – My first husband is identified as such in the first part of the book from when I was a teenager until we divorced. Again, this is in the first section of the book.

George Staples entered my life after the part of the manuscript dealing with the D.B. Cooper case when I left California, returned to Ohio, married him and began my State Department travels. There is no possible way he can be confused with George Brooks, who I met when I was 13 years old and who appears in the first part of the manuscript.

James Smith was a man I dated when I worked in Cincinnati, Ohio. James or Jim is clearly identified as a sporting goods manager, skeet shooter, and someone who I had a romantic relationship with before moving to California.

Jim or Jimmy Fuson was my brother and mentioned often until his death. He was my oldest brother and sometimes in the manuscript I refer to him "Brother Jim." It should be clear that this Jim, my brother, is hard to confuse with Jim Smith.

Introduction

Well, my memoir is finished, and you're holding it in your hands—but why did I write it? Very simply, I wanted to leave something of myself in this world. I have a deep love for books and the written word, but I am not a philosopher like Marcus Aurelius. Years ago, when I first discovered his writings, I realized that his thoughts on how to live one's life were timeless, and perhaps I could write a story that would be passed down through time.

There has been, up to now, no written history of my maternal family. Things were told to me through oral history, mostly from my grandmother. However, I wanted to leave a written history to the present. I grew up in the mountains of southeastern Kentucky, and I wanted to share what happened in my life, both the good and the painful. I've lived what some may consider an exceptional life that took me to Ohio and California, and then overseas to Central America, South America, Africa, the Middle East, and Europe. I saw with my own eyes the good that we can do to help others but also the harm that humankind can do, as in the Rwandan genocide.

Some family members and friends have told me my life was interesting and that I should share my stories. To die, never having shared them would be a shame. I've made great friends along the way, and I hope these stories will enrich and help readers to make better decisions.

Be very careful in giving your heart. I gave mine to Robert Wesley Rackstraw. He was suspected of being the alleged skyjacker D. B. Cooper. I have written in this book about my life and time with him. Robert and I lived a short time in Iran, and I gained an understanding of how Ayatollah Khomeini came to power.

I eventually married a Foreign Service officer, who is my husband of forty-three years, and we went on a journey of government service that lasted twenty-six years. I have a daughter and a beautiful granddaughter. Most things I've written about came from my life in the US Foreign Service. I experienced living in two war zones, overcoming malaria and lots of danger. After surviving all this, we retired to Kentucky in 2007, and later, I survived a grizzly bear attack in Alaska. Tragically, I lost Eva Lewis Taylor, my best friend forever (BFF), to COVID-19 on July 23, 2020. We were friends for fifty-seven years.

I've tried to tell my story in an honest and open way so that my readers might say, "This was a strong woman whose life was well lived."

Go well, be safe (old African saying).

Chapter 1

I've always enjoyed being awakened early to the sounds of nature. When I was ten years old, I used to jump out of the bed I shared with my sister, Pauline, who was nine, and check on the time. Saturday morning was my favorite time of the day and week. My sister and I had shared the same bed since we stopped nursing from our mother's breast. I would go out the front door and close it very carefully because I didn't want to disturb my mother, sister, and brothers. I could view the huge mountain with hundreds of trees in front of us. The front porch was often the center of activity, and I wanted to have a few minutes to be alone and feel the morning before all the noise started.

As I remember, it was a cool morning one Saturday at our home in Greenbriar Hollow, and a cover of fog had settled in between the hills. I sat in the rocking chair with a warm blanket and checked out my world. The chair had airplane propellers carved on the back. A man periodically came by in a truck with rocking chairs, and my mother had bought the ones with the carved propellers. The chairs are now antiques and no longer sold.

Across the field, smoke came from my grandmother's chimney, as she still cooked on a wood and coal stove. Mary Liz North was my grandmother. Her grandchildren called her "Mammie." She was old for her years and not in the best of health. Everyone in the hollow knew she was "the boss" of her family. She had six children and twenty-five grandchildren. We loved and feared her because you didn't want to get on her wrong side. Even at a young age, I knew my grandmother had lived a hard life.

My grandmother was a great storyteller. I loved to sit with her in front of her fireplace, eat sweet potatoes baked in ashes on the hearth, and listen to her stories. Sometimes they were so scary, I was afraid to go home when it was dark outside. For example, Mammie would start with, "When your grandfather and

I were first married, he had to walk across the mountain and down the other side to go to work at the sawmill. One evening, he was coming down the side of our mountain, and he could hear a baby crying. He followed the sound, and as he got closer, he saw a baby all alone under a tree. He was concerned because something didn't feel right. After a bit, he moved in closer, and when he tried to touch the baby, it disappeared. For many years, he walked the same trail, but he never heard the baby again." She also spoke about a witch putting a curse on her cow because she refused to give her milk. All the milk was bloody until my grandmother asked the witch to remove the curse.

Mammie didn't come out on her porch, so I couldn't holler over and wish her a good morning. Very few people in the hollow had a phone. Everyone was still sleeping that morning, so I went inside and turned on the TV, grabbed a blanket, and secured my place on the couch. It was time for Saturday morning programs. My favorite show was *Western Theater*, starring a horse named Fury. I hoped that maybe one day I could have a horse.

Later, I'd go to my mother's bedroom and kiss her to wake her up. She was beautiful, with gorgeous dark red hair and blue eyes. Janie, my mother, loved me so very much and depended on me to help with the house and take care of the younger children. Mommy hadn't had an easy time since my father died in an automobile accident when I was seven. Three weeks before, my grandfather died of lung cancer. My mother was very sad, lonely, and overwhelmed with too much responsibility.

Mom would go to the kitchen and prepare my favorite breakfast of fried pork chops, eggs, gravy, and homemade biscuits. This was a Saturday morning tradition and my mother's way of spoiling me. There was not a lot of money since my father's death, but I was spoiled with love. One day in the future, I would not be able to look at pork chops without crying. I stopped eating them for about ten years after my mother's death. In our home, everyone usually ate at the table, but on Saturday mornings, Mommy let us eat in front of the TV because we didn't want to miss a minute of our programs.

After breakfast, my mom started getting ready for the Saturday morning trip to town. I was fascinated with my mother and loved to watch her dress. Her panties, bra, and slip had to match. Her nails were long, with bright red polish. She'd tell me that she worked hard but took a lot of pride in beautiful nails. She always pin-curled her hair on Friday night, and when it was combed out on Saturday, it was full and beautiful.

In the kitchen, washing the dishes, I'd look down the road, dreaming of a trip to Indiana to visit my cousin. I had never left my home in Pineville, a small town in southeastern Kentucky. I wished she would come and get me, but she never did. Mom had a boyfriend who came to visit from Ohio, but I never left my hollow except to go into town for shopping and a movie with friends.

I had a great friend and neighbor named Ailene. We rode the school bus together and were caught up in the same situation. We had real live babies to carry on our hips. Her stepfather, Murph, didn't treat her as he did his biological daughters. Ailene's sister Loraine still lives down the hill from me. Ailene died during my time in California, a few years after I had moved there. I decorate her grave on Memorial Day. We were young Elvis fans, and once every so often, we'd get to go into town. I can't remember if she was with me to see his movie *King Creole*, and when Elvis got shot, I cried. Years later, my daughter, Catherine, gave me my all-time greatest compliment. She said, "Mom, if Elvis could have seen you, Priscilla would not have had a chance."

I knew that one day, I would get into a car, drive to Interstate 75, and go north to Ohio, where some people I knew had gone to find work. But on Saturdays, there was cooking to do and floors to be waxed, and I had to take care of my brothers and sister. I waxed the linoleum rugs with Johnson Paste Wax. My sister, Pauline, and brothers, Jim, Alvie, and Bill, were happy because I pulled them on an old wool army blanket to shine the floors.

Later, Mommy returned from town with food for the week. Friends, aunts, and uncles arrived with beer, moonshine, and musical instruments. I was always hoping there would not be a fight as the evening evolved. In our family, people worked hard and played hard. On the weekend, they drank too much, and that was the way it had been from my earliest memories. By Sunday morning, our beautiful clean house would be trashed. I knew the same scenario would repeat the next week.

Growing up, I had time to go into the mountains and pick wildflowers for flowerpots for the dining and living room tables. I loved Queen Anne's lace and ironweed. I would spray the arrangements with Mom's hairspray. Uncle AY, my mother's brother, always teased me about flowers. He'd say, "They are damn chigger weed and will make you itch." I didn't care because they were pretty. I also liked dogwood and redbud branches for flower arrangements. I didn't have a pretty flower vase, but there were always quart glass jars. One day, out there in the future when I had Waterford and Baccarat crystal vases to use for flower arrangements, I would remember these days.

Later, I would go out on the porch and look for Uncle AY, who lived with my grandmother. I can still see them across the field at their house. Uncle AY would have a cigarette on the front porch and watch his mother work in her flower garden. No one had a flower garden like my grandmother. She also always had a vegetable garden, as well as apple, pear, and cherry trees with lots of fruit for eating and making jelly and preserves. She canned peaches and blackberries to make cobblers for special occasions.

I didn't realize how wonderful and important those days and memories would be in my life. The strength and teachings of these strong mountain people with pioneering, spirited souls helped me overcome many challenges. They gave me the courage to face hurt and pain, and I would be tested many times. I have asked these questions: *Why do some people get all the shit to deal with in life? How do some people go through life almost untouched?* I've never gotten a satisfying answer from anyone.

Chapter 2

I'm from the beautiful but poor part of Kentucky. Southeastern Kentucky has always been the forgotten part of the state. Lots of coal comes out of my part of the world, but very little revenue comes back. I often think about who I am and how my life will end. Will it be unfulfilled? When I try to remember my father, Ben Fuson, I have very good memories. He was handsome with beautiful teeth; I can remember watching him brush his teeth with a glass of water in his hand. We were very close and loved driving fast. I was his first child. People would talk about him for years after his death. Uncle Bill and Uncle Joe spoke nicely about him for years. Uncle AY would never say one negative word about my father as long as he was alive. He loved his brother-in-law and visited his grave every Memorial Day. Uncle AY is buried near my father, three graves above his friend. People would tell me many years later, "Jo Ann, your father's funeral was the largest in my memory. The funeral procession was many miles long with no room in the church for most of the people."

I can recall the last day of my father's life in detail. He worked in a coal mine as an electrician. The money was fantastic in those days because coal was booming in Kentucky. He was very black from all the coal dust when he came home, and I liked to wash his back after he got into the tub. One day, two of his cousins came by and wanted him to take them to town. He loved beautiful fast cars and was happy to do a favor for anyone. One of my earliest memories was sitting in between his legs in his Jeep and pretending I was driving. On his last day, I was outside filling coal buckets from the coal pile, expecting that when my father returned, he would take me to buy candy. My mother's sister, my aunt Della, had a grocery store about two miles down the road. Mommy said, "If you want to go for candy, finish with the coal so we can heat the house."

I heard a big noise but continued to break large lumps of coal into smaller ones with my hatchet before putting them into two buckets. Then my mother would carry them for me. I was excited about dinner because my mother was making Daddy's favorite meal: Jell-O with fruit, fried chicken with gravy, and biscuits. My father was always playing tricks on me at the kitchen table. He would say, "Look, there's a mouse." When I looked away, he would take my plate away and pretend it disappeared. Of course, it reappeared when he distracted me again. We also played a game with Jell-O by seeing who could balance a large piece on a fork the longest.

On this particular day, a neighbor suddenly came up the hill to the house, and then other people started arriving. I learned the noise had come from the crash of my father's car. How could my father with the beautiful white teeth die and leave me? I washed his back. He took me for drives in his beautiful fast car. We passed cars and laughed with excitement when we went over bumps. I would say, "Daddy, pass that one and another one for me."

I had seen my first television show the week before in a bar while my father drank beer with friends. Many years later, I tried to remember if I cried at his viewing, but I couldn't. At the funeral, someone held me up to the coffin and I kissed my father for the last time. I decided to hate and never forgive the two cousins who came and got my father out of bed. They survived the car crash with only minor injuries.

My aunt Della had seen my father's beautiful green and white Studebaker pass her house. She said, "He must have been going over a hundred miles per hour. The car was like a streak of lightning." The road was about a mile straight in front of her house and store. I never planned to write the following details because they still hurt to think and write about at seventy-five years of age.

My dad lost control going into a curve. He hit the right side of the bank, then swerved left and right in a figure eight pattern, and then went over the hill into a big drop down the bank. Remember, this was before seat belts. His two cousins stayed in the car, but my dad went out the driver's side. The car came down on his head. I still remember the conversations about what a great job the funeral home did with reconstruction and how he was positioned for the viewing.

On the day of the accident, I helped my mother, sister, and brothers change their clothes and wash their faces and hands. We walked down the hill, crossed the road, and turned left onto the railroad tracks. Aunt Della lived about two miles down the road, close to Pine Mountain State Park. She was Mommy's only sister and was ten years old when my mother was born. On that tragic day, I wasn't thinking about candy or going behind the counter to slide open the wooden door on the display cabinet, with the glass front for customers to see all the candy and chewing gum. This grocery store was one of my favorite places in my small world.

Many, many people started to arrive. Everyone was crying, talking all at the same time and wanting to know how this could have happened. They were talking about my father in the past tense. He was a man's man. Women thought he was wonderful. He loved and paid a lot of attention to children. Ben would do anything he could for anyone in need of help. He took his Jeep to the top of mountains where there are no roads to drive old people to the doctor or to go vote if they had no transportation. How could God let this happen? Ben had survived the Second World War, came home to marry a beautiful woman, and had gorgeous children. He left us too soon and certainly too young. He was just thirty-two years old.

My father's death was the first hole in my soul. I went across the road and up a hill to a cool spot in the woods. There was green moss, flowers, trees, and running water. The water ran over large rocks that could be very slippery, and I had taken more than my fair share of falls. The water is very cold in Pine Mountain. I didn't know it yet, but I had just developed a pattern that I would follow throughout my life. When life hurts too much, I look to nature for help and acceptance. Nature is my religion, teacher, and strength, never the church. I tried church on several occasions but was always disappointed. The ripple effect from my father's bad choice still hurts after all these years. Why had he been so reckless with a young family, now left with no protector?

Chapter 3

Life went on in our hollow, and times were good for my family. My friends and I had the mountains to play in, trees to climb, and big rocks covered in lush green moss that I made into pretend furniture. Sometimes, in heavy rain, I would be caught on the hill behind our house, but the foliage was so thick, I could stay still, look out through the leaves and limbs at our house, and not get wet. In the winter, when it snowed, my friends and I would pull an old car top up a hill and then, with lots of whooping and hollering, ride it down like a toboggan.

My fourteenth birthday was fast approaching. People would say even then that I was very pretty, but I didn't pay any attention until later in life. I can remember meeting a man many years later named Laus Goodin, who said to me, "You were the prettiest young girl I had ever seen." I heard that a lot from others, especially those of the opposite sex. I weighed 113 pounds, had great skin, beautiful thick brown hair, and blue eyes with black eyebrows and very long eyelashes. I had gotten used to stares and comments about my eyes but wished my bust size could have been a bit smaller. I was self-conscious, and boys had teased me since the fourth grade about my breasts not being real. I didn't pay attention to most compliments because I had observed that men always seemed to have a hidden agenda, especially those who came around my mother.

My sister, Pauline, was not like me in appearance, but we were very close and looked out for each other. Pauline was slender, shy, and very pretty. She hated mother's drinking and partying and was afraid Mom would get hurt. Pauline's way of dealing with her fears was to escape into sewing doll clothes. She loved our mother, who was our whole life. Even today, we are both old enough to still miss our father. I was seven and Pauline was five when he died, so we all had to look out for each other. Everyone knew not to mess with Jo Ann's sister and brothers. I'm overprotective to the extreme, and that has never changed. I will fight if pushed but will never start any trouble.

Every Saturday, my mother went to town to go grocery shopping with her neighbor lady friend, who was Ailene's mother. While they were gone, I scrubbed our front porch because it was dirty from dog hair and mud. We had to work to keep our yard clean because we had no grass, only sand. I threw water on the porch from a pump in the yard, then sprinkled washing powder to make suds and scrubbed the floor with a straw broom. I made it fun for us to play in the water and pretend we were skating. This was a normal Saturday part of house cleaning.

I loved my dog, Tag, because he had been a gift from my father when I was very small. At this time, Tag was about twelve years old and was going blind. He had mange, which made him lose his hair. We didn't know about veterinarians, so everyone treated their animals with home remedies. One day, when I went to school, my mom had Cousin Bill Doc take him to the mountains and shoot him. That was the first time I ever told my mother I hated her. I can only remember one other time later in life.

The relatives and neighbors had clean homes. I was old enough to understand we were called "hillbillies," a term for those who lived in my part of the world. I wasn't sure what it meant, but I came to understand that it was used to describe people who were dirty or backward. In contrast, my family members cared about their appearance. Shoes were polished, clothes were ironed, and everyone had a lot of concern about their hair. I was proud of the way we dressed and looked. We weren't dirty hillbillies. If a hillbilly was a dirty and unkempt person, we didn't fit the stereotypical image.

One day, as I finished my work, a very shiny, late model station wagon pulled up to the fence. A man got out and said, "Is this the home of Janie Fuson?" I said yes, but she wasn't home. He said, "My name is Robert Gambrel. What time do you expect her home?" I said about 6:00 p.m. or a little later. He told me he would return in the evening. I didn't know I had just met the devil! If I had known, I would have gotten my grandmother's .38 pistol, shot him dead, and buried him in the woods. I'm very serious. I didn't get any good energy from him. From that moment, my life was changed forever, and my peaceful hollow would never be the same. My world was over as long as Bob Gambrel was alive.

Bob looked good at first appearance, but he turned out to be a serious drunk. He was kind of handsome and dressed in a suit and tie. In my family, no one wore a suit except the minister at the church, my principal at school, and some people who wore suits for funerals. A few men in suits would stop by before Election Day to pass out their campaign cards. However, I had a bad feeling about Bob Gambrel.

After he left, I thought about him. We were off the main road—how did he find us? I remembered an old woman coming to visit my mom previously. Could she have been the connection because she was Bob's stepmother. We called her "Old Nor." No one liked her. Why had she sent this stepson looking for my mom? Could she have been trying to be a matchmaker? People in our area were always suspicious of strangers.

When she returned, I told my mom a stranger who wasn't from around here had come by. Later that same day, Bob returned with some other men. Mom invited them in. She told me to make them food and drinks. I cut cheese and baloney about an inch thick for each sandwich between two slices of Wonder Bread. I didn't put mayonnaise, lettuce, or tomato on their sandwiches. Why should I show any hospitality to these strangers? Mom would be mad later because I used too much food and I was rebelling because I didn't want to feed them. The men also smelled of unwashed underarms. It turned out that the shiny station wagon wasn't Bob's but belonged to one of the other men. People would come with a couple of friends. There was safety in numbers in unknown places.

That evening, the partying went on until the early morning. When I got up, people were sleeping in chairs and on the couch. I looked out the window and saw my grandmother coming through the field in front of the house. I knew she wasn't going to be happy because a car she didn't recognize was parked in front of our house. She made it up three steps, grabbed the porch post, and pulled herself up. My mother came out, sat huddled in a passive position in a corner of a rocking chair, and said, "Good morning, Mom." All her life, Mommy had been made to mind her mother. She could never fight for herself. It wasn't in her to raise her voice or stand up to her mother. It was built into the culture.

Mammie told my mother in very harsh words, "Janie, I want these men out of here and right now. I will not have these carryings-on in front of my grand-children." Everyone was awake now, and the strange men came out on the porch. My grandmother told them to leave. One man said, "My car wouldn't start last night." Mammie told them, "Push it, then, but get it out of my sight."

They hesitated, and Mammie pulled her pistol out of her apron pocket and shot three times off the porch into the front yard. They left quickly. I was very pleased but hated to see my mother cry. My mother had cried too much, and Bob Gambrel would bring many more tears and heartbreak before his life was over.

Bob Gambrel didn't leave, and two weeks later, he and my mom married. I had a stepfather, and for the first time in seven years since my father died, there was a man in the house. Bob had wormed his way into my mother's life because of Old Nor, his stepmother. We didn't know Bob, but Mom had met Old Nor previously.

I had many arguments with Bob about his behavior before I moved to Cincinnati. I saw lots of drinking and fighting in our house, and he would even throw things at me. I picked my battles and waited for my time to get even. Bob liked to run around the house in some very short white shorts. Once when he passed out on the bed, I went to the kitchen and got a wash pan of water. I got on the bed, took a razor and some soap, and shaved one leg that was very hairy. He paraded around all summer with no hair on his leg.

After Bob and my mom married, I got to know a high school basketball player. He was good-looking and lived close by, and we started dating. George Brooks played the forward position, and the coach told me many years later, "You can't have a good team without a player like George."

My mother always said, "Ann, the most important thing in life is a satisfied mind." Would I ever have that "satisfied mind"? I know she never found it in this life. My beautiful mother left me when I was twenty-four years old due to domestic violence.

Chapter 4

During the seventh grade, I met Eva Lewis. Eva was very popular, had a great personality, and knew how to tell a joke. She was from a similar background as mine, and we both were raised in hollows, about ten miles apart. Eva had a wonderful mother who was very religious and a father who was not so nice and played around on her. Eva's family was in the coal business. From the beginning, Eva and I became friends, and our friendship lasted fifty-seven years. We both were cheerleaders for basketball teams at different schools.

During this time, my home life was terrible because of Bob. His drinking continued, and it was very clear that he was an alcoholic. He was mean to my mom when he had too much to drink. He was also a pervert and a child molester, but my mother made excuses for him and believed anything he told her. My mother was just too weak, and her religion had taught her to work within her marriage and not to divorce. I remember screaming at her, saying, "I will never love a man so much that I can't turn my back on him, walk away, and never look back! I'll never stay with a man who hits me!" I remember asking her, "How could you do this to yourself and your children?" I told my mother that because of a stupid religious belief, she was going to get us all killed. I said I was leaving as soon as I could find a way out of the mess that was our home.

Soon afterwards, I learned that things weren't going well for Eva. Her wonderful mother had been diagnosed with ovarian cancer. Eva was working at a restaurant and staying with her mom at the hospital while trying hard to keep her grades up. Eva hated her father, who wasn't nice to her mother, even when she was so sick. Eva and I spoke of leaving home together, getting an apartment, and having a better life. But I also hated the thought of leaving my sister and brothers alone to deal with Bob and my mother, who by now was also starting to drink too much and not take care of her home and children.

I found out later there had been another run-in between my grandmother and Bob. Mammie had seen bruises on my brother Alvie. When she asked what had happened, he said, "Bob beat me with a belt and used the buckle part." Mammie threatened to shoot Bob with her trusted .38 pistol.

Years later, Alvie told the story to me. I said, "Al, why did he do this terrible thing?"

"I ate a doughnut!" He never elaborated.

Eva's mother died after a long battle with cancer. We left Pineville but not as we had dreamed. Eva drove off in the car her mother had left her to live with her aunt Opal in Covington, Kentucky. Meantime, I married George and prepared to leave Pineville. I had dreamed of this day for so long, and I thought my heart would burst from excitement. George and I stopped for burgers, cokes, and fries before heading north on I-75 to Cincinnati, Ohio, where he had been working for two years. We were very young, in fact too young, looking back. George and I loved each other, and even though we traveled different paths after five years, we never stopped loving each other.

As we drove north through Lexington, I saw for the first time the fencing of the larger horse farms. When we reached Covington, we could see the Cincinnati skyline. Seeing my first big city took my breath away. I loved books; they kindled my interest in traveling. I wanted to see the whole world. We crossed over the Ohio River and continued north, past Crosley Field, where the Cincinnati Reds baseball team used to play. I learned about baseball from my uncle AY, who was a big fan.

George had found an apartment for us in the Norwood section of Cincinnati. I knew we were getting close when we passed the Twin Drive-In movie theater. George told me we would be going there often to see the latest movies.

After moving to Cincinnati, I read Donald Trump's book *The Art of the Deal*, in which he talked about hillbillies who lived in his father's Swifton Village apartment complex. While I suppose I could have been described as a hillbilly because of where I grew up, labels stopped bothering me many years ago. In the years and months to come, I'd get a job at a linen supply company. Later, I went to work at Kmart and took some adult education classes in English and writing. Eva also settled in Cincinnati, went to beauty school, and started a good job at Kmart as a personnel manager. Life for us both looked promising with endless possibilities for a bright future.

Chapter 5

In Cincinnati, Eva was happily married to Jack Taylor, a man from Pineville who had gone to a different high school. Eva told the story about how he was leaning up against a parking meter in town, tanned and handsome, just back from Florida. Love at first sight! Eva and Jack married on Halloween and would talk for years about who got tricked. Jack would later be drafted into the army and serve in Vietnam.

Judy was Eva's neighbor from down home, and she came from Kentucky to live with Eva while Jack was overseas. Judy, Eva, and I would go shopping, and Judy took us to a very nice ladies' shop. The owner let us pay monthly on our purchases of very nice suits, dresses, coats, and so on because we didn't have credit cards. These were great, fun times for three young women. Although I didn't meet Judy until she came to live with Eva, she would become a very important person in my life. Judy said, "Because we share our clothes, we can dress for special events." Judy had a diamond and emerald ring that she referred to as "my ring." I would wear it on special occasions when I came to visit her. She would say, "Want to wear your ring tonight?" I own it now and wear it sometimes, which makes me feel close to Judy.

After being in Cincinnati for a few years, I met Marian Bichelmeir at the pool in the complex where I lived. I didn't realize this woman would become a lifelong friend. She was very strong emotionally and started helping me with cultural awakening. She took me to my first opera, and while I didn't like it too much, I did enjoy the stage settings, costumes, and so on. Marian also enjoyed going with me to the art museum and art galleries, the playhouse, and participating in other cultural activities. I had loved art since my third-grade teacher introduced me to landscapes and watercolors. My interest in art has been a lifelong exploration that has taken me to art exhibits and museums around the world. Some of my most pleasurable moments have come from a passion for beautiful things and collections of art objects.

After my arrival in Cincinnati, I found "the Strip," with its jazz and blues music and met mostly local entertainers. There were piano bars and supper clubs where famous personalities often appeared. I especially enjoyed meeting Randy Crawford, who later sang with the Jazz Crusaders.

The only problem for most of us from our part of the country is our attachment to the mountains and the culture back home in Kentucky. This lonesome, homesick feeling is very difficult for an outsider to understand. It's an attachment to a place and a group of people that few will know, especially those in relationships with men who aren't from that culture.

Chapter 6

After a few years, I found myself unable to remain with George. We had grown apart and wanted different things in life. I had met a wonderful man named James Smith, who worked with me at Kmart and was the manager of the sporting goods department. He became my first love after George, and I decided to divorce. He would later become a very important person in my life, and I loved him very much. I still think about and miss James so much. He was eventually transferred to another state. In the beginning, I would try to see him during long weekends and holidays. We made love, went dancing, and made love again and again. I was young and didn't understand at the time how precious and valuable this love was, and I was hardheaded. Time taught me some hard lessons. *How did I let this happen?* I had a problem giving completely in relationships after observing my mother's problems with men.

James was crying before I went to the airport. I was on my way to Germany, where George was serving in the army. I remarried George because we thought it might keep him from going to Vietnam. Eva's Jack was already in Vietnam, and we were always worried about him. We prayed George wouldn't be assigned to Vietnam.

Before I boarded the plane, I was paged. When I answered the phone, it was James. He said, "Jo Ann, please don't go. Please turn around and come back." I said, "I have to go because this is what my mother and grandmother want me to do. They feel we'll never have anything together because of your previous marriage and family commitments. I want more than working to help pay child support for your three children. I love you, but I just can't decide what is best for everyone."

George and I lived in Bad Hersfeld, a two-hour drive from Frankfurt. We lived in a small apartment in the city, and I was left alone a lot while George went on maneuvers. I had no transportation and felt isolated. One night at the enlisted men's club, I met three ladies who became friends. One of them, Ursula, whom we called "Ushi," took me to a guest house, where I spent my twenty-first birthday. These friends helped lessen the isolation, but it wasn't enough.

I stayed in Germany for about six months before returning to Cincinnati. I couldn't remain married to George, even though I had no doubt about his love for me. When we first married, he was a very hard worker, working two jobs. I was working also. On weekends, however, he got drunk. I had lived that way most of my life back home. He wanted to make money and later would become very rich, but without me. He never understood! I wanted to go dancing, listen to good music, and travel.

In Cincinnati, life resumed with my friends from Kentucky. Judy was bartending and making a lot of money from tips. She suggested I help out and earn some money for my car payment. I learned how to make drinks and got to know the nightlife. Life was wonderful except for missing James and for worrying about my brothers and sister. My mother continued to be abused by my stepfather and continued her drinking. She wasn't cooking or keeping up her house, and my brothers were old enough to start fighting with Bob.

I confronted my mother, who by then was living across from Cincinnati in Newport, Kentucky, but she just cried because she had sold our old house to her brother AY. Mom tried to buy it back, but he would not sell it to her. He said, "As long as you're married to Bob, I won't let you have it back. We don't want him back here."

Mom took the money and bought two houses on land contracts. Following her death, this proved to be a very bad mistake. Mom blamed her brother AY and told me, "You left me, and I moved here to be closer to you. I have all my money invested in these two apartment buildings. If I leave, I lose everything." Mom knew her two houses had been designated to be taken eventually by the state for a freeway ramp. I believe she died with a belief that she had to suffer in this life for her sins. Today when I drive the bypass around Cincinnati and see the ramp leading to Newport where my mother's two old houses used to be, I want to scream for the great loss and pain I still feel.

Chapter 7

James was glad I had returned from Germany and came to visit. He tried to convince me it would be better if I moved to Detroit with him. We had a wonderful evening, with a great dinner and dancing at one of my favorite places. I knew all the band members because they stopped to have a drink where I used to be a cocktail waitress.

The next day, James took me to lunch. When I returned to work, I got a telephone call from Mom's next-door neighbor, who was a nurse. She told me my mother had been shot. James drove me to the hospital. I was totally out of control because I loved my mother so very much and felt sorry about some of the cruel things I sometimes said to her about the way she lived her life.

I thought back to the month before, when I had received a call that my mother had been beaten and locked out of the house. I drove there alone. When I saw my mother and how Bob had beaten her beautiful face, I ran at him and leaped like a lion to get to him. During the fight, we broke a lamp and the coffee table. I knew since they were first married that if he was drunk, I could get the best of him. I tried to be a nice person, but I had a terrible temper and would fight anyone who hurt the people I loved. Bob called the police and went to sit on the front porch. When they arrived, he said I had come into his house and attacked him. I said, "Yes, and look at my mother." The police put me in my car and made me leave. They followed me until I crossed the bridge back to Cincinnati.

And now my mother had been shot. At the hospital, I ran to the emergency room door. I wanted to see my mother. James and I talked with a doctor, who told me, "Your mother has been shot twice in the back." We were taken to see her. Mom was crying and said, "I knew I would never live to see my grandchildren." Then the doctor told me, "Your mother was shot once; the second hole is the exit wound."

I cried as James and I held my mother. She'd been crying and said, "I'm going to die and never live to have grandchildren."

To lighten the scene in the emergency room, James commented about Mom's feet and said, "Look, Janie, how ugly your feet look." We all laughed, and I took Mom home with me.

Bob had been arrested. We got a restraining order and had photos taken of Mom's face for the judge to see when we went to court.

A month later, Bob talked Mom into forgiving him and let him return. I had an exchange of words because I couldn't believe she would take him back.

Mom said, "He's promised to stop drinking. I don't have enough education, and I don't want to be dependent on my children. I have to take care of my property. It's my only income. We're going to church and stop drinking."

I didn't believe Bob would ever change. I never stopped worrying about my beautiful mother, with the auburn red hair and bright red fingernails. Oh, I almost forgot her freckles. But what could I do but hope and pray he would never hurt her again.

James Smith returned to Detroit, and we never saw each other again. We just stopped communicating and began to date other people. Later, he called. I needed him so very much, but I couldn't ask him to come because I was dating someone else. My life at this point felt so confusing and out of control.

Chapter 8

A few weeks after my mother had been shot, my life began to change for the better. I had a sales job at a linen supply company, friends, and a very busy social life. I was very happy for the first time in many years. My sister, Pauline, had finished high school and had come to join me. She got a nice job in retail, and we moved into a beautiful apartment. I very much loved my sister, and we had a wonderful year together. Later, Pauline was transferred for work to another state. Our only worry was our mother and her marriage to Bob. He was drinking again, and we knew his promises would once again prove to be false. We helped financially support our three brothers, who were living with Bob and Mommy, and felt guilty because they were suffering and caught up in a terrible situation.

Once when Mommy was drinking, she told me not to worry and said she would have my brother Jim kill Bob if he ever hurt her again. I lost all patience with her and screamed at her, "Mom, you are disgusting! How could you ask him to kill for you?!" Later, I remembered these words and wished I wouldn't have been so hard because I knew she didn't really mean it.

Through all the years and conflict, I never doubted my mother's love for her children. All her children were exceptionally beautiful, and she would say, "Ann, don't you know pretty people have pretty babies?" I heard her say on many occasions, "I would gladly give my life to save your life. There is nothing like a mother's love." Then, teasingly, she would say, "I didn't want any of my pregnancies. I cried because I got pregnant and vomited the whole nine months. But the moment I saw all of you for the first time, it was instant love." She told me how handsome my father, Ben, was after he returned from WWII. Mother laughed and said, "Every time he put his pants on the bedpost, I got pregnant." My mother told me I was conceived in her father's barn loft in a bed of hay. I loved this romantic story. It made me feel better to know my mother was once loved and protected.

I tried many times to analyze my mother's circumstances, and I felt a lot of anger for the Southern Baptist religion. Mommy believed her abuse was God's punishment for her liberated lifestyle after my father's death, but she would still go to heaven when she died. I had many horrible dreams because of those hellfire and damnation teachings. I am still very confused about religion and the guilt that comes with these church teachings. I got very angry with people who told my mother that she should live this way, do these things, and so on. Who were they? Where did these beliefs come from? I will always look at a belief, give each one lots of thought, and decide to accept or reject it based on life experiences and research. My childhood could have been better, but I was loved and happy, and I never lose sight of those two facts.

If I could change only one thing about my childhood, it would have been to have had more reading material in our home. Why didn't my mother think about having books, magazines, and newspapers for her children? But when these resentments enter my mind, I know the answer. Mommy didn't have a lot of education, maybe up to eighth grade in a one-room school. Books were also a luxury her own mother couldn't afford. Mommy's priorities were food, clothing, and paying her bills at the beginning of each month. As an adult, I was consumed with buying and reading books.

From growing up in this environment, I seemed to be always looking for a strong male influence in my life. Most times, I was disappointed. The men who have gotten close to me usually were disappointing when I got to know them better. When I realized they needed me more than I needed them, that was the time to leave the relationship. I tried to lower my expectations, but I am such a dreamer—he must be out there someplace. This idea has caused me lots of problems with lovers and husbands.

The small amount of Cherokee blood in me must be what makes me strong in times of need. Maybe my love for music, food, and dance came from the Irish part of the family. I love to sip on "good moonshine" or a great glass of French champagne. I am always saying to myself, "Jo Ann, Jo Ann! Please remember moderation is the key to a happy life."

Chapter 9

I loved Cincinnati. I loved going up into the park and looking down on the Ohio River. This was such a dreamy place. I had my favorite bench, high on the hillside that slopes down to the edge of the water. There, I could watch the tugboats as they pushed the barges loaded with coal down the river. Maybe one day, I'll have enough money to take the *Delta Queen* riverboat all the way to New Orleans, especially with my love of blues music. The fall would be a lovely time of year for this adventure, with all the trees turning and cool evenings on the river. Marian and I have talked about making this trip for years. If a dreamer lives forever, then I will have a long life. It's time to stop dreaming and return to my story.

While working at the linen supply company, I had a company car. I had to make sales calls and exceed my quota for the month. The job was interesting, but it wasn't really a career. I had first started out in the production manager's office, with a move to the general manager's office after about one year, and then to a job in the sales department. The work was easy when compared to the hardworking ladies who worked in the production department. The production manager didn't care about people. He cared only about making quotas and his numbers at the end of each day. However, the salary and benefits allowed me to have a comfortable apartment.

Jack had returned from Vietnam, and he and Eva moved to Columbus, Ohio. She had a five-month-old little boy named Jackie. I adored him and wished they lived closer, but Jack had his work in Columbus. I would have liked to relocate to some other place, but there were lots of reasons to stay close to Mom. I couldn't understand why my mother continued to stay with Bob. I went to live with Judy.

One day, I checked on my new restaurant account, made a couple of calls on companies that I would have liked to take from the competition, and returned to my office. Two messages awaited me. The secretary informed me, "You've gotten the new accounts at the brewery and an interview with the manager of the Sheraton." I was excited because I had to write some new business; this would put me over my sales quota for the month. I called Judy, who said, "Get your prettiest dress ready. We're hitting the Strip tonight."

I put the top down on my new MG and went north on I-75 to the Reading Road exit, turned right, and went to Swifton Village. Judy opened the door with a glass of wine and told me, "We have reservations at the Wishing Well restaurant." Was there time for a bubble bath? Judy said I had one hour as I rushed for the bathroom.

We were dressed and ready to go out the door when the phone rang. Judy said, "Let it ring." But I answered the phone, and on the line was Robert, the owner of the bar where my brother Al worked after school. He told me to get to Newport right away. Had Bob hurt my mother? Robert told me, "Jo Ann, your mother is dead." I started to scream and threw the telephone receiver against the wall so hard it broke. The next year was a living hell for me and my family.

Judy called a friend, and he came to the apartment with medication for me. Judy and I drove to Newport to be with my brothers Jim, Alvie, and Bill. I was very worried about my brothers and wanted to know what had happened. My mother wasn't capable of making good decisions. I should have taken her home to Pineville. Damn those old apartments. I once again questioned God about why some people have so much pain and some people escape with very little pain in their lives.

I left Cincinnati, crossed the bridge to Newport, and went to check on my brothers. I pulled into a parking spot in front of Mom's house and tried to get some control of myself for the sake of my brothers. They were nineteen, seventeen, and fifteen years of age.

As I entered the house, my youngest brother, Bill, ran into my arms and told me, "Sis, he shot Mom, and I saw it all happen. Mom told him to put the pistols away because people were coming to pay their rent and having two old pistols nearby would make them nervous. Bob got mad and picked up one of the pistols and started shooting. Mom tried to run but fell on the bottom of the bed."

I wanted to know where they had taken my mother. Jim, my older brother, said, "The ambulance took her to Saint Luke Hospital." I wanted to kill Bob, but I couldn't get to him because he was in jail. Why hadn't I killed him years ago?

I called Pauline in Louisiana, Eva in Columbus, and all the family at home. I worried about my grandmother. How would she be able to handle Mommy's death? She had always been a source of strength for the whole family but was now seventy-five years old. Eva came the next day, and all of us traveled together to southeastern Kentucky. I took care of all the arrangements to send our mother's body home. Mom died on May 23, 1971. In July, we were going to have a family reunion, and Mom had been excited because Pauline was planning to be there.

During the drive, I thought about my last trip to Kentucky with my mother. It had been just two months before, when we went for my mother's uncle's funeral. I thought about the fried chicken, homemade biscuits, and thermos of coffee Mom had packed for the five-hour drive. The plan was to eat as we drove to save time. Mom fed me every bite I ate during the drive. It was so nice to be without Bob. We had a perfect excuse not to take him; my MG had seating for only two people.

I remembered some of our conversation during the drive. Mom said, "Honey, your mom has never had the opportunities to do all the things you have done. I've never had a real vacation. Oh, I might have had a few good experiences, but they weren't so great now that I think about those times. I thought I was having fun."

I told her, "One day, Mom, you and I will go on a vacation to Florida. I'm taking you to Daytona Beach. We will go shopping and walk on the beach, and you can have a manicure and pedicure."

I now understood hate, real hate, for the first time. I would never forgive Bob. Never! Never! Never! Not in a million years!

I've experienced too many traumas. When I hear the siren of an ambulance, my mind goes back years to my mother's last thoughts. Did she die instantly? Did she die at the bottom of the bed? Did she die in the ambulance? What were her last conscious thoughts? These are thoughts that torment me, never to be answered. I miss our all-night movie-watching times. We would see four or five movies, eating and drinking until the morning light came through the window.

Chapter 10

After my mother's funeral, I returned to Cincinnati but didn't immediately go back to work. Mom's death was so very hard on everyone, especially my grandmother. She told me, "I've outlived two husbands, all my brothers and sisters, parents, sisters-in-law, brothers-in-law, friends, and so forth. But there are no words to describe the loss of my child." I was just numb and still can't come to terms with my mother's death.

I had to take care of every detail of the funeral, even polishing Mom's nails, those beautiful nails that were polished bright red every Friday night for her Saturday shopping trip. I will never see my mother's hands again. Mom's body was taken to the family cemetery for burial.

I couldn't help but think about how my grandmother had planned to live one day with my mom. She would have had her own room, decorated with nice furniture, purple curtains, and a bedspread that I had already prepared for her. She would have loved it, but now it was not going to happen.

Bob called twice, and I refused to take his calls. The bastard even sent flowers to the funeral home. I immediately took them to the garbage can. How dare he send flowers. I hated him with a vengeance and wished I had a connection to have him killed. It would take many years and lots of therapy before I could trust any man.

After a while, I returned to work and went through the motions, being alive but suffering so much pain from the loss of my mother. No words from anyone from her church, family members, or well-intentioned friends brought comfort to me. There was once again another hole in my soul. A few months later, I found by accident a copy of *Think and Grow Rich* by Napoleon Hill. He explained how matter can go through various stages of change, but it can't be destroyed. This helped me to cope with not having Mom's presence in my life.

My brothers, Jim, Al, and Bill came to live with me. Pauline and her husband went back to work in Shreveport, Louisiana. It was a big adjustment having my brothers to take care of in my two-bedroom apartment. Al and Jim were doing better than Bill and I. Bill was the eyewitness to the shooting. He was only fifteen years old and was not doing well emotionally. I wondered how he would hold up when we had to go to court. I didn't have a good feeling for the Commonwealth attorney who would be prosecuting my stepfather. Bill was in his own world most days. I tried to talk with him, but he would not or could not answer. I would scream at him, "Bill, answer me! Why won't you answer when I call your name?!" He went to a place somewhere deep inside, and I couldn't always reach him.

Sweet and gentle Alvie, who was only seventeen years old, had gone to work stocking shelves at a sporting goods company. He wanted to feel he was helping. Jim was working in sales at a store selling rifles, pistols, and fishing equipment. Jim broke monthly sales records. He was a born hustler and created stories about fishing lures he used. He knew a lot about hunting, weapons, and ammunition. He spent most of his life in Kentucky, where he grew up with people who knew a lot about the woods and animals.

My friend James Smith called often from Detroit, but I hadn't seen him but twice in six months. One time, we went to my favorite place in the park for a small picnic. The other time was to stroll through the Cincinnati Art Museum and see my favorite paintings.

My favorite painting in the museum is *Last Flowers* by Jules Breton. It's part of the museum's permanent collection. My beloved Dick Davidson, my platonic friend since I was nineteen years old, had sold insurance to an art school. Dick asked one of the best students to go to the museum on a Saturday and paint the picture for me. Dick gave it to me, and it hangs by my bed. What an act of love!

I've loved painting and sculpture since the third grade. This love has been with me nearly all my life and brings me a lot of comfort. But despite James's sensitivity to my love of art, the long-distance relationship wasn't going to work.

Chapter 11

Soon I was preparing for Bob Gambrel's trial. After one year from my mother's death, we had a trial date. This was my first experience with the judicial system, and it was a learning experience. Bob had gotten out on bail soon after shooting Mommy. How could he have been out of jail for such a long time before a trial date was set? How could he have continued living in her house, collecting the rent from the apartments, and being free?

The day of the trial, everyone was feeling good because they believed justice would finally be served, but I worried about my brother Bill. How would he hold up under cross-examination? The last year had been very difficult for my family, especially Bill. I thought about James and wished I would have accepted his offer to be with me. Dear sweet Eva drove down from Columbus to be with me. She was a big help during the trial.

When the trial began, I couldn't go into the courtroom because I was on the list as a possible witness. Eva kept coming out and updating me on how things were going. She told me everything was going well, and things were going our way. She came out again and said that Bill was doing great under cross-examination. Bob's attorney tried to confuse him with stupid questions, but it didn't work. For example, the attorney asked Bill, "Why did you throw a banana split at Bob? Had the ice cream melted?" I was so relieved that Bill maintained his composure. The prosecuting attorney didn't seem so competent, but just maybe he had a chance to win and have justice for our mother and our family back home.

Eva then informed me that the coroner would be the next witness. She returned to the courtroom, and I had to wait. After a while, Eva returned with a worried look on her face. She said, "Jo Ann, everything has gone wrong. The judge has called a mistrial." I wanted to know what in the hell was a mistrial.

Eva explained that during the cross-examination of the coroner, he was asked, "How many bullets did you recover from the victim's body?" He answered, "Five in total: three from the shooting that killed her and two from an undetermined time." The courtroom went crazy, and the defense attorney screamed, "You can only try my client for the one shooting! You're bringing evidence from another shooting!" Our attorney responded that he didn't know about the other shooting or bullets.

I was in shock and didn't understand. I told our attorney, "There was another time when Bob shot my mother." When I got to the hospital after the shooting, the emergency doctor told me she had been shot twice in the back. Then he left to check the X-rays. Upon his return, he said, "I was wrong. The second hole was an exit wound." I explained this to our attorney after the mistrial.

I said to the emergency room doctor, "Are you telling me my mother lived for more than two years with two bullets in her back that we didn't know were there?"

He said, "From the evidence, that looks to be the case."

The defense attorney told me I would be notified when another court date was set. I was angry and confused. When another trial happened, the evidence would be the same. There would always be five bullets recovered from Mommy's back. My whole family was very upset about the mistrial and the possibility of having to do this all over again. I especially had had difficult moments with Bill over the past year, and I was worried about his mental well-being.

A few weeks later, I was notified that the judge, defense attorney, and Kentucky Commonwealth prosecuting attorney would like to meet with me. On the appointed day, I met them and was asked if Bob pleaded guilty to second-degree manslaughter, would I agree to his serving seven years in prison? I quickly said, "No. No way."

They had a conference and returned with another offer. The judge asked, "Would you agree to ten years?"

I thought about my brother Bill being so young and having to deal with another trial. I felt I should take the ten years but asked one question: "Will he actually serve ten years?" They said, "If he goes before a parole board, you will be notified, and you can appear."

I agreed, then discovered that nine months later while awaiting a new trial, Bob was back living in the apartment building my mother had worked for and died trying to keep. No one had ever notified me about a trial date, and Bob never faced justice. This was my first experience with the court system. It was a hard lesson to learn. All my lessons in life have been learned the hard way. Bob later died in a fire in one of the apartments.

After the mistrial and Bob's release on bail, I was no longer a naive young twenty-four-year-old girl. I no longer believed right wins out in the end. Bob's sister had money and connections that may have helped him escape doing serious jail time. I understood there are two justice systems depending on which side of the social ladder you fall on: one for people with money and one for people without. I always believed there had to be a way to avenge my mother's death. Somehow there had to be a way to find the justice I didn't find in the court system.

Immediately after the mistrial, I went to my car. I wanted to see my mother's two houses with rental apartments. I pulled into the curbside parking and wanted my mind to return to happier days, but it was impossible. The properties had not been maintained. The storm doors had been ripped off, a window was broken, and strange people were sitting on the porch. I cried for Mommy, the sobs of a small child. I wanted someone or something to take the pain away. I pulled away from the curb and vowed never to return to that house.

Had I made the right decision on the ten-year plea deal? Would my family back home be supportive of my decision? It didn't matter! It was over and done. There was no way to change the outcome. I never got over the need for my mother. In small and big hurts in life, I wanted my mother. She wanted to see her grandchildren. She had had her faults, but we had home-cooked meals and ate at the table together. I don't ever remember being hungry. I miss my mother's sheets, dried on a clothesline in the sun.

Chapter 12

Hard work has always been an important part of my life. Good physical work helped in many ways, both mentally and physically, to bring success and well-being to my life. When there was a lot on my mind, I liked to do some kind of hard work. I believe this thinking must have come from Mammie and Uncle AY. He said to me, "Jo Ann, if you would get out in the garden and do some work, you wouldn't have to go to the gym." It was hard to break that pioneering mentality. My aunt Irene, who was my father's sister, had a son, Bill, who was my favorite first cousin who came to California after I moved there. Aunt Irene told me I would pay later in life with physical pain from doing too much hard work. Time would prove her words to be true. After my mother's death, I returned to my job and my love of nature to keep my sanity.

My job had lost its meaning. I was making my sales quotas, but I was just going through the motions. Pauline was still living in Shreveport, Louisiana, with her husband, Jim, and asked our brother Bill to come and live with her. I hated to see my baby brother go, my first baby, whom I had carried on my hip and for whom I made his bottles and washed his shitty diapers. But I felt he needed a man's influence. Pauline's husband turned out to be a hard disciplinarian. Bill worked at the skating rink, finished high school, and joined the navy. He retired after twenty years.

I didn't know it then, but my brother Alvie would be leaving me soon to live with friends from home who were living in Louisville, Kentucky. Brother Jim had been a rolling stone; he would spend time with Mom, have problems with Bob, then leave and spend time with me. After a while, he'd go home to the hollow and live with Uncle Bill before returning once more to live with me in Cincinnati.

Years later, when I lived in California, Jim came for a visit. He was very mischievous and enjoyed tricking me. For example, one time, I arrived an hour early at the airport to meet him. It must have been a full flight. The passengers kept exiting, but no brother Jim. I was near tears, but then, here came Jim! He was laughing and flirting with the cabin attendants. I said, "Damn you, Jim, that was intentional." He was laughing and said, "Sis, I wanted to make you sweat."

In Cincinnati, I was alone, and Judy wanted me to come and work again in the cocktail lounge. I needed the money but also wanted to be around people. I always liked the bar business. My customers were very interesting, and I liked to watch people. I'd get ready for work, iron my black skirt and white blouse, and polish my black shoes. I had been to the Playboy Club in Cincinnati and Chicago and seen how the "Bunnies" dressed. I thought the ladies were beautiful, but I would feel uncomfortable in the skimpy clothing.

I had been working with Judy for about six months. There were men at work who were interested in me, but I couldn't get past dinner with any of them. One night I went to work, not realizing that my life would change forever. An interesting man walked in and took a seat at the bar. He ordered a rum and Coke. Judy was on her dinner break. I made him a drink, and I got busy. I tried not to think about this handsome blonde with the long hair and leather jacket. He said, "Mama, when you get time, I would like another drink." No one had ever called me that before.

Judy returned, and the piano player started her first show of the evening. The lounge got busy, and there was no time for conversing with my customers, but I kept glancing at the blonde Adonis. I did have time to check out his body when he removed his jacket. I went to the bar to get a drink order for one of my tables. He went to the bathroom and introduced himself to me. "I'm Ken Spraggins from California. I know your first name but not your last name."

I told him as I served my table a drink order, "I'm Jo Ann Fuson from Kentucky."

He left me a note and a ten-dollar tip on the bar ledge. The note said, "*You're beautiful, sunshine.*" He had drawn a happy face with a big smile with his address and telephone number on the bottom.

I drove home, thought about him before I went to sleep, and wondered if I would ever see him again. The next day, I made a couple of sales and left my office at five. There wasn't a lot of time before I left for the Music Lounge. I took extra care with my hair. Makeup wasn't a big deal because I used a little powder and lipstick. My eyelashes are naturally long and black. I worked all evening, and Adonis didn't make an appearance. At midnight, he came through the door and took his place at the bar. There wasn't much time for talking, but I asked about his day and what had brought him to Cincinnati. He was in town for a repair on a computer system. He left. I finished the cleanup and went to my car. Ken was leaning against it. "Mama, may I buy you breakfast?" That's all it took, and I said, "Sure, if you will help me take the top down."

We got into my car and went out to I-75. His hair was long like mine. I had never been with a man who had long hair. What fun to mess up his hair. We went to a late-night place across the river.

I suffered the next day as I had to be at work by 8:00 a.m. I arrived late at 9:30. No one said a word because I was never late. My sales were up, and that was what made the general manager happy. I felt a little hungover and sleepy, but I left work early and took a nap. It helped because it was Friday night, and I didn't have to work at the lounge.

I picked Ken up at his hotel, and we had dinner at my favorite restaurant. He was charming and knew just what to say to get close to me. We returned to his motel. I went with him to his room, and we had no doubt about what was going to happen. Our lovemaking was wild and savage for the next two hours. We couldn't get enough of each other. I waited on him, and he waited on me because we both had a lot of control over our bodies. In the early morning hours, we fell into a deep sleep. We repeated the same thing for the next five nights. Of course, there was no love involved like the love I had shared with James.

Ken finished his engineering work. I took him to the airport, and he promised to keep in touch. He called every morning to wake me up. Letters started to arrive, and he expressed himself beautifully with words of shared passion. He would say time and time again, *"Mama, please come to California. There's lots of sunshine and happiness here for you."* Ken promised to help me relocate and to find an apartment and new job. There seemed to be so many details to work out. I went a bit crazy for the next month and started giving my things to Judy and Marian. I arranged a drive-away service to take my car, bought ten-foot lockers at Kmart, and shipped them to California by Greyhound bus. Then I flew to San Francisco.

It was hard leaving my comfortable life for the unknown. California wouldn't be forever, but I knew I would be free for the first time in my life. I had always felt responsible for taking care of my sister and brothers. Pauline and dear friends Eva, Judy, and Marian thought I had lost my mind. What would happen with me? I wanted to experience a different kind of life that Ken told me existed in California.

Overlooking a small part of my hometown. Pineville, Kentucky, during a hike at Pine Mountain State Park.

Mom with her five children. Left to right, Jo Ann, Jim, Pauline, Mommy with baby Bill, and Alvie.

My parents, Ben and Janie Fuson, at the fire lookout tower, Pine Mountain State Park.

Mammie and me standing on her back kitchen porch.

Uncle AY North who lived with Mammie directly across the field from us.

Uncle Porter Partin walking with brother Jim to get a bottle of moonshine for a customer.

Standing with my aunt, Della Partin, the matriarch of our family.

My Cousin Bill Larimore on a visit home to Kentucky.

My first-grade picture.

My mother decorating graves at our
family cemetery.

Judy Miller, my friend from Pineville who helped
me so much when I lived in Cincinnati, Ohio.
Her home was my home whenever I needed
her the most.

George Brooks, my first husband.

Judy, Jo Ann, and Eva. Three young women, together in Cincinnati, Ohio, ready to meet life's challenges.

One of my favorite photos taken before leaving for California.

Chapter 13

I arrived in San Francisco, and Ken was at the gate to meet me. We ran into each other's arms, and we both were scared. His friends and ex-wife had told him that he had rushed into something without thinking it through.

We crossed the Golden Gate Bridge. Everything looked so different. Ken lived in what people referred to as the Silicon Valley. He told me the drive would be about one hour. I closed my eyes and took a few deep breaths. Nothing looked familiar. There were no green trees. The hillsides were bare, brown, and dry. What had I done? Would this work, and would I be happy? Ken took my hand and said, "Mama, don't worry because I will take such good care of you. I will never let anything hurt you."

Although I was nervous, I felt a freedom I had never experienced before. Ken's home was beautiful with lots of warm colors, lush green houseplants, and wonderful music. He was true to his word and quickly spoiled me with trips to the ocean and shopping for clothes and ski equipment. This was my first opportunity to try snow skiing. I felt loved and protected by this wonderful man. I was so happy to be in California. We shopped for short dresses. He could sew! We would have a drink at the kitchen table while he put another two-inch hem in my skirts and dresses. He said, "Mama, one of these days, you won't have these beautiful legs." Years later, I would remember his words, sobbing like a baby when I looked at my leg after the wounds from a bear attack.

Life was good in the valley, but this wasn't my valley. My hollow would always be in the hills of Kentucky. There were no thunderstorms to watch moving down the hollow. I needed the warmth of being in front of my grandmother's fireplace, with a fire and sweet potatoes baking in the ashes that had been knocked through to the hearth with a poker. But my soul was crying out for this freedom from family responsibility in my life. I was twenty-four years old, and for the first time since age seven, I felt less responsible for my brothers, who were now sixteen, eighteen, and twenty, or for my sister, who was twenty-two. Mommy's soul had gone to another place. I understood that energy can go through changes but can't be destroyed. That was how I coped with her loss thanks to Napoleon Hill's book.

Ken eventually knew a lot about my past. He felt I needed a few sessions with a good therapist. I agreed and started therapy on a one-on-one basis. There were also weekend group seminars. They were wonderful experiences for me. I went deeply into my childhood and adulthood, faced some old fears, and did away with some belief systems. Why do we buy other people's beliefs? As adults, we must think for ourselves. I wondered, *Who in the hell are "they"?* "They" say you should be this way, think a certain way, and live a certain way. I thought I was an enlightened woman now. What would the future hold for this Kentucky woman?

I found a job with a scrap metal company and enrolled at a bartender's school. Soon it was time to have a place of my own. I would have to tell Ken I wanted to look for an apartment. It wasn't going to be easy. He reluctantly agreed to help, and it was the right thing to do. Of course, he was only ten minutes away. There would still be a lot of beach, skiing, and overnight time together. He had a terrible temper that I had seen directed toward others, but it had never been directed at me. He also had a pistol that made me a little nervous. I had grown up with rifles and pistols. Every household in my family had several for hunting and protection. There was still the pain of my mother's death. That's a pain no therapist can ever take from my mind and body. I often talked in my mind to Mom, and I felt her presence.

Life took on a rhythm for the next few months. I found a lovely apartment in Sunnyvale, California, and made a successful transition to life in the Santa Clara Valley. I'd meet Ken for breakfast and go to work.

He was still very protective of me. Once after we left a restaurant, he reached in the window and fastened my seat belt. He told me, "Mama, you'd better learn to fasten your seat belt." I quickly drove away and merged onto the freeway but didn't notice that a fool had stopped in front of me. I accelerated and rear-ended his car, but I wasn't injured. Once again, Ken and my guardian angels had saved me.

Chapter 14

While still working at the scrap metal company, I went to bartender's school. I soon began work at a very nice restaurant with a great cocktail lounge, and I loved my job as day manager. The owner and his wife made me feel like part of the family. I watched as the hostess greeted a very interesting group of men. One especially caught my eye.

I had just finished another weekend therapy seminar. I had been told that until I learned to let go and trust someone, I would never have the love I hoped for in my life. They called me a fence rider. I believed that meant I needed to let go and jump over the fence and to hold nothing back. That was so hard for me to do with my background and what had happened to Mom. *Maybe*, I thought, *I'll give it a try*.

I watched as the group of men came to the bar while I moved through the dining room and talked with my customers. Most of them were regulars, and I knew them by their first names. I made a point to say hi. When I returned to the bar, I made a point to say hi to the rugged Charles Bronson-like one in the group. He asked, "Angel, may I buy you a drink?" I answered, "Sure! I'll have a Shirley Temple."

He wanted to know if I was serious. I went behind the bar and put some 7 Up in a glass with a splash of grenadine. I was in a good mood after the seminar and receptive to his charm.

His name was Robert "Bob" Rackstraw. He told me he had a helicopter service close by, and the other guys in the group worked for him. They stayed about one and a half hours, asked to be served lunch at the bar, and made a lot of noise. I was near the hostess station when they started to leave. Bob said, "Angel, would you like to have lunch with me tomorrow?" I quickly answered,

"Where should I meet you?" He told me he would meet me tomorrow at the restaurant.

I went home and kept thinking of Bob all evening. What will I wear? Where will we go? Everything happened so quickly. What had gotten into me? Must have been the seminar.

I got up early the next morning. There were chores to be done every Saturday morning. I had to run my clothes to the cleaners, water my plants, and clean the balcony. My hair, eyes, and legs are my best features, or so they say. I decided to wear my hair down, with a chambray blue shirt to match my eyes and a white pair of jeans with espadrilles shoes that tie around my ankles. My hair was brown and hung about four inches below my bra strap.

I arrived at the parking lot about 1:15 p.m. Bob was waiting for me, and he was wearing jeans. Great! He walked me to a dirty pickup truck and opened the passenger door for me. So far so good! He had a bucket of fried chicken and a small cooler on the front seat. He didn't ask where I would like to go but proceeded to the airport and took me out on the tarmac to a red and white helicopter. I carried the cooler and bucket of Kentucky Fried Chicken. He didn't know his passenger was a Kentucky woman. My hometown is thirty miles from the original KFC. He said, "Come with me, Angel. We're going on a picnic." This would be my first helicopter ride. Later, I would think back on this moment and realize I didn't have any fear but experienced lots of excitement with this total stranger.

I felt like I was in a bubble. The view was wonderful both inside and outside the helicopter. Bob was very focused on his flying. He put on my headset and adjusted the volume. It was difficult to have a conversation during the flight, but I was happy just to be having a new experience. The landing was textbook perfect as far as I could tell. We were in a completely isolated area with nothing around for miles. It was time for the greatest picnic of my life.

We talked and got to know each other. Bob explained we were on about 350 acres that belonged to a man without an easement access to his property. The owner came in by horseback. He was an old, eccentric professor from Stanford, and Bob was helping him with some supplies. I was having a wonderful time with great company and perfect weather. I stayed close to Bob because I kept thinking of the wild boar I had seen on the wall in Carmel at Clint Eastwood's bar, named the Hog's Breath Inn. I didn't feel in danger because Bob had a rifle.

He told me he had been a chopper pilot in Vietnam. He had served two tours and asked to go back for a third, but the army refused his request. Move over, Mr. Bronson, because I had found a real-life man better than those Hollywood movie types. I also ate the truly best fried chicken I had ever tasted. Maybe, just maybe I had found the man who would make me feel safe. Could I do what the psychologist said I must do to experience the feelings of being in love?

On the way back to pick up my car, Bob started to sing. He had a great voice. We shared musical interests and discovered we liked a lot of the same artists. We liked Gerry Rafferty and especially his song "Baker Street," and we were both big Eagles fans. We agreed that it doesn't get any better than Bob Seger.

Bob took me back to my car and gave me the softest kiss with the warmest lips I had ever experienced. He promised to call, and I gave him my phone number. What a great day! What a man!

Chapter 15

What a wonderful world I was experiencing in California. I loved the beach, and I couldn't wait for the weekends. It had gotten to be a routine to leave after work on Friday, pack Ken's camper with rum Dinger, rum, cheese, Triscuits, and breakfast makings. We would drive over to Route 7 and head for Santa Cruz. I feel like crying when I think of all the years without the ocean in my life. The ocean would become my retreat in good and bad times throughout my life. Mom was often in my thoughts as I walked the beach alone and said out loud, "Mom, where are you now? Can you see me? Do you know what I'm feeling?" The sound of the ocean was always louder than my words, and no one heard me cry for my mother. Maybe God was listening.

Trouble was coming, and I could feel it was unavoidable. Ken had fallen in love with me. He wanted more than I could give. There was no doubt that I loved him but not enough to marry. There was another complication because Ken and his first wife had decided not to have children. He'd had a vasectomy several years before I met him. There was also no doubt in my mind about wanting children eventually. Why can't relationships be uncomplicated? Maybe it was my fault because something was missing that kept me from loving and trusting deeply.

Robert came to see me at work. I was excited to see him but didn't let him know. He couldn't just walk in the door again after three weeks and say, "Angel, I missed you." I looked into his green eyes. There was a lot of mischief in them. I could feel his gaze as I went about my work. There was an unspoken energy between us. He had a way of filling up a room. He seemed to dominate all conversations, especially with men. They wanted to hear his war stories. I understand what the word *macho* means. He was my dream come true.

Bob left with, "I'll see you later, Angel." I made out my work schedule for the next week, then checked out my register, and everything was balanced for a change. I hated spending time looking for a few dollars. I left two hundred dollars in the register drawer for Saturday's cashier. The balance was locked in the safe, and I headed home for a Friday night alone. All that was on my mind was a gin and tonic with two limes and putting up my tired feet.

I headed to my car and saw Bob leaning against the trunk. He said, "Angel, where are we going?"

I replied, "Home for a gin and tonic."

He said, "Do you have a rum and Coke?"

I answered, "With or without lime?"

He helped me put down the car top and snap the boot cover. We drove to my apartment. There wasn't any conversation. It was a beautiful and sunny afternoon as I entered the freeway. The wind caused my hairpins to come loose. I held my hair to the side with my left hand to keep it from blowing into my eyes. After exiting the freeway and coming to a stop, I looked into Bob's green eyes, and he looked into my blue eyes. From that moment on, we were lost in each other, and I knew in that moment, my life would be changed forever.

I parked in my open-covered garage, then went up the wooden stairs to my safe haven. This was my space that I had not shared with many people. It was small because I didn't need a lot to move back to Kentucky or Ohio. I had never planned to stay in California forever. My apartment included books, music, family photos, and framed prints. I had no expensive paintings, but one day, I dreamed of buying art that I loved. Boston ferns sat on three white pedestals. I couldn't be in Kentucky to feel the green forest, see wildflowers, and hear running water, but I did my best to recreate those feelings in my apartment. Everything was white and green. What was Bob thinking?

I put on violin music, which filled the room. I wanted to be Bob's Scheherazade and weave a story that would keep him curious for a thousand and one nights. We shared a drink and made small talk for some time. Then I excused myself and went through my closet and into the shower. The shower curtain was pulled partially open, and Bob entered the shower. What was a woman to do? I said, "Would you like to wash my back?" Any control I might have thought I had was lost at that moment.

Bob dried my back, but I couldn't turn around and let him see me. I have always been shy. He took my shoulders in his big hands and turned me toward him. At that moment, I wished all the women I loved could have seen what I was seeing. My head was facing the most hair I had ever seen on a man's chest. His shoulders must have been forty-two inches over a thirty-inch waist-line. He gently kissed me with his soft lips, but the gentleness didn't last long. Quickly, too quickly, everything got very hard. He gently put me on my bed. We were still wet from the shower. For a moment, I thought about my green silk bedspread and how much I had paid for it but not for too long. At a certain moment, I lost all outside thoughts, and there was no one in the world but Bob and me.

Later, both of us were shocked by what our two bodies could do together. Bob would write to me several years later and say, "Angel, we were just two kids who didn't have a great start in life, but we created the most beautiful love together." He left the next day with a promise to return soon. I wasn't too worried because I knew he would. We had started something that was like a drug for both of us. In the meantime, I would go on as usual with my work. It amazed me to know so much about him, and yet I knew so very little. Was he married? Did he have children? How could I find him again? I wouldn't look for him because he knew how to find me.

I was the great-great-granddaughter of Mary Goodin, the great-grand-daughter of Polly Jones, the granddaughter of Mary Liz Jones North, and the daughter of Janie North Fuson. Before these women were my Cherokee ancestors, with some English and Scots Irish too. My courage came from these women, and when things went wrong, I turned to nature and these women for help. They have been there to help me, and I have a strong belief in angels. Men came to us; we didn't chase them.

It had been a month since Bob had left me after a night of lovemaking that touched my soul. When the door opened at work, I looked for him. I had started a gradual separation from Ken. He was dating other people, and I hoped for a friendship. He called me and invited me to dinner. I desperately wanted to stay close to him, but I had doubts.

When I left for Ken's, I had mixed emotions. The evening was progressing nicely, but he was getting very angry. He wanted to argue with me. We went to the bedroom, but for some unknown reason, he wanted to go to the guest bedroom. I thought, *If he gets really pushy for sex, I'll go through the motions to avoid a bad situation.*

He started raging and said, "Mama, I gave you unconditional love, I loved you for who you are, and I still love you. Why can't you give me the same?" He wanted an open relationship. This was a new concept for me, and I had to say no. He became enraged and held me down on the bed. I didn't know he had his pistol nearby. He kept holding me down and crying as he put the pistol to my temple.

I had never been so frightened in my life. I flashed back to my mother's last few minutes. Had she known the bullets were coming? What were her last words and thoughts? I was crying, and I said, "Ken, please don't kill me. I don't want to die like my mother. Please don't do this to me."

Ken was sobbing as he put the gun down beside the bed. I just put my arms around him, and we held each other and cried together. I felt some responsibility for this out-of-control situation. Maybe I had given him unrealistic expectations that we would have a future together.

Chapter 16

I was numb for days about the incident with Ken. I still joined him for breakfast. He would come by my apartment to see if I needed anything. He would take my car home with him, leave his car for me, and do general maintenance. We both knew things would never be as they'd been before. I had started to seriously look at myself and whom I let into my life. Trying to let go of the past and focus on the future, I made plans to return to Cincinnati. Home was calling to me, and I started planning to leave my beautiful apartment. It had been the first place that was mine—wonderful California and my ocean.

It was April, and I promised myself this would be my last birthday in California. On April 8, just two days away, I would be twenty-six years old. I arrived at work to find a bar full of men. I received lots of long-distance calls from friends and family, but my grandmother's call pleased me most.

I had a dental appointment in the morning and came to work at lunchtime. There was Bob and his friends having a great time. He came to me quickly and asked how I had been since he'd last seen me. I didn't want to talk because my mouth was still numb. He mistook that as a rejection and went back to the bar. I had never chased a man in my life, and now wasn't the time to break my rule. I would never call to check on someone or try to find him. That wasn't my style.

Bob paid the bar and food bill and left with his friends. He walked by the hostess desk and winked at me. I checked out his hips and remembered what they felt like in my hands. Tight was the word that came to my mind. I have always liked butts.

I went to bed the night of the seventh and thought about my birthday the next day. Ken had asked me to dinner, but I had lied and said I had other plans. The day would be free because I had asked my boss for the day off. I had learned early in life that it is okay to be alone. I didn't have the mountains, but I had the ocean. I packed my car by 7:00 a.m. The morning air felt great with the top down. I loved the drive to Santa Cruz. It felt good as I drove through the area with all the trees. So cool and calm, it soothed my soul. The ocean was near; I could smell it. My heart rate went up as the sign came in sight to turn north onto Route 1. Ken was right; there is lots of sunshine and happiness in California.

I could never pack lightly. Friends and family had complained about my overpacking for years. The front seat of my little MGB was full. It took two trips to carry everything down to my favorite spot. No one was there. It was going to be a good day. After I put the windscreen in place, I ate lunch in a cool spot with books and magazines spread out on my beach blanket. I settled in for a nice day in the sun. My white bikini still looked nice, but my little tummy would never go away. On my back, I could see my hip bones, and my stomach was concave then. I thought, Not a bad body for a twenty-six-year-old woman who was having a birthday today.

The day was over too soon. It was time to leave for home, though California wasn't my real home. The Safeway store was a good place to buy a bottle of Robert Mondavi red wine and something quick for the oven.

During the night, I was awakened by many knocks on my door. I picked up my Ruger pistol and went to the door. I asked, "Who's there?"

It was Bob, and he said, "Angel, let me in." I pulled the door open with my pistol in my hand to a drunken and shocked Robert. "What do you want at two a.m.?" I asked.

"I want you," he said.

I invited him in because I knew in his present condition, he would never take no for an answer. There wasn't any rum or Coke in my apartment, but I had half a bottle of wine left from my dinner. We sat at my little bar and finished the wine. I thought this might end up being a birthday to remember.

A little voice told me not to let Bob drink too much. His hands were wonderful, big with wide fingers and wide nails. When I met his children, I noticed his beautiful daughter had her father's nails. His hands weren't soft, but I could feel the calluses as he took my T-shirt off over my head. I could tell a lot about him from his hands. He worked with his hands, and I noticed his nails were clean. His lips were soft but not too soft. They didn't say a lot in words, but touch told me what I needed to know. He started to unbutton his shirt slowly. I put my hands on his big, hard shoulders and kissed the hair on his chest at the same time. He had his fingers in my hair and put pressure on both sides of my head. Then he kissed every spot on my face. There was a rush to get our bodies together. I was already nude because I liked to sleep in a T-shirt with no panties.

Bob said, "Angel, I tried to stay away from you."

As two bodies melted into one, I thought about letting go and really loving someone for the first time. My mind told me to be careful. This was a man in my bed and arms.

When I opened my eyes, he was gone. I jumped out of bed and went to make coffee. On my bar was a note that said, *"Angel, I had to go to Hawaii to finish a contract. Love, Bob."* Later, I received a postcard from Hawaii. I still have it.

I didn't know how to find Bob. If I had, I would not have called. I had my job and the ocean until he showed up again. He would return to me, and I would ask more questions next time. Who was this man who had invaded my life and mind? Maybe I could go out to where he had his helicopter. No! I wouldn't break my rule. Let him come to me. My way would work if I were patient.

Chapter 17

I had always called home to check on everyone, especially my grandmother. All my grandmother wanted was for me, her favorite grandchild, to come home to Kentucky. She wanted to give me some land in the upper field by her house. She would say, "We will buy a car, and you can drive me." Of course, my grandmother wanted short trips. Long trips for her would have been within the state of Kentucky. She said, "Jo Ann, all your folks are here."

My grandmother was an herbalist and a deliverer of many babies, including me, before the doctor arrived. She couldn't read or write, but she was the matriarch of our family. She was very proud that she could sign her name and keep up with her money. No one could cheat her out of one penny, and she would mention that often.

One of my favorite stories was about a day in town with my grandmother. We had stopped to talk with an old couple she had known for years. This was my first time meeting them. The old man hugged Mammie with a warm greeting. The wife said, "I've wondered for years about you."

My grandmother said, "Well, honey, if he hasn't told you by now, we'll just leave it in the past."

What could the woman say after that answer? We walked on, and my grandmother and I never mentioned it again.

While still in California, I called to check up on my friend, Bob Madon, the mayor of Pineville, my hometown, who had mentioned he had a friend named Eddie who lived in Nevada. Bob thought I should go up to Lake Tahoe to meet him. His family had a car dealership there. I made my reservations and went to Tahoe. What an unexpected pleasure. Eddie was so happy to meet me. He had many friends and connections. Eddie arranged VIP treatment for me to see Frank Sinatra at the Sahara. I could put my hand on the stage. I thought if he would only sing "Send in the Clowns," he would do it just for me. And then he did, and I was thrilled!

Eddie's wife, Diana, had a couple of friends who were Romani. They made jewelry, and I had them design a gold pinkie ring that I've worn many times over the last fifty years. It has remained my second favorite piece of jewelry.

Diana and Eddie are dear friends to this day. Eddie has had many problems from his Vietnam days. I think a lot was caused by his exposure to Agent Orange.

After returning home one day from work, after my trip to Tahoe, I heard a knock on my door. Who should be there, but Bob Rackstraw, with a television in his arms. I guess he must have noticed on his last visit that I didn't have a TV. Those were the days when Walter Cronkite was king of the news. I wasn't a serious news follower then, and I could trust the people in power would make good decisions for Americans. I had decided not to buy a TV and to enjoy my books, music, and magazines. How could I be mad at Bob? It had been just four months since his birthday visit. Under his arm was also a cheap bottle of Boone's Farm wine. What was a woman to do but let him in out of the heat and humidity?

Bob stayed for three days. He would take me to work and pick me up in the parking lot. The second day was a Friday. I was free on Saturday, and we planned an outing together as we ate carryout pizza and watched my new TV. Slowly Bob started to talk about himself. He was a real war hero with a construction company and three children by his ex-wife. I felt there was something he wasn't sharing, but I didn't press him to tell me his life story. I certainly wasn't ready to discuss my whole life in three days. One should keep some mystery in a relationship. My grandmother had told me, "A woman doesn't have to tell everything she knows. You should have some money that no one knows about hidden away." I will never forget that good advice.

Our time together was over quickly. It had been the stuff that dreams are made of, things that a woman will remember when old and in a rocking chair. My friend Eva once said, "We will have lots of rocking chair memories for the front porch to talk about when we are old." I was sure that once a woman had known a man like Bob, he would affect her whole life and relationships with other men. My fence-riding days were over. I would jump over to the other side and try loving someone with no holding back my love and my feelings. I hoped my psychologist's advice was right. This was unchartered territory, and I was scared. If only Mom could have lived. I needed my mother.

Bob had my phone number and knew where I worked. Now and then, he checked in but would only say he was traveling. One day when I left work, I saw his truck beside my car. "Do you know a place where I can spend the night?" he asked in a very weary voice. There was something wrong, and I could feel it in my stomach. That old feeling was back, and I was worried.

"Sure. I have room for you in my bed" was all I said as I opened my car door. I went up the steps, and Bob followed me.

When I opened my apartment door, I looked closely at him for the first time. The right side of his face was a mess. He had been in a fight or something worse. There was something wrong with his shoulder. I could tell from his face he was in a lot of pain. I helped him remove his shirt and get to the bed. I asked, "Robert, what is wrong with your shoulder? Why do you have a bandage on it?"

He said, "I've been shot."

"What are you telling me? I want to know right now."

He said, "I was doing other work, working undercover in Los Angeles, and I got shot, but I'm okay."

There wasn't much else to do but try to take care of him. I knew I would get no more information out of him until he was ready to talk.

During the next week, he recovered with my good care. I took a couple of days off, and we went for long rides in my car. Much of our time together, we talked about our mothers. Bob was the product of a WWII romance. His parents were very different from each other, but not so different that they couldn't make a son together. Bob told me his mother, Lucille, wasn't sophisticated enough for his father, a WWII pilot. He eventually took off and left Lucille alone with two small children. She worked as a waitress and eventually had a bad relationship with a construction worker and truck driver named Phil. Bob loved his mother but had an intense dislike for his stepfather. He had been abused by Phil's trucker drinking friends. Bob and I had had similar experiences, but Bob still had his mother, and Phil and Lucille were still together.

I missed Bob after he left, but I was ready to have my space to myself again. I went back to my usual routine. My work and trips to the beach filled my life. I didn't have any California lady friends. I hadn't planned that; it just happened. When I needed a woman's advice, I called my sister Pauline in Louisiana and my dear friends Judy in Cincinnati and Eva who was still in Columbus with her two children. Dear friend Marian was always there to listen and give sound advice. Such is life!

Chapter 18

That fall, I called my grandmother on October 9 to wish her a happy birthday. I was so pleased to talk with her. Mammie had never had a phone. Whenever she called me, she'd walk up the hill to my uncle Ned's house, and his family would place the call for her. Uncle Ned, Mammie's son, had worked in the coal mines and had been injured; to what degree I never knew. He always dressed smartly while sitting on his front porch with a flyswatter he used on anything flying or crawling nearby. He also liked to dance, whatever the occasion. In the neighborhood, however, Ned was most famous for walking up behind his house every New Year's Eve and setting off a charge of dynamite. Others stepped outside and fired their pistols, but Uncle Ned topped them all!

Every time Mammie called, I was so touched by this expression of love, I cried with joy and wanted to be home. Before long, however, my grandmother was living with my aunt Della, my mother's only sister. Mammie could no longer take care of herself as she was now eighty-five years old. She had once said, "As long as I can scoot my feet on my floor, I'll stay in my own house." But she couldn't stay there any longer. I decided to go home to Kentucky to see about her. That night at work, I asked my boss for a couple of weeks off. He agreed and wished me safe travels.

Robert was out of town, so Ken took me to San Francisco to get the flight to Cincinnati. I called everyone with my flight information. My friend Dick had always said he would be there for me, and he agreed to meet me at the airport. Dick had been a close but platonic friend since I was nineteen years old. We met at a bowling alley and that was a beginning of a wonderful friendship.

As a successful Cincinnati real estate professional and a mason, Dick was scrupulous about always being courteous and eager to listen. He would check on my mother and brothers to make sure they were okay and had what they needed. My family thought the world of Dick, and I'm sure he had a crush on me. But he was never someone with whom I could have a romantic relationship.

The flight was good, and Dick was there as I entered the terminal. He took me to the Avis counter and insisted on paying for my car rental. We went for a drink and lunch at the Quality Court Motel. This has always been one of my favorite restaurants. The restaurant was on the top floor and revolved, offering a magnificent 360-degree view of Cincinnati and Northern Kentucky. The food was always great. We ate quickly, and as soon as I finished, I headed south on Interstate 75 to get home as soon as I could.

As the Cincinnati skyline receded in my rearview mirror, I thought back to my first view of the city with George, my first husband. My mother was no longer alive. God, why me? I wanted parents like other people. I just wanted my mother. I checked myself in the mirror and wondered how my life had reached this point.

The excitement was building as I got closer to home, and my hands were wet on the steering wheel. My hands always perspired when I got nervous. The curved mountain road would be my next turn. My aunt's house was five miles away, and there have always been horrific accidents on this road. My dad and a cousin died on this road. As I came over the hill, my aunt's grocery store and house came into view. I parked by the chain-link fence. This was like home for me. My hollow was just about ten miles from her house.

When I entered the house, my grandmother was sitting on the sofa. She had on a bibbed apron that I remembered from years back, with an ashtray, her snuffbox, and cigarettes in her lap. She had started smoking in her sixties and had a way of lacing a cigarette through three fingers. I don't think she ever inhaled. I gave her a soft kiss on her cheeks. There was such a look of love in her blue eyes. Mammie said, "I love you so good," and I said, "I love you so good." These words were just for the two of us. I never used those words with anyone else until years later with my daughter.

Aunt Della came from the kitchen and gave me a big hug. She treated me like one of her four daughters, and we became especially close after my mother's death. She was comforting and reassuring just to be around. I was proud of her forty-nine-year record serving as an election volunteer. Handling her country store, election work, and church treasurer position while still helping her husband, my uncle Porter, with his bootlegging business, Aunt Della was someone uniquely special in the community.

My timing was perfect as dinner was almost ready. When I raised the lids, I saw that the pots were full of chicken and dumplings. A pan of cornbread was in the oven. Green beans with potatoes cooked in them were the vegetables. On the other burner was another kettle full of blackberry dumplings. There was no doubt in my mind. I was home, and this wasn't a dream.

There were many family members to see in the next two weeks. There was music, dancing, and lots of storytelling. Of course, there was lots of laughter, hugs, and kisses. My family was very affectionate. Until I left these mountains, I thought this was the way most people behaved. At one point, Mammie asked Aunt Della's son Fred, my cousin, to help her up so she could dance. She could only move her hips a little, but everyone was pleased with her effort.

I was disappointed because I didn't get to sleep with Mammie. My aunt had put a hospital bed in her own room for her mother. Mammie could reach out and touch her during the night. I had slept in my grandmother's feather bed hundreds of times. Uncle Porter didn't mind his mother-in-law being in the room with them. Through the years, other aunts had stayed with them until they died. We took care of our old people. That was our culture.

The next morning, I could smell breakfast cooking in the kitchen. I was staying in one of the upstairs bedrooms. I dressed and got in line for the bathroom. The rule had always been to comb our hair and wash our faces before going to the table.

My grandmother made an announcement at breakfast. She looked at me and said, "Jo Ann, I'm going home today, and I want you to take me."

Aunt Della was quick to say, "Mom, you're too sick, and your house doesn't have a bathroom."

Mammie said, "You hear me, Della, and listen carefully. I'm going home today. Pack my grip." That was her word for tote.

I wanted to see my home, my uncles, my aunts, and Uncle Bill, so I said, "Aunt Della, with your permission, I will take Mammie home for a visit, and I'll take care of her to the best of my ability."

We left for Greenbriar Hollow, where I had grown up, as soon as we could pack.

I watched my grandmother's beautiful old face as we turned up the hollow. There were no emotional outbreaks, but that didn't surprise me. She could be gentle, but she could also be as hard as nails. I remembered a conversation when Mammie said that when she was young, everyone was mean and carried a gun. "Jo," she said, "if you thought you were mean, your neighbor was just as mean."

Brothers fought to kill each other. Mammie's father was shot in his front yard by a man as he put out his hand to shake and settle a feud. My great-grandfather made his way to the porch, sat on the side with his feet on the grass, and said, "Cal, don't shoot me again. You've already killed me."

Mammie was nine years old at the time. She told me, "Jo Ann, you may be a strong woman, and I'm not saying you aren't, but back then, you had to be strong to survive. Life was very hard. Those weren't the good old days. These are the good old days."

This whole story of the shooting is on microfiche at the library in Pineville, Kentucky. There were no executions by electric chair in Kentucky until 1913, only hangings before then. I know the man named Cal Miracle, who killed my great-grandfather, Matthew Jones, was one of the first to be electrocuted in our state.

When we arrived at Mammie's house, I pulled up to the walkway, got out, and went around to open her door. I had to pull her up because she was very weak. With the help of Uncle AY, who had been living in the house, I did manage to get her up the wooden walkway on the back porch and into her kitchen. We put her in her rocking chair and got her ashtray, cigarettes, snuff, and lighter. Then we saw a very big smile, but she spoke no words.

We stayed for four days and slept together in Mammie's feather bed. We shared talks about my life in California and what she was feeling now. I asked, "What do you think about when you're in that small bedroom at Aunt Della's with your back to the door and facing the wall? People say that you're hurt because your son Bill [another uncle] doesn't come to see you very much."

Mammie said, "It doesn't matter anymore. My mind isn't in the present. It goes way back, back to your grandfather when we were young and the kids were small. I see my grandmother who raised me, and my mother, father, and all my brothers and sisters who have died. All my girlfriends are gone. All my aunts and uncles. Everyone is gone but me. If you live long enough, you see everyone leave you. That was a lot of hurt, but nothing hurt me like losing your mother."

I asked her who she had loved. There was a long silence before she answered. "Well, I loved your grandfather well enough to live with him until his death. I had his six children and was good to him. He was my second husband. My first husband was my great love. His name was Murph. We had only two years together and one child, your uncle Ned." She added, "I can remember standing in the back kitchen door and looking down the hollow for Murph. I could make out a small spot and watch until it got bigger and bigger. Then I could tell it was a person as he got closer and closer to home."

"What happened to him?" I asked.

Mammie said, "He played baseball one day, got a fever, and died!"

Mammie looked at the Big Ben clock on her stand table and told me it was time to go to sleep. I scooted up close to my grandmother's back and put my feet next to hers. I wonder what happened to the old clock. Her feet were always cold because of poor circulation. I remembered an earlier time when I was so small, I couldn't touch her feet. For a moment before sleep came, I was seven years old and sleeping again with my grandmother.

The next three days were very busy. Many people came to see Mammie, and all were pleased to see us both. They stopped on the road to talk or came on the porch to visit. A few Mammie knew and liked were invited inside. They all respectfully asked her how she was doing and reminisced a bit before leaving. These were country people, dressed nicely, pleased to know Mammie had returned to see her home again but aware she couldn't stay for a long time. I hollered from one porch to the other for my brother to come for a visit. He came through the field with his coffee cup in hand and a face full of joy at seeing Mammie back in the house that contained so many memories.

One person in particular who visited and stands out in my memory was Uncle Cal Lawson. He had been married to Mammie's sister Maude. He was ninety-two and very wise about weather patterns. Cal and Maude had been Mammie's neighbors for years. After Aunt Maude's death, Uncle Cal made an unexpected visit to his sister-n-law and said, "Mary, I think I should move in with you." He was chewing tobacco and spit on her hearth in front of the grate where she built fires. My grandmother, who didn't take nonsense, got her straw broom and drove him out of the house. How dare he insult her! Aunt Maude was the last of Mammie's brothers and sisters to die.

On the second day of our visit, a big, long black Lincoln pulled in front of the house. It was a neighbor and old boyfriend of mine. K.T. as slender with very black hair, and some women would say he was handsome. When we were younger, there had been some serious love play between us, but nothing happened. Mommy thought he was too rough, with a bad reputation for fighting and driving too fast. KT told me he was a very successful builder with a contract to build many restaurants for a famous chain across the US. He had married a school friend of mine who, like me, had been a cheerleader. He visited with us for a couple of hours. Then he hugged and kissed my grandmother and said, "Aunt Mary, it was great having you home again." I walked him out to his car. He told me we should have married because we shared the same culture and religion.

On the fourth day, it was time for us to leave. It had been a wonderful visit for Mammie and me. I took the rocking chairs out on the front porch. We sat and enjoyed once more the sight and sounds, catching the early morning sun as it crossed the mountain ridges.

No one in the whole hollow had a flower garden like my grandmother's, and Uncle AY had done a good job of maintaining it. It was an old-fashioned garden with some raised beds of daisies, poppies, mums, bachelor buttons, and hollyhocks. No Miracle Grow or plants from a nursery here. Mammie used a small hand sickle that she called a reaping hook, and nearby was an old push lawnmower. The bright varieties of flowers plus the old purple roses my grandfather had planted forty years before warmed my soul.

I went inside to finish the breakfast dishes and do the packing. Then I left my grandmother to her thoughts as I walked through the field to the old house where I grew up. Brother Alvie lived there now. I looked up on the mountainside to see if the old oak was still standing, and it was. It was a landmark in my hollow where I was born, a place where people stopped to rest when walking over two ridges at Pine Mountain to get to Aunt Della's country store. People walked because the roads were so bad; only a few people had cars, and the distance was shorter. Food was carried across the mountain along with jars of moonshine. The oak tree was also a hiding place for a few pint bottles of moonshine available to those making the walk. Drinks were taken on the honor system, mostly by family members.

Uncle Joe, Uncle Ned, and Uncle AY helped their mother to the car. Brother Alvie was waiting at the end of the lane to kiss and hug us. He is such a gentle soul, too gentle, like our mother. He gave each of us a small, abstract wood carving. I kept looking over to see signs of tears or emotions on my grandmother's face, but there were none. She didn't cry or look back. Aunt Della would later tell me that her mother never asked to go home again. I was so pleased with myself for giving this visit to a dear soul.

The yard was full of cars for our arrival back at Aunt Della's. There must have been seventy people in the store, yard, and house, most related to me and all happy to greet Mammie as we helped her into the house. When all the hugs and greetings and a few hard-to-hide tears were finished, I went across the yard to the store. The store was one of my childhood special memories. About ten customers were there to just hang out, others had come for food, and some had come to buy moonshine and beer. We lived in a dry county, and it was illegal for Uncle Porter to sell moonshine and beer. He had to be very careful because the sheriff's men were always around and, in the mountains, looking for stills. They had undercover people trying to catch people by selling to them. You had to know your customers very well. Nothing was ever sold to a stranger.

I helped in the store while my aunt Della got her mother settled. Some customers wanted baloney sandwiches. I made them to order and wrapped them in wax paper. Whiskey, moonshine, and beer were ordered to go. No one could hang around and drink in the store. This had been the rule for as long as I could remember, first because one of the customers could be an undercover agent, and second because some customers were very religious and would be offended or, even worse, turn my uncle in to the sheriff's office. When I made a sale, the money was put into a wooden drawer built into the counter. My aunt had never gotten a cash register. At the end of the day, the money was put into a cigar box. Aunt Della used the end of the kitchen table to separate the tax money from the store money and kept her money separate from Uncle Porter's.

The last ten days had gone by quickly. The day before I left, I went to look in on Mammie, who had gone to the bedroom to take a rest. I said, "What are you thinking about?"

She answered, "My death."

I was upset and said, "I don't want you to die. I'm not strong enough. You can't leave me."

"Now, Jo Ann," she said, "you have to be strong and face facts. I'm going to die soon!"

I started crying, but I saw just one tear slide down my sweet grandmother's cheek. I put my head on her stomach below her left breast and held her hand. When she was asleep, I left the room and went upstairs to finish packing. I loved my mountain family and my heritage. No matter where I was in the world, I didn't want to be away from home for too long.

After a while, I joined Uncle Porter on the side porch swing. He said, "Jo Ann, your aunt Della doesn't want to have sex anymore."

I said, "I don't know what to say."

Then he said, "I don't understand. She doesn't have to worry about getting pregnant anymore!"

I didn't know if he was pulling my leg, but his demeanor never changed, and he didn't smile. After he died, I told Aunt Della about the conversation. She laughed and said, "Oh, he aggravated me but couldn't do anything because of that old blood pressure medicine."

The thought of leaving my family, especially Mammie, was hard. Before departing, I walked across the road to one of my favorite spots in the woods. Twenty years ago, I had gone to this place to calm myself and be alone after my father's death. It was so cool from the flow of the cold mountain water. I picked up some dry pine needles, broke a small branch from a nearby pine tree, and rubbed it in between my hands to smell. I took off my shoes and walked on the slippery moss-covered rocks underneath the running water. How many times as a child had I been told not to do this because I could fall and hurt myself badly? There had been lots of bloody knees. It was a challenge to test fate. Sometimes, I had won, and other times, I had lost. But as Eva would always say, "You'll be all right."

The next morning, I left for Cincinnati but first took the winding mountain road to Pineville and made the circle around the courthouse to check out my hometown. Lots of small shops still bustled with business. Our regional hospital was operating, as well as two banks and a couple of pharmacies. Not bad when you think about it for a small town of about two thousand with two traffic lights. Pineville, however, was bigger in my memory. Was that because I had been smaller? Maybe it was smaller now because lots of people had to go north to bigger cities to find employment. Many of my friends had gone to Cincinnati, Lima, and Dayton, Ohio. Detroit, Michigan, was the destination for those wanting to work in factories for the large carmakers.

I got onto Interstate 75 and headed north as I had done so many times in my life. The tears came, and I wiped them away as I drove. *Mom, where are you? Do you see me? Do you know about my life? Are you somewhere out there watching me?* There were so many questions and no answers. When will I have that satisfied mind my mother always talked about? A few years later, I bought a wooden sculpture from an artist friend, Doris Munson. When I looked at the abstract wood carving with a woman's head tilted back and her eyes closed, she gave me a feeling of a woman with a satisfied mind. Doris's sculptures have traveled the world with me. They were prominently displayed in all our homes later in our lives after we began our diplomatic travels. They bring calm in a sometimes-restless world. I'm the proud owner of three Doris Munson sculptures.

Once again, I saw all the beautiful horse farms and their large barns. The huge homes would be impossible to keep clean without lots of help. I always wondered about the women who lived in them. Were they in love with their husbands? I didn't know then that in the future there would be many big homes overseas with large staff for me to manage. I kept driving until Cincinnati came into view. Seeing the Cincinnati skyline was still just as exciting as my first time. I called Judy to meet me when I got into town, and we spent a quiet night together before my early flight to San Francisco. I was headed back to California with all its sunshine and happiness.

Chapter 19

When my flight arrived, Ken was waiting for me and looked perfectly groomed. At that time, you could meet people at the gate. Times have changed.

I wanted to go to my safe haven. I was so excited to be back in Santa Clara. Everything was just as I had left it. Ken had kept my plants alive. He was born and raised in California, and, like his father, had served in the navy. California had everything he needed. I had previously asked him to go home to Kentucky for a visit with me, but he had no interest.

Robert was different. I asked him to go home to Kentucky with me, and he did. We hiked in the mountains with Uncle Joe and brother Jim. Bob loved photography and took some beautiful photos of butterflies—so macho and yet so sensitive. We rented a plane and went flying with Jim and his wife, Tina. They had never had the opportunity to see our hollow from the air. Bob helped Uncle AY build a storage building for his winter coal. He even went hunting with Jack, Eva's husband. I was told he shot three squirrels.

The most important person to meet was my grandmother, and her approval was very important to me. Bob got down on his knees to be eye level with her. Mammie was sitting in the corner of Aunt Della's couch. Her legs were very weak. She studied him for a while, then said, "I like the look of you." That was all I needed to hear. I would be loyal to Bob through thick and thin, as the saying goes.

One of favorite customers that came to the bar and who was very close to me in California was originally from Kentucky. Johnny had three wives who had left him. He had been a hobo and loved betting the horses. If he won, he would come through the door saying, "Angel, I won. Rowdy-dow, how sweet it is." Through the years, I have used his words. I became his family. I never knew where he lived. For his birthday, I had a cake baked with a horse running on the top. We had a cake-cutting on the bar top. One day, I told him I was going to get a tattoo. He said, "Oh no, Angel, you'll be marked for life."

Soon after I returned from Kentucky, lo and behold Bob Rackstraw, my knight, returned, not in shining armor but jeans and a T-shirt. We went to my apartment and locked out the world. That was the way we lived for many months, even when I moved in with him. Yes, I gave up my beautiful apartment for Bob. The commute was getting too much for both of us.

One day, Bob came with a truck and two guys who worked for him and moved me to the mountains in Valley Springs, California. Of course, I went, with my king-size waterbed, clothes, rocking chair, and plants. Bob had bought an A-frame and put it in my name. He was very, very good to me. I felt loved and protected. I said, "We don't need four bedrooms." He would arrive with a load of lumber, put on his nail apron, and go to work. I asked for a deck to be built around a tree, and it happened. I made a comment about my memories of my father's Jeep. I had seen a pink Jeep somewhere, and I told Bob it looked sharp. Next thing I knew, he pulled into the driveway pulling an old CJ-5 Jeep for me, and he'd had it painted pink! We enjoyed driving the Jeep, and we got some looks. It wasn't the image for a man who looked like Robert. He didn't care.

I missed my restaurant job and my favorite customers, but I loved living and working together with Bob on construction projects. We would bid on a job, and when we got the contract, it was a lot of work. One that comes to mind was an Army Corps of Engineers project. Bob had to extend a boat launch ramp because the water level had gone too far down. We also built two houses, but not with a good ending because there was a shortage of R19 insulation. We couldn't meet the contract deadline and lost money on that job. We had some wins and some losses, but I was having fun, and there was lots of laughter. When we made a profit, life was good. Robert would rent a plane and fly us to Tahoe. We'd see some shows but didn't gamble. It was about the music and who was performing.

Chapter 20

During these times, Bob got a logbook to start teaching me how to fly and record my progress. He was an instructor in fixed-wing and rotary aircraft. I had only a few lessons but never had the chance to do takeoffs and landings or solo, as we were busy with other projects.

We would take the pickup to Stockton and buy supplies for our jobs. The drive was about an hour. During these drives, Bob would sing to me. He had a beautiful voice. He knew I was a serious Elvis fan and sang lots of Elvis songs to me. I loved riding along with him. We were partners. I paid the workers, checked on how things were going on job sites, and met our workers before they started work, sometimes with Bob's instructions.

Bob and I created a beautiful home together. I thought we were in love and very happy together. During these times, I felt so protected. I had never had that feeling before. At some point in our relationship, Bob told me he'd had a vasectomy. He had three children by his first wife. I had assumed we could have a child together. I was very disappointed.

I remember the first time I met Pam, Bob's first wife, and his beautiful children. I remember driving to Santa Cruz and picking up Robbie, Shelene, and Patrice and taking them home with me. I have photos of those glorious times. We went to the community clubhouse, had train rides, cooked out, and killed snakes, skinning them to put on a board. Shelene was like her dad and wanted a photo taken of a dead snake in the yard.

Difficult days were ahead because Bob's mother, Lucille, had breast cancer. I met her and liked her very much. I went to help her and vacuum her floors. I didn't care for the stepfather because of the things Bob had shared. He wasn't good to Lucille, especially after she had the double breast mastectomy. She had not had reconstruction surgery. Lucille was pretty, and I'm sure she was a beautiful woman when she was younger. She told me her husband wanted no sexual relationship with her after the mastectomy. There were rumors he had a girlfriend. If so, she didn't share that with me.

Bob loved his mother. She was a Jehovah's Witness. Bob didn't share her belief but paid for her trips to Mexico for alternative cancer treatments. But they didn't work. A couple of days before she died, I gave her a bath. Both of us were worn out by the time I got her back to bed from the bathtub.

She hemorrhaged at some point, but Phil, Bob's stepfather, didn't come and get us. Bob was furious with him. Bob's sister, Linda, came to the funeral. I think I had met her once before. It was a very simple service and a quick burial because of no embalming. Bob and his mom had been through rough times together.

Phil just disappeared after Lucille died. Bob told me this was a pattern with him. He would leave them and be gone for months, only to reappear as if nothing had ever happened. He was drinking before Lucille's death and more after she died. I remember an incident when he got into an argument with the telephone answering machine thinking he was talking to a real person. I had also experienced delusional events with my stepfather when he was very drunk. Maybe Phil had gone to Hawaii. Bob said he had done this before.

Robert and I went camping in Yosemite Valley. We hiked Bridalveil, saw El Capitan, and took lots of photos. It was a day to remember and a favorite memory after all these years. Sometimes, I felt guilty because it was too good! I didn't know what was coming just around the bend. We parked our little camper in the big redwoods. We put a blanket on the ground and got on our backs to get a feel for these giant living trees. It felt as if they touched the stars.

How do I write about this next part of my life? I received a call from home. My grandmother had died. I flew to Cincinnati and went home. I called to talk with my sister. Pauline and her husband, Jim, met me in Pineville. Baby brother Bill was there in his navy uniform. Brother Alvie came from Germany and was dressed in his army uniform. I think my brother Jim was already in Kentucky when Mammie died. I have blocked out parts of the event. I must have gone through the funeral. I just can't remember! I do remember lots of love and support from family members and a host of friends and neighbors. I had sat with my grandmother at the service in our family church when Mommy died. Mammie held my hand and said, "Jo, you be strong for me, and I will be strong for you." When Grandmother died, dear sweet Eva was seated with me in our family church. She was strong for me and held my hand in hers.

My Mammie was taken to our family cemetery. No need for a headstone. Years ago, she had bought double stones for my grandfather and herself. When she was older, we managed to get her up the hillside. It was very steep, and she would sit on her headstone and tell us what to do and where to put the flowers on the family graves. Down from her grave, my mother and father had been buried. I would return there too many times through the years. So much pain, hurt, and loss. Thank God, I had Bob at such a difficult time in my life.

I can remember after I moved to live with Bob and he said, "Angel, do you remember the D. B. Cooper story, about the guy who jumped out of the plane? The FBI has been trying to prove I was that man." I didn't really care or think much about it at the time until a couple of years later. We were living in a bubble created by love. On New Year's, we made resolutions and sealed them to be opened the next year. I opened mine later, and it said, "I promise to make Jo Ann Fuson the happiest woman in the world if my past doesn't get in the way."

Why didn't he just let me go and take me back to Sunnyvale, where I could get another job and apartment? I belonged to the bartender's union and could have found a good job. But he loved me too much, and I didn't want to believe he was D. B. Cooper. I would like to think Bob felt the FBI would leave him alone because they didn't have enough evidence. We could keep our bubble of happiness going. He was Robert Wesley Rackstraw. His birth name was Jones.

Bob was a highly decorated Vietnam veteran. I'm sure he was very patriotic before, during, and after the war, but I'm not so sure after he learned the truth about Vietnam. Like a lot of young men, he was angry and disturbed when he understood the lies and politics after the war. I was awakened by his terrible dreams. I am from the Vietnam era, and friends from my hometown were drafted. My first husband, George Brooks, and Eva's husband, Jack, had been drafted. Fifty thousand of my contemporaries are named on the Vietnam War Memorial in Washington, DC. What a loss to my country.

Chapter 21

I once asked Robert, "Have you ever found anything in life that you didn't get bored with?"

He said, "Yes, war, and they stopped it."

I thought, *"What a strange answer."* He was referring to Vietnam. When I went to live with him, I made an office in an extra bedroom. I framed some of his certificates from psychological warfare school; desert, armored, and guerilla warfare training; underwater diving school, where he learned how to plant explosives; and how to make night jumps out of airplanes. These trainings made him a perfect suspect for being D. B. Cooper. In his second tour, he was a helicopter pilot for a General Jones. I share this because of Bob's comment about war. Maybe Bob thought he was the best man for the job in a war zone.

Bob would master anything in a short time and then get bored. When he had an opportunity to go to work for Bell Helicopter to teach Iranians how to fly them, I went with him. This was during the time of the Shah, about a year before the revolution. I later realized I was very, very naive. Before going to Iran, we went on vacation to Hawaii and then to Dallas for a short time. I don't remember much of a briefing from Bell Helicopter officials on how to respect the Iranian culture. We stopped in Tehran for a short time and then went on to Isfahan. This was my first time in a Muslim country.

A young man named John, who worked for Bell Helicopter, helped me find housing, buy furniture, and get my personal effects moved to our new home. I had shipped several trunks. Bob started work immediately, and I had to do everything else. I loved the different culture, buying food, and going to the incredible souk, the central market. Incense, spices, every kind of brass object, and much more abounded. I loved this new experience.

I made new friends, and we all went out together for food. Everyone appeared to be happy with the Shah. Every shop had a photo of the Shah and his wife. However, we were told not to go into a shop where there was a black flag; that meant the people there were opposed to the Shah.

Bob and I went to a bar called the Long Branch Saloon, and alcohol was served. Iranian women were wearing Western clothing and trying to make hamburgers. I didn't know there was unrest below the surface among people who felt their conservative values were being disrespected. I later understood why Ayatollah Khomeini could take over so quickly.

After a few weeks, we had to leave the country as a result of the FBI's search for Bob as part of the continuing D. B. Cooper investigation. We had, as I remember, twenty-four hours to pack. To use an unladylike expression that Robert used often, "the shit hit the fan." That's no exaggeration. The FBI escorted us to the airport, and in Paris, the French police came on board to see if Bob and I were in our seats.

We landed at JFK, and Robert told me to leave the plane before him, go to the baggage claim and get our luggage, and buy a ticket to Kentucky. That didn't work out for me. The FBI got me at the luggage carousel. They took me to see Robert. I didn't understand what was happening. I wasn't wanted for anything, but Bob had been arrested. I didn't know at that point exactly why.

One of the FBI agents took me to LaGuardia Airport. He helped me with my luggage, and I bought a ticket to Knoxville, Tennessee. The Knoxville airport is the nearest one to my home in Pineville.

Judy had returned from Cincinnati to our hometown for family reasons. She had bought a nice mobile home, but she missed her life in the big city. Her home was beautifully decorated, which didn't surprise me since she always liked to have the best for herself and her son, Jason. She always had nice clothes, furniture, and cars, preferably a Mercury. On special occasions, she liked to use Joy perfume.

Like Scarlett in *Gone with the Wind*, I could always go home and stay with Judy wherever she might be! When I walked in, she said, "You know where your bedroom is. Take your luggage down the hall. I'll have a drink ready for you." Bless her heart! There were no cocktail lounges or nice restaurants in Pineville.

Judy's father, Charley, had owned the local taxicab company for many years. Judy had started driving for her father. We were strong women, but she wouldn't be strong forever. Her family never treated her right after she got pregnant with her son. She was married but wasn't happy and came home. With her mother's help, she was a good mother to Jason. He was about five when I arrived in Pineville, and she loved her son. Judy and Eva came from the same hollow. Judy was an outstanding bartender. She liked the best for herself and her son, Jason. She was a great daughter and loved her mother.

Meantime, I had to think about Robert. He was in jail in New York, waiting for extradition to California on charges of shipping explosives through the mail and unlawful flight to avoid prosecution. I sent my lawyer from Pineville, Steve Cawood, who had helped me with some local legal matters, to get him out on bond. I wanted to know what had happened. Steve went to New York and met with Bob. I could make Bob's bond, or so I thought. But a hundred thousand changed to two and half million in a few days following the discovery of Bob's stepfather's body. Steve came back and said, "He is very intelligent but could be the biggest con man I've ever met."

In a very short time, I found out that Bob's stepfather's body had been found in a grave on Bob's mother's and stepfather's property in Calaveras, California. Bob's sister, Linda, had been persistent that something was wrong with her stepfather Phil's disappearance and pressed the authorities for further investigation. Bob was soon thereafter charged with Phil's murder. I was numb and scared for the first time. The other charges seemed minor. They weren't so terrible because he had a permit to buy explosives. They were probably left from the Army Corps of Engineering project, and he just had the caps with no sticks of dynamite. Bob sent them to a friend from his Vietnam days who lived in San Antonio. Phil's disappearance and, as I later learned, his murder changed me forever.

After a few weeks, Bob was extradited to California, and I flew to see him. When I saw Bob in an orange jumpsuit, it broke my heart. He held a yellow legal pad to the window and had written the name D. B. Cooper so no one could hear. He said, "Do you remember what I told you?"

I said, "I remember the talk at the A-frame, and you told me they were holding you because they thought you to be the famous skyjacker. Now you've been arrested for Phil's death." I wasn't interested in the skyjacker story, but I was very concerned about the circumstances of Phil's death.

I would spend months trying to get Bob out of jail. Life became pages and pages of legal pads with things to do and people to contact. Letters from Bob were arriving daily with instructions on who to contact and what to do next. I began hating yellow legal pads. I had no experience to fall back on and was in over my head. I got Bob a famous San Francisco Bay Area attorney. Dennis Roberts had a name for trying famous cases. I sold my house to help with the defense. The lawyer got Bob's Corvette. The gun collection went to his sister, Linda, but I didn't know that until years later. Meanwhile, I had to find money to pay Bob's legal fees.

I loved Bob, and I would not run out on him. I was taught not to abandon someone in trouble. He had no one else to help him. My knight in shining armor had become badly tarnished. Little did I know that more troubles lay ahead. My heart was broken, and I started to question our lives together. Why didn't Bob leave me out of all these past troubles? I wished I could be back in Sunnyvale, in my peaceful apartment.

Dennis and Robert didn't want me in Stockton for the murder trial, so I returned to Pineville. I don't remember how long the trial lasted, but Bob was acquitted. I flew back to California and met our friend Pat. I had met Pat and his first wife several years earlier. I met beautiful Patricia, who became Pat's second wife. He rented a plane, and we flew to Folsom Prison to pick up Bob. Bob and I flew away very happy with our first real contact in a long time. We waggled the wings to say goodbye to Folsom Prison.

We arrived back in Laguna Beach, California. Bob and Pat had prearranged during our time in Iran to buy a beautiful trailer. After all these years, some things are very vivid to me, and some lost to time. I can't remember everything, but sometimes, I remember too much. Bob had promised me a home with an ocean view and had kept his promise. It was in a very nice private park for mobile homes. We owned the structure but not the land. I had seagulls flying over the deck. That was the start of my love of this bird. I bought the book and video of *Jonathan Livingston Seagull*. I have wished many times I could be like Jonathan, but I couldn't fly away from this disaster.

Now Robert and I were back together, living the dream in Laguna, in a small but beautiful space in a trailer park by the ocean. During those fun-filled days, I was very happy. At the laundromat, I met the actress Lillian Bronson, who had played a judge in the *Perry Mason* TV series. She played the grandmother in *Spencer's Mountain* and the Fonz's grandmother in *Happy Days*. We enjoyed sharing sunsets at our rock down by the ocean. We stayed friends until her death some years later. I loved this old, fragile, and exciting woman, who, I thought, was about eighty years old. She was so poised and sophisticated. I still have a postcard from a billboard she appeared on titled "Old Lady of the Freeway." I also have a postcard of her in front of the locks in Lockport, New York, which celebrated Lillian Bronson Day.

At the trailer park, I met another neighbor woman and my nutrition expert, Kory Curtis Hartfield. Kory introduced me to books and lectures about the importance of staying healthy. One book that's remained a favorite is *How to Get Well* by Paavo Airola. It's about good health, vegetarian eating, dry-brush body massage, and more. Both women were older, but I have always had friends of all ages.

One day, when I was jogging on the beach, I was drawn to a woman sitting alone. I stopped and started a conversation with her. That was the day I met dear, sweet Doris, who became a lifelong friend. She had a nice husband. I introduced Craig and Doris to Robert. Everyone liked Bob, especially women. I had new friends, sunshine, and the ocean. Doris was an artist and sculptor of driftwood burrows. She referred to them as redwood burrows. Our friendship has lasted over fifty years.

Bob did some construction jobs with his friend Bill while Pat was working eighteen hours a day, trying to get his own business up and running. I was studying nutrition, and we were eating lots of salads, steamed vegetables, brown rice, and fish. I had Pat, Bob, and myself taking colon cleanses. What fun and laughs with one bathroom. They were good sports to help me with my new interest. God, what a relief after all the trauma since we had left Iran and the horrible mess in Calaveras. I was still in love with Bob.

Later, when I was married to George, my current husband, and we were in DC for training, Bob sent me a card with a butterfly. The card said, "*Poopie* [a nickname], *if you would not have cared so much, I may not have made it. Thank you for being you and caring so much about me. Love, Poop.*"

Chapter 22

Robert was always trying to teach me something new. We had successes and failures, and I remember one particular failure I'll never forget. Bob decided he would teach me how to scuba dive. He got out all the scuba equipment, and we went to the pool where we lived. He put all the gear on me: a wet suit, full oxygen tank, mask, and fins. It all felt awkward at first, but I did well with his instructions, even though I was uncomfortable with clearing water from the mask.

A couple of days later, on a bright, pristine morning, we took the ferry to Catalina Island, a historic Southern California tourist destination. The ferry, with its wooden-bench, open-air seating, had for years run multiple times daily and was a tourist destination in and of itself. The Wrigley family that owned the Chicago Cubs baseball team and produced chewing gum had an estate on the island, which included a private zoo. Cars were not allowed, and most residents motored about in golf carts.

We rented a boat, and off we went scuba diving. I sat on the side of the boat, and when we reached a good spot, I was supposed to fall backward off the boat into the water. Bob helped me dress, checked the tank, and put me in position to go. But when the moment came, I froze and couldn't muster up the courage. Bob tried to explain I was missing another world below the ocean surface. I didn't want to disappoint him, but I couldn't leave the boat. Bob should have taken into consideration that I've been claustrophobic all my life. Later, in DC, I bought a silk screen by a Chinese artist. It made me feel like I was viewing underwater vegetation, but that was as close as I got to experiencing what Bob had described. I learned from my Catalina experience that I'll always be a snorkeler, close to the surface, rather than scuba diving in unknown deep water.

Not too long after that experience, Bob asked if I would be interested in skydiving. It has been a lifelong problem for me that I say yes without all the information I need. We flew from Laguna Beach to Elsinore in Southern California. Robert and I went through a two-day training session. He sat through everything with me and must have been bored or amused because he never mentioned to anyone that he was a qualified parachutist. He'd had thirty-eight combat jumps in Vietnam and some night jumps with full scuba gear. In Valley Springs, Robert showed me some reel-to-reel footage of the sky filled full of men parachuting into Cambodia. This operation was denied by the Nixon administration but later proved to be true and caused a political firestorm.

I gave all this information to Bob's attorney, Dennis Roberts, when the FBI was trying to prove he was D. B. Cooper. I thought all the certificates of training would show Bob to be a patriot who loved his country and served it well. Later, however, his military records would work against him and be used by critics to prove he could indeed have been D. B. Cooper. Bob later said, "Jo Ann, just burn it all." His attorney never gave all the certificates back to me, but I wouldn't have burned them. The years of harassment never stopped until Robert's death on July 9, 2019. He was getting very tired of the harassment and had told me it would only stop after his death.

To get ready for the jump, I learned how to know if I had a low-speed or high-speed malfunction, how to check out the apex, and how to look for the windsock to determine how to face the wind when preparing before hitting the ground. The training sessions were good, and I paid careful attention, but when I stood in the door to jump, I said to myself, *What has Rackstraw gotten me into this time?!* At that moment, I knew, as with so many other times in my life, that I was alone and Robert couldn't save me.

People asked me later what my skydiving experience was like. I told them I didn't have time to think about it. I thought before jumping that I would float along and enjoy the scenery. However, as soon as I left the plane, my mind was calculating about what I had to do to survive and land properly. I didn't float like Jonathan Livingston Seagull. The chute opened properly, I pulled on the toggles to correct my turn, and I got into landing position. I panicked, looking for the windsock, but I found it and landed without breaking anything. I quickly pulled on the lines to collapse the parachute. Another wonderful day with "Poop" in paradise. Those damn names have stuck for many years.

Sometimes, we called each other "Poop" and "Poopie." Those names came from Bob's son Robbie when he was five years old. Bob could never stop creating upset, trauma, and just plain old shit and getting me involved.

Soon Bob was facing another trial for unlawful flight to avoid prosecution, shipping of explosives in the mail, and check-kiting. I didn't know what that meant until much later, but I would find out after the fact when he got into trouble. I knew he was thinking about not going back to face the charges. He understood law enforcement people don't always tell the truth. I was aware of that from personal experience.

Bob said, "Angel, it would be better if Robert Rackstraw just disappeared." He was concerned about going behind bars again on trumped-up charges. He believed the FBI couldn't be trusted. They never let up on the D. B. Cooper case. I didn't know the full extent of Bob's plan. Later, when he returned to Laguna Beach, he told me what he had done.

Bob had gone to Northern California, rented a plane, called in an SOS, threw some clothes and cushions out the window, and made it look like the plane had crashed. He flew under the radar and took the plane to a Podunk airport in Southern California. He sure hadn't thought this through. What a disaster! I was very upset because Pam, Bob's ex-wife, and his children had been notified he was missing. I found out they were very upset. Maybe he thought he would call Pam later. What a terrible thing to do to them.

Bob could no longer use his name or mention his aviation experience or military and work record. He went to a printer to get a new identity. The man became suspicious and called the police. I got a call from Bob that he had been arrested for trying to get a false ID. I called a local attorney to meet me at the jail. I got anxious and went inside, looking for the attorney.

The police immediately took my purse and put me in a cell. Five policemen were talking to me, three local officers and two from Calaveras County. They wanted to know what Bob had done with the plane. I couldn't tell them anything because I didn't know where it was. I remember sliding down a corner in the cell and trying to stay calm. I was sitting on the floor. At a certain point in the interrogation, I started talking about nutrition. I told them about being a vegetarian. The cell door wasn't locked, and I heard one officer tell another that he didn't think I knew anything. Thank God, they believed me.

They brought Robert and me together in a room. To this day, I can't remem-ber if I cried. Bob said he would tell them where the plane was if they would let me go with no charges. I wasn't charged with anything. I went home, got into my waterbed, and had a long, hard overdue cry. From the time I had gone to meet the attorney until getting home, it had been ten hours. Pat, our room-mate in the trailer in Laguna, didn't know where I was because that was before cell phones, and he couldn't contact me.

Robert was sent back to Folsom Prison to await trial. I tried to do what I could for him. I got in touch with Dennis Roberts, his previous attorney. Bob asked me to get into touch with some friends and ask for financial help to pay Dennis.

I flew home to Pineville. I needed my family. I met a man named George Staples on a return flight to California. I was flying out of Knoxville, Tennessee, and dear friend Eva and her children took me to the airport. George told me later that he had seen me enter the terminal. Eva couldn't go to the gate, but she walked me to the security screening point. George said he saw me get stopped by security. The X-ray machine showed something strange in my carry-on luggage. George said he wanted to come back to try to help me. He told me later that I was beautiful and that men sometimes meet lots of pretty women in airports but never get a chance to talk to them. Eva had made blackberry dumplings for me and had put them in a Tupperware container, which looked suspicious on the machine.

George saw me again when I boarded the plane. He later told me he thought, *There she is again.* I came down the aisle and stopped by his seat and said, "Excuse me; I have the window seat." We had a couple of drinks and talked about our grandmothers. His grandmother lived in Knoxville, and Mammie lived across the border in Pineville, which was about eighty miles from Knoxville. We were on the same flight to Dallas, where we transferred to other flights. He was going to San Antonio. He was still in the air force and was a captain. I was on my way to Laguna Beach. He asked for my number, and I gave him Eva's because my life had been turned upside down. Eva was always there for me, and I could be reached through her. God bless Eva! I hope she is cheering me on and telling me to get this memoir finished. She said, "Jo Ann, you were always the smartest. You can write this book." She believed in me.

Bob was taken back to Northern California. I remained in Laguna Beach with my friends and had to tell them about my life with Bob. They knew Bob liked all of them very much.

During those difficult days, an FBI agent working on the D. B. Cooper case came to see me. He wanted information about my knowledge of the case and asked if I had a twenty-dollar bill that could be connected to the skyjacking. I said, "How would I know? Do you have a list of serial numbers?" They were sent to me later, and I didn't realize that a list of two hundred thousand numbers could be quite a stack of paper. I never had any of the money.

The agent and I decided to go for a walk on the beach. He said, "If you were my daughter, I would tell you to get away from this man. We don't have anything on you, but if you stay with Bob, you will eventually get into trouble." This gave me a lot of food for thought. I had already started to have some second thoughts. When I climbed to the top of my very large rock on the beach and looked out at the Pacific Ocean, I thought about the past and all the love and support I had given to this relationship. I was starting to have doubts about our future together.

I could go on and on with this saga of Bob and Jo Ann, but I must move forward. After being convicted of the less serious charges after the second trial, Bob was given three years and served eighteen months. I was there when he was released. Pat rented a plane, and we flew to Folsom to get Bob and go home to Laguna Beach. What a pack rat! The cargo area of the plane was filled with boxes of mostly books and legal paperwork. What a brilliant mind to waste. Why didn't he put that energy into another direction? I think Vietnam was partially to blame. The US government created war machines—men highly trained for combat. But after a war has ended, what do you do with them? This was not true for some soldiers, but Robert couldn't sit behind a desk and be a good boy. He craved the action he got from war. If someone was ready for a fight, he would give it to them. I could tell it in his green eyes. I was a witness twice, and those fights were about me.

Bob and I came to a point where the love was still there but couldn't endure without trust. He had destroyed a beautiful dream, but we had been there once in a special moment. I will not call it Camelot, but rich and powerful people think they have an exclusive on love. That just isn't true. Beautiful love can be felt by people in every walk of life. I have looked for it and have seen it in many acts and gestures by simple folks.

I called my sister, Pauline, and asked her to come to California to help me move out from Bob's place. Robert helped us pack, and we both shed tears. I told him, "Poop, if I ever think I made a mistake, I will come and get you."

He said, "If that time ever comes, I will be waiting."

As Pauline and I drove away, I looked in the right-side mirror and saw Bob standing in the street.

A year later, in 1979, I started a new life and married George Staples, whom I had met on the flight from Knoxville. He likes to call it "the magic plane ride," as we would refer to it for many years. George had tried to find me through Eva. When he first called, I wasn't in any shape to talk with anyone. My wonderful grandmother had died in October. George had cleaned out his briefcase during New Year's and tried calling me again. Eva gave him my number, and we connected. That was the beginning of a new life completely different from what we both expected.

George resigned from the air force, went to work for the Procter and Gamble Company, and relocated to Cincinnati. I was still in Laguna Beach. Later, I moved to Cincinnati and went to work for my old employer Abbot Linen Supply. George bought us a beautiful home, but it was too far from the city.

George had grown up in Los Angeles, California and, after college, had joined the air force and traveled a lot. But the military had changed for him after the Vietnam War, and he no longer felt that he would be able to have a successful military career. After working for two years for Procter and Gamble, he changed jobs to the Federated Department Stores headquarters, also located in Cincinnati. Despite doing well in the private sector, George missed government service.

One Sunday, I was reading the *Cincinnati Enquirer* newspaper. There was an advertisement about taking the Foreign Service Exam in Chicago. I encouraged George to take the entrance exam and seek employment with the State Department. He knew what it was about but not completely. I knew nothing about this life, not even from the movies. But George was recruited immediately because he was needed, had all the security background checks from his air force service, and spoke a foreign language fluently. He had spent a year in Monterey, California, learning Turkish before being assigned to a NATO job in Turkey. George was off language probation as soon as he entered the State Department. Since family members are also assigned overseas and eligible for language training, we still had to spend six months learning Spanish before going to our first assignment, where George would issue visas and report on economic developments of interest to analysts and investors.

So, we went to Washington, DC, on a journey that would take us to places and experiences we could not have imagined. First stop was Spanish language class, then area studies, and a lot of security briefings. Little did we know that the first assignment would be El Salvador in Central America, where a war was going on. What the hell!

Ken Spraggins, the man who talked me into going to California.

Robert (Bob) Rackstraw, on vacation in Kentucky preparing to fly over Pine Mountain.

Getting ready for Bob to show me my hometown from the air.

Bob relaxing on vacation at Yosemite National Park.

Vacationing with Bob in Yosemite.

With Eddie Bates, my friend from Pineville, who arranged for me to see the Frank Sinatra show at Lake Tahoe, California. Here at my home after retirement, Eddie and I are standing in the foyer in front of the American flag presented to me by Secretary of State Condoleezza Rice in recognition of 26 years of government service.

Mammie wearing her beautiful sweater. Content at Aunt Della's after the brief return visit to her home.

My dear friend, Lillian Bronson, enjoying one of many sunsets at our rock in Laguna Beach, California.

My wedding to George Staples at Nellis Air Force Base, Las Vegas, Nevada. George was an active member of the Air Force Reserve before beginning a career as a Foreign Service Officer.

Chapter 23

El Salvador was our first overseas assignment. No dependents were allowed there at the beginning of our assignment because a civil war was in progress and Americans were targeted. After language training, I went home to Pineville until it was determined that it was safe for me to travel to the embassy. Just when I had gotten a nice, comfortable place fixed up behind my uncle Joe's house, I was off and running against the wind once more. As I remember, I was the first US government spouse to be allowed to enter El Salvador who was not employed by the US embassy. Later, other ladies started arriving, some with kids. I never understood that decision, as a civil war was underway.

I arrived in San Salvador, the capital, in the spring of 1982, after George had been there a few months. I remember the drive with George from the airport to our residence. The drive into town felt very tropical, with lots of lush green vegetation outside the window. It was not that different to me from what I had experienced in Hawaii. George told me we were on the airport road where Catholic nuns had been killed a few years earlier. When we arrived at our house, the staff greeted me, food was ready, and my bags were taken to the master bedroom. This was the beginning of having live-in household staff. I learned to love having a cook, housekeeper, and gardener. The residence was very nice, and the house plan was great. We had all-new Drexel furniture. My air freight and surface shipment had arrived earlier.

I got to see my first embassy and meet other Americans and local employees. I also met my first American ambassador, Deane Hinton. I felt as if I had met someone very special, and he made me feel welcome and secure. He would remain my favorite ambassador for several years until I met Ambassador David Ransom, who selected George to be his deputy ambassador in Manama, Bahrain. Back to San Salvador. The embassy was sometimes referred to as Fort

Apache because we had fifty US Marines securing the perimeter to protect us against rocket attacks from communist guerillas. This Kentucky woman didn't fully understand the situation she had gotten herself into. Even after forty years, I still can't get a complete grasp of what happened in El Salvador, part of a lifelong pattern of getting myself involved without all the information.

Sometime after getting settled, we were invited to dinner at Ambassador Hinton's residence. El Salvador is in a volcanic region of Central America. We experienced numerous tremors, even during dinner. From my view in the dining room, I could see the swimming pool's water sloshing around. During one of the many social events at the ambassador's residence, I made a decision for George and me—one of these days, I would be the ambassador's wife and live in a beautiful residence. Of course, everything comes at a price, but I could overlook the dangers of health issues, kidnappings, and earthquakes. I was ready to do the work to get there and could handle the management of dinners, receptions, and other public appearances that would lead to promotions. I had been an assistant restaurant manager, bartender, and salesperson for linen supplies to restaurants, motels, and so on. Plus, I had grown up in Kentucky, and there had been lots of cooking, parties, and cleanup at my family's homes, especially my grandmother's. I loved to entertain and to plan events. My grandmother would say, "It's a scandal to brag about oneself." I shouldn't brag too much.

During those early days as a diplomatic spouse, I thought our foreign policy was made because of communist threats to our country. If countries' presidents were anticommunist, we supported them no matter how corrupt they were. That was our policy in Vietnam and elsewhere. In Central America Area Studies at the Foreign Service Institute, we learned about Nicaragua, its corrupt former president Somoza, and the Sandinista rebels. Nicaragua, like El Salvador, was also at that time experiencing a civil war.

My friend Doris Munson Leverault, originally from Montana, was our only visitor daring enough to come to El Salvador during our eighteen-month assignment. She had also visited me in Kentucky. Doris had at one time been an underwater ballet performer, and later, as I mentioned earlier, she became a talented driftwood sculptor. We Montana and Kentucky girls are friends forever. Her three sculptures I owned traveled with me to all our postings.

Doris and I share many memories before my Foreign Service life, like the time we traveled to Mexico together. I can see her now, sick on the train to

Veracruz, with her head close to the window, as our first-class tickets turned out to be for third class. We were packed into cramped seating with poor people carrying chickens. We had no food and experienced every odor imaginable. Later, after the trip, when I got back to Laguna Beach, I had lice in my hair!

When we returned from Veracruz to Mexico City, I used my American Express card and got us into the plush Gran Hotel. I had asked Doris to stay outside with our backpacks so the hotel staff couldn't tell we had traveled like hippies. We had bubble baths and room service. So much for Doris's idea to see Mexico on twenty dollars a day! I was a five-star, minibar-type woman when I could afford to upgrade. Now I could treat Doris to first-class service when she visited us in San Salvador. We had access to a beautiful beach house, swimming pool, and white sand beach to take walks. I liked to say that if I can't go first class, I'll stay home. I guess that's an exaggeration because our family traveled in economy many times during our early years in the State Department.

I made new friends in El Salvador. There was Rosa, a beautiful woman who owned a restaurant; we shared nice times together at my residence. I hope she made it through the war. I never had news of her life after we left. George and I were also friends with Carlos and Yolanda, who had two beautiful daughters. We went to the beach together. There was black as well as white sand beaches, but not as black as the beach in Cameroon. I had a wonderful friend named Salvador Ananya, a successful coffee grower. I knew him through John and Philicia Collins. John was our administrative officer, and Philicia had permission to work at the embassy. They became great friends, and we have remained close for forty years.

The man named Salvador would become a very important part of my life. He was there for a very special moment. I saw my first Mario Escobar painting at Salvador's home. Salvador had an amazing art collection. I never imagined there would be an opportunity to have an Escobar painting. Salvador called and said he had been visited by Escobar's brother, who wanted to sell two paintings. Salvador came by my residence with the paintings. He said to think about it overnight and make a choice. I chose a beautiful portrait in vibrant orange of a local woman sitting in a simple chair. When I took a closer look, I could see she was pregnant. I became the proud owner of a Mario Escobar painting. I made a friend who loved art, and George got a chess partner. Can't beat that!

Later, Salvador picked me up to go see another artist. He said I shouldn't appear to be connected to the US embassy, as there was a war going on. I wore big sunglasses and a scarf. I was a little concerned because we were leaving the city. We went through a small overgrown path that led us to the artist's home. The name was hard to read, but I loved it.

Both paintings are in my condo in Cincinnati. I had my sculptures and a few paintings before my time in the Foreign Service. In San Salvador, my art collection started to grow, and with most of our postings, I could afford to buy more paintings.

Chapter 24

There were days in Escalon, the area where we lived in San Salvador, when bodies would be found in the morning that had been murdered by death squads and tossed out during the night at the roundabout. I was also possibly the target of a kidnapping. It was the same pattern we were told about in Washington during our security training. I had taken a short walk up the street. I saw a van pull over to the curb and the sliding side door open. I was being watched in the side mirror. I quickly took a walkway to a house and waited for them to pull away. I ran home and called the embassy. Was it for real? I will never know for sure, but that was the end of my walks.

After I had been in the country for a while, I asked the regional security officer about permission to carry a handgun. I went with embassy personnel to a Salvadoran military base to prove I could handle a pistol. I shot every weapon they would let me shoot, and I was approved to carry a weapon.

I watched journalists come from the US to write about the situation in El Salvador. They stayed for two or three weeks. They tried to learn about the situation but never stayed long enough to become authorities. I lived there for almost eighteen months and left without a complete understanding of the situation. I just knew the communists were trying to take over the country. Today, Central America has different security problems, and many people want to go elsewhere for a better life. However, most people don't want to leave their homes if they don't feel forced to do so. I really believe that corrupt politicians and greed destroy lives. How sad for the people of these poor countries.

El Salvador is a beautiful country and even hosted the Miss Universe pageant before the war. I have seen a few beaches in my life, and nothing compares to the white sand beaches in El Salvador. El Salvador was the fourth largest coffee producer in the world before the civil war in the 1980s. The climate was lovely, with a tropical mist rain that watered my garden. El Salvador left a permanent imprint on my mind. It was a learning experience for me. I think the first diplomatic assignment will always be special for anyone.

In El Salvador, I did my first work with the American Women's Club. Other women and families started arriving sometime after I arrived. Ambassador Thomas Pickering followed Ambassador Hinton, and soon I had my first meeting with his wife, Alice. The new ladies wanted to know about the commissary, whether there were Pampers and Sara Lee. I asked how many knew how to shoot a pistol and had practiced using the embassy radio to get in touch with the marine on duty. A couple ladies started crying. Gee! What had I done?

We did a lot of good work helping different groups, especially children in the orphanages, with Kwell shampoo, mattresses, and so on. There were many abandoned children. We visited different locations. I was told women left their children because boyfriends didn't want their kids, and it would be easier trying to get across the US border without them. Children were left outside the gates at Salvadoran military locations, and we saw abandoned children left with Father Meir, a Catholic priest. Children and women are always the greatest casualties in war. I believe history has proven that to be true.

Chapter 25

I asked George, if I ever saw a little girl I felt something special about, could we consider adoption? He quickly said yes, but he didn't think it would happen. He has been accused through the years of trying to get me anything I wanted if he could. Once or twice, Coronel Nunez, a friend and Salvadoran Army officer, went with me to visit places caring for children, but on this special day, it was dear Salvador. We went to an orphanage called Rosa Virginia. Now I was actively searching for a baby girl. This was no longer about an American Women's Club project.

The orphanage had two levels. Salvador and I went upstairs to a room where there were smaller children. We saw a little girl in a highchair. I saw my Catherine at that moment. Her head had been shaved and medication applied to her forehead. That inner voice said, *She is the one.* Salvador agreed.

I went home and told George about my day. I asked him to come back with me to the orphanage and see her. When we arrived, the ladies in charge brought the little girl to us. I held her, and that special baby girl gave George a long look. He was hooked and would start helping make this little girl ours. George had met the judge of the children's court earlier. We went to see the judge, and I told him about this little girl at Rosa Virginia. I asked to take her out for medical treatment. He gave me the proper paperwork to get her released to us.

George arranged for a driver to pick me up to go get her. The orphanage was in a dangerous part of the city. The special armored car with a driver and man with a rifle stuck through the right side of the car drove me and Sylvia, my cook, to the orphanage. Sylvia and I had found a dress with no buttons on the shoulders to dress her. The driver took us home quickly.

Sylvia quickly went up the street to find something for my baby to wear to her first doctor's office visit. The embassy nurse was also there to meet me. Our little girl was sick with terrible tummy cramps and horrible diarrhea. The doctor was very nice, and he did all the measurements: body weight, height, and so forth. He had been a pediatrician for thirty-five years. With love, a clean environment, and healthy food, the baby would be perfect in a few weeks. The embassy nurse was wonderful.

My baby's name is Catherine Desiree, and we chose it for a reason. I liked Desiree, Napoleon's great love, and George liked Catherine because he admired the Russian monarch Catherine the Great. Catherine had been abandoned or lost about three weeks before I saw her. She was picked up by the Salvadorian equivalent of our Red Cross. The good or bad part of this is that there was no name and no birth information for her.

Catherine never cried and expressed no attachments upon leaving the orphanage. She put her arms around my neck, and I held her. In the days and weeks following, she showed no hint of sadness. We listened to music, and I put her legs around my waist so we could dance together. I had none of the normal baby highchairs, beds, toys, and so on. We had a second sitting room by the master bedroom. I had Sylvia put a love seat in the master bedroom next to my side of the bed. The mosquito netting was big enough to cover both bed and love seat. The love seat was level with the mattress, and I could pull her close to me. For several years, Catherine slept next to me. This continued even when she had her own room. We called it "sneaky time." She would wait for George to fall asleep and then come and touch me, and I would pull back the covers for her to slide in beside me. George would wake up in the morning and be surprised to see her in our bed.

Other Americans and Salvadorans brought their children to play with Catherine. We had several piñata parties. Catherine didn't like sharing the candy. I didn't know what a piñata party was; there was no such thing in Kentucky!

When the driver dropped George at home, Sylvia would say, "Your papa is home." He would spend some time with her after changing his clothes. We had dinner at the dining room table. We never used a highchair. I used the wing chair with pillows for Catherine to sit on to eat.

The adoption was a long and expensive process. We had to get an attorney. Catherine's photo had to be published for three days in the newspaper, and we were so frightened that someone might come forward and claim her. The judge let me know that if a family member came forward, we would lose her. These were very emotional days.

I tried everything to get help so I could keep my baby. I asked the embassy protocol assistant to arrange a call on the First Lady of El Salvador. I remember the driver taking me to the presidential palace. I wasn't scared because I was on a mission to keep my baby. When I was shown in to meet Mrs. Duarte, I explained my situation. To my disappointment, the First Lady said she could not intervene on my behalf. She was very religious and said she would pray that everything turned out well. If it were meant to be, then Catherine would be mine.

In the meantime, while waiting for the adoption process to be completed, we had to have a home study interview, and this service, required to be from a US agency, wasn't available for us in El Salvador. However, we located a service that handled regional adoptions, and two people flew in from Mexico City to interview us. The interview went well, and we were approved. We got a lot of help from our embassy. All Catherine's paperwork, including passport, shot records, and travel tickets, was arranged after the judge finally approved our petition.

In November 1983, our assignment was over, and it was time to leave. Catherine was traveling on a Salvadoran passport. Going through the airport and security check, I was scared that a last-minute snafu might delay us from flying to Miami. When the wheels went up, I knew we had made a long journey, and we breathed a big sigh of relief. We didn't have to worry ever again that Catherine would be taken away from us.

Chapter 26

We flew to Knoxville in November 1983, to spend time with George's grandmother. We were anxious for Grandmother McDade to see Catherine Desiree Fuson Staples. We were there for Thanksgiving and Christmas. George's father, Clyde Staples, and his second wife, Ruth, were very nice, especially Ruth. I now have a forty-year-old Christmas cactus in the entry of our home in Kentucky that Ruth gave me when we first met. George stayed in Knoxville with his grandmother while I drove to see family in Pineville. My baby was a little celebrity. Friends and family came to see Catherine, and for all, it was love at first sight.

However, since first arriving in Knoxville, I hadn't been feeling well. I was admitted to the hospital but released with no diagnosis. When I went to Kentucky with Catherine, I continued to be sick and couldn't get out of bed. Brother Jim put a bucket by my bed. Brother Bill was there with his son Billy for the holidays and to see his niece, Catherine. He took me back to Baptist Hospital in Knoxville. I was readmitted with a team of doctors looking for a diagnosis. Since there was still no diagnosis, I was put in isolation with blood precautions. Doctors were in touch with the Centers for Disease Control in Atlanta. Lots of tests were coming back both positive and negative.

George brought Catherine to see me daily in a little stroller, but he was very concerned he might have to raise a baby without me. I was so very scared. George didn't know a thing about babies, but I'm sure Grandmother was advising him. George's mother was her daughter, but unfortunately, she died while George was still in military language training in Monterey, California. Mrs. Staples never got to meet me or see her granddaughter, Catherine. She had been a devoted schoolteacher and would have loved traveling to visit us at our new assignments. Life is hard!

My group of doctors called in a specialist. After seeing a very sick woman, the specialist started requesting blood work every six hours. He had been a doctor during WWII and Vietnam and had seen a lot of malaria. Malaria was cycling in my blood. He made the diagnosis, and treatment started immediately. Things began turning around quickly, but without an early diagnosis, there were problems. I had red cell destruction. They called in a pathologist to do a bone marrow test. As I remember, I had no storage of iron in the bone marrow. Our next posting was Montevideo, Uruguay. I saw a hematologist for six months. Doctors told me later they had never seen a malaria case since a missionary couple from overseas had been treated at Baptist Hospital. The lesson of this story is to never get malaria in the winter with snow on the ground in Knoxville, Tennessee.

Before I move on to write about our next assignment in Uruguay, I must mention an event of major importance. As a State Department family, we received assistance in getting Catherine approved for expeditious naturalization. We took her to the federal courthouse in Nashville, Tennessee, where she was sworn in and became an American citizen. I was holding Catherine and said, "Baby girl, raise your hand." This was one of the proudest moments in our lives. She was given a little American flag to wave.

During that first visit to Kentucky after returning home from El Salvador, my sister-in-law, Tina, could not keep her hands off Catherine. She put a Barbie doll plastic bathtub in the middle of the kitchen table for her bath. Everyone loved my little baby! It hurts to say too many are no longer alive, such as my uncle AY, whom she loved, and he loved her. He had never been married, and he loved Catherine more than all his other nieces and nephews. We would stay with him when we got home to the hollow. He taught her to eat sardines and mustard on Wonder Bread. He had Cracker Jacks and other sweets that Catherine would hide in his sofa. Upon returning to the house six months to a year later, Catherine would find her hidden treasures in the same spot where she had left them. She would climb up in Uncle AY's lap and listen to his pocket watch, grab a piece of peppermint candy from his green candy jar, and watch all of his favorite soap operas with him. Catherine now has her uncle AY's pocket watch.

How do I love my daughter? Let me count the ways. I love Catherine in a thousand ways. She has been the almost perfect child, young daughter, and beautiful woman. Now she is the mother of a beautiful daughter. I have a good son-in-law. A few years ago, Catherine and I were watching on TV about the massacre at Sandy Hook Elementary School. All those beautiful children. There was an interview with one of the mothers who talked about her daughter, Grace, and their last morning together. I said to Catherine, "If you ever have a daughter, would you think about naming her Grace?" A few years later, we were blessed with a little granddaughter. Catherine remembered our conversation. Now we have our Grace Ann, and she is amazing. I would like to meet the mother of Grace, the child who was killed at Sandy Hook Elementary School. She has to live without her Amazing Grace. When will the change come that stops senseless violence?

I thought that the Sandy Hook tragedy would be the beginning of serious gun legislation. Things are now worse than before. People have let the National Rifle Association (NRA) have too much power and influence with leaders in government. We let the NRA buy people in office with money. I'm a simple person, but anyone with a pea brain can figure this out. People listen to sound bites and take them for the truth. There are too many sheep and not enough leaders in the Senate and the House of Representatives.

I believe in ownership of guns. Everyone in my family owned a pistol, a .22 caliber rifle, and a shotgun for killing food and protecting our homes. Who needs an assault weapon besides the military and police officers, and perhaps collectors who are carefully vetted with background checks? But most others buy them so they can brag and show them off to their buddies. Try finding what was left of a squirrel or rabbit after being shot by an assault rifle. These weapons are meant for war.

Chapter 27

After El Salvador came an assignment to Montevideo, Uruguay, and the beautiful Río de la Plata. It wasn't the ocean, but I couldn't see the other side of the river. I could walk across the road to the Rambla, an unrestricted sidewalk that runs for miles parallel to a road where people can walk and bike. In Montevideo, it also ran parallel the Río del Plata River. Catherine could learn how to ride her tricycle there. From our new home, I had an oversized window on both levels, with a view of a huge palm tree and the Río de la Plata.

Our home in Uruguay required a complete makeover. These were the days before the State Department helped pay for gardening services. The backyard had a *parillada*, but I couldn't see it for the overgrown brush and uncut grass. A *parillada* is a fancy barbecue made of brick and about four feet by eight feet, with a metal roof, a grill area made into the brick, and a buffet serving area. Uruguay was known as the land of beef. The consumption of beef was huge, and few people ever ate fish. Many well-off Uruguayans eventually go to the US for heart bypass surgery.

I was always struggling with Spanish because the accents in Uruguay were different from El Salvador. My teacher at the State Department Language Institute was from Cuba. Her Spanish accent was different, and some words were hard to understand. I had an accent from the Kentucky mountains. Everything was against me!

George had very interesting work. Uruguay was transitioning from a military dictatorship to a democracy. I had a lot to learn about the two political parties: the Colorados and the Blancos. George worked in the embassy's Political Section, which had the primary responsibility for reporting on the transition from military to civilian rule. I wanted to always have a general knowledge of events for conversation purposes.

We met a wonderful American couple at the embassy named Larry and Lucille Palmer. Lucille said she could "run with me," enjoy being friends and discovering Uruguay. Lucille and I took Catherine and her son, Vincent, to Uruguay's Punta del Este resort area. A funny thing happened at the hotel. We were on the twelfth floor of the hotel, having dinner and wine. Lucille had a hundred-dollar bill in her hand. A strong wind came up and blew it away. We had to watch it slowly sail down into the trees. Ours would be a forever friendship. We would laugh about this story many times.

I have always given great parties. One memorable party happened at our residence. Friends from the embassy and lots of other people came. The house was full. George was in charge of the music. Then the Palmers entered! The ladies had never met Larry. He was the most beautiful Black man they had ever seen. Larry never gave up his Afro, and when it turned gray, he would still stand out in a crowd. The ladies lost their composure. Later in his career, Larry would become ambassador to Honduras and then Barbados. Lucille was by his side all the way. People forget the State Department gets two for one. Lucille came to Catherine's wedding. The years have gone too fast. We were young and beautiful.

While in Uruguay, I got a call from my friend Judy. She was sick but felt she wasn't going to die, and I didn't have to come home. George was going to see his grandmother in Knoxville. Pineville was eighty-six miles from Knoxville, so he went to see about Judy for me. He called and said, "Make a reservation and get home right away." I got there before Thanksgiving and left after Judy died on January 2. We were able to spend two holidays together. For Thanksgiving, Judy's nephew George Clyde made food for her. I gave her a shower and brought her prettiest set of lingerie to the hospital as well as one place setting of her china, silver, and crystal to set up nicely on her hospital tray with a rose.

Judy had lung cancer and a brain tumor and went back and forth from intensive care about four times. We left one of her vehicles in the hospital parking lot. We got a gurney and loaded it with her things when she went to intensive care. When she went back to another room, we unloaded her Suburban and brought her things to the new room. We had her coffee maker, coffee, toilet paper, personal things, and the calculator she used to do her paperwork for her taxi business, which hauled railroad workers from one station to another.

Eva was there with Judy some of the time, but she had two children now. Brother Jim and his wife, Tina, also looked after Catherine. The doctor said

Judy would be passing on soon. I didn't believe him. She was talking and giving instructions as usual, but then she took a turn for the worse in a short time. Earlier, we had told her son, Jason, to go home and get some rest. I was on one side of her bed with Eva on the other. We were holding Judy's hands. She was squeezing mine. She gritted her teeth, and I watched one tear slide down her face. She was gone. How would my life be without Judy? Eva and I were the two left from the three who had hit Cincinnati with a bang! I returned to Uruguay with a heavy heart.

In Uruguay, I employed a lady named Mirta to be our housekeeper. Lucia was a second housekeeper, and her daughter, Marianela, baby sat with Catherine. I will never forget a visit to a rural area to meet Mirta's family. It was right out of a storybook. I often pull photos off the shelf and reflect on this time with Mirta. Her family was beautiful in spirit and hospitality. Her father was dressed in his gaucho clothes, worn by South America's version of our cowboys. He did not wear them only for festive occasions but were his usual clothing. He was so interesting. I was meeting a family I thought were out of the past. Mirta's sister, Catherine, and I went by horseback to round up the sheep. The land was flat, and I could see forever. What a contrast to life in the Kentucky mountains.

The family made a semiformal dinner for me. They closed off the door to the dining room. It had not been used recently, so it took a little push to get it open. They made me feel very special. Mirta looked like her mother. I remember the peace and calm she projected with an incredible smile. I was born in a place like this, different but with some of the same feelings. We met Mirta's brother, who seemed out of another time, wearing his gaucho clothes. He came by horseback and tied his horse to a hitching post. This was one of those unforgettable moments I will have as long as I have my memory. I've lost a lot thanks to aging and accidents, but I pray to God that I never lose my memory and sight.

Remates (auctions) were common in Uruguay. Running buddy Lucille and I couldn't bid on much, but if one had money, it was a shopper's market. The open-air markets for fruit and vegetables were great. Antique cars were seen on the streets, and rolltop desks from Italy and crystal chandeliers were common sights.

Some people spoke about Uruguay being a European country in South America. Almost everyone was descended from Spanish and Italian immigrants. Some of the people looked like they could have starred in gangster movies from the thirties. Some men wore garters on their socks. The seasons were reversed from the US in South America, with November and December being the summer months while June and July were the coldest. George bought me a full-length mink coat made from Russian pelts, a nutria coat, and a fox jacket. I have to laugh about how many years of storage we paid on those coats. Once, Mirta had a ticket to the theater, and I wanted to help her dress nicely; I loaned her my mink coat.

Our baby girl was now about three. We enrolled her in a Montessori school. I loved being Catherine's mother. I prayed to God many times never to fail as her mother. I had some failures in my life but not as a mother. Catherine has confirmed both verbally and in a scrapbook of letters that I'm a great mother. I want to be a great grandmother to Grace Ann, time permitting. Recently, she told me she hated me but loved my heart. What an interesting statement from a four-year-old.

We made trips inside Uruguay but also crossed the river to Buenos Aires for my first hydrofoil experience. The city had the widest streets I had ever seen as well as world-famous shopping, though it was too expensive for my budget. However, we always managed to have a nice hotel. About halfway through our assignment, George, Catherine, and I made a trip to southern Brazil. It looked like Bavaria in Germany. Maybe it was because of the Germans who had left Europe and settled in this part of Brazil after World War II. We have beautiful photos of the resorts Gramado and Canela. We also made a memorable bus trip to the hot springs in Argentina. We sure did enjoy our time there with our new friends Larry and Lucille Palmer. We were also accompanied by Uruguayans from the embassy who participated in a local soccer tournament. I don't remember the score, but a good time was had by one and all.

I left Uruguay with three paintings and a brass sculpture of a gaucho about one foot tall. One beautiful painting was of a young woman George had bought for me on a Saturday morning trip to the Port of Montevideo. Another day, a lady who worked at the embassy invited us to visit her father-in-law's gallery. We walked upstairs, and the door was open to his office. I saw something of interest behind his desk. I asked the embassy worker to talk to him and see if he would sell the painting. She came to me the next day and said he would sell it to me. It was a country scene of a cookout with gauchos, dogs, and meat eaten from skewers. I still love the painting.

I would often take a bike ride along the Rambla and watch the morning fishermen go out for the early catch. The boats were piled high with orange netting. I loved these times with my baby and George. I have a watercolor of this scene painted by E. R. Carino, a very famous watercolor artist. In Spanish, *carino* means love. I have strong memories of almost all the pieces in my art collection, but I haven't been able to recall how I found this work of art. George and I have different tastes in art. I like traditional works by the old masters—landscapes and self-portraits. I don't care for still life. He likes wildlife scenes and etchings. He sometimes complains about my purchases. But after he's lived a while with a painting, he always seems to say, "Jodi [some family and friends call me Jodi], you were right. It's a real treasure."

On a visit to the Outer Banks in North Carolina, I saw a very interesting painting. It was a restored 1850 oil painting from the Dutch period of a family in traditional clothing at the ocean. I asked George what he thought, and he said, "If you feel something for the painting, then buy it." If he commented on something that he liked, I would return and buy the piece—painting, swords, or engraved wooden boxes—for him. Daughter Catherine would comment sometimes on a purchase. Of one painting in Zimbabwe, she said, "*Que triste,*" which in Spanish means "how sad." "Mom," she said, "I don't know who you bought that for, but it wasn't me." The painting is of a suffering, hungry street child. I have learned through the years to please myself. I learned to bargain; it is expected. Most of the time, as in Uruguay, the dollar was strong and the exchange to local currency gave me buying power.

I can remember one special magical night in Montevideo. It must have been the result of a navy invitation through the embassy to us. I remember my beautiful dress as I entered a large room for ballroom dancing. The music was perfect. A very handsome uniformed Uruguayan military man asked me to dance. He led me out on the floor, and I felt as if I were living a dream. I felt I was a good dancer, but together, he made us great. It seemed I was floating on air. There will never be another dance like that one in this life.

Chapter 28

Little did I know what was to come for an ongoing assignment. We were going in the summer of 1985 to Equatorial Guinea, a country on the west coast of Africa. Part of the country is located on an island close to the equator. We would be living in Malabo, the capital, which was on an island. The other part of the country is on the coast and is called Río Muni. We lived in Equatorial Guinea—at the time one of the poorest countries in Africa—for two years, and it was designated a hardship post, those embassies in countries with poor infrastructure, hazardous health conditions, poor schools for children, and other difficulties.

The president was Teodoro Obiang, who came to power by killing his uncle Macías, the country's first president at independence. I don't approve of killing to take power, but there are always exceptions. As my grandmother told me many years ago, some men deserve to die. There are many stories of Macías's cruelty to his people and the destruction of his country. Government officials would be killed at meetings if they spoke against his policies. He destroyed the fishing boats to make it difficult for people to flee the island. He also destroyed the infrastructure and public services to the point that when we were there, the only source of electricity was generators. My housekeeper told me that after the electricity went off, it came back on nine years later. The country lost a third of its population during the years of Macías's rule.

The country had an interesting history. It was originally called Fernando Po, a Portuguese colony. It was passed to the British in the mid-1800s as an antislavery outpost. At some point, ownership was transferred to Spain, and the name was changed to Equatorial Guinea. During Spanish colonial rule, the country became prosperous. Macías literally took the country back to the bush. In the heyday of Malabo, it was rumored that Frederick Forsyth wrote the famous novel *The Dogs of War* from the patio of the Bahia Hotel. The hotel had a view of the ocean but no beach, and the coast was black sand.

George's career adviser had suggested this assignment as a good choice, but he was not a favorite person of mine. At times, I wished I could have punched him in the face or shot him for assigning us to Malabo. This post was not the place for a family with a young child. Other diplomats would come and ask for caskets from our warehouse to bury their dead, who usually were malaria victims. We denied their requests to make sure we had the caskets if a member of our staff died. It was especially eerie for me to see the small coffin that could be used for a child, and we had the only American child at the embassy. There were deaths within twenty-four hours from malaria, and we took antimalarial medicine for our entire two-year assignment. We could never be sure we wouldn't be stricken.

We attended an African area studies seminar before leaving for post. We had a stopover in Paris and then a flight to Douala, Cameroon. I can't remember if there were some rest periods in between flights, but I can share one thing from my memory. We were treated differently after Colin Powell became secretary of state. He knew how to treat people. If an overseas flight was more than sixteen hours, we could stop over en route to our destination. In some cases, we could be upgraded to business class, and we could be given credit for our frequently traveled miles. In the days before Secretary Powell, we could, with few exceptions, fly only economy class.

Our ambassador in Malabo was Frank Ruddy. George was the deputy chief of mission, commonly known as the DCM. Sally and Ted Nest were there in administration positions. Monica Frantz and her husband, Hal, worked for the US Agency for International Development (USAID). I was hired as a contract employee to fill a job in a General Services position, overseeing distribution of supplies and housing essentials while also providing maintenance support to embassy operations, vehicles, and facilities. Our daughter, Catherine, at age six had no security clearance, but once she was spotted in Ambassador Ruddy's office copying her hands on the printer with his help.

Ambassador Ruddy and his wife, Teri, were late meeting us at the airport when we arrived. We connected on the airport road. I looked at Mrs. Ruddy's legs and saw red spots from blood coming through her stockings. These were from bites from tsetse flies, commonly known as no-see-ums. Malaria was very prevalent in the country. Where had George brought us to on this assignment?

We were taken to what would be our home for the next two years in a compound of four houses. The Shaliffs were in one of the houses. Herb was an embassy communication specialist. Spanish businessmen from Las Palmas lived in the other two houses. There wasn't a blade of grass in the yard. The guards swept the sand with straw brooms. All I could see across the fence was the one-lane dirt road. There was nothing to see but dense jungle all the way up to a large and thankfully inactive volcano. Gabon vipers lurched across the road. They didn't cross to my yard because the guards killed them. They have the nickname of *quatro pasos*, or four steps, meaning if you were bitten by these snakes, you might make four steps and then die.

A part of newcomers' introduction to a new country would normally be a windshield tour in which a driver would take you around to get a feel of the city and what was available. It provided a quick overview of where to shop, points of interest, and supermarkets. But not in Malabo! The drive lasted about fifteen minutes. Nothing was there but a small minimarket run by a Lebanese family. Spanish was the official language as the country was the only former Spanish colony in sub-Saharan Africa. My Spanish was improving but never rose to the level of George's. I did have a more extensive vocabulary, though. I knew all the words for domestic work, food, and keeping us alive. The boiling of water was essential. I was told that Equatorial Guinea was the poorest of the poor in Africa. We settled into a routine that was pleasant, considering the circumstances. My baby girl went to the Spanish school run by nuns while I went to work at the embassy and tried to come up with ideas to help local staff and Americans in the country.

We took monthly charter flights to Douala, Cameroon, for supplies, especially food, which was a priority. We stayed at the Novotel Hotel. My Catherine loved the pool, and there was a gift shop for treasure hunting. The restaurants had great food and no worries about getting sick. I had never seen prawns that big. I had couscous for the first time. We shopped at a local store that imported American products, but the prices were sky-high. For example, on a trip to Douala he took without us, George bought a package of Oreo cookies for the equivalent of ten American dollars and promptly ate the whole thing before the night was over. He told us what he had done later. He has been known to hide cookies in his computer drawer.

At the embassy, we had no storage for classified information. We took sensitive materials by diplomatic pouch to our consulate in Douala and brought back similar pouches containing supply items and food. The planes were flown by French contract pilots based in Douala, who sometimes had a bit to drink before the flight. We had no choice but to get on the plane and hope for the best. We never gained much altitude, as the back-and-forth flights were brief, and sometimes, I could look out the window and see fish in the ocean.

I made friends with Ramona Edjan, who was from Malabo and had two young girls, which was nice for Catherine. Ramona had once been married to an American. She had a small beauty shop, so I had a place for manicures and pedicures. Life was getting better! I had a job at the embassy and really did enjoy the American staff and Foreign Service Nationals (FSNs). I very much liked a special local employee named Tomas Dickens and his wife, Trudy. Tomas was a great help to me because if I needed to negotiate a contract, he was fluent in reading and writing Spanish and French. I would do or say something, and he would say, "Mrs. Staples, it was too good." I still use those words forty years later.

On a USAID project, I went with their staff to give medication to chickens to prevent parasites. On the given day, we had many people bring their chickens. This project is embedded in my mind forever. A woman came down a path with chickens in both hands. To this day, I have never seen a more regal woman. Her shoulders were back, and her body was held straight. She taught me a lifelong lesson: grace and dignity can be seen everywhere. Not often, but it is always there. It's something that money can't buy.

Malabo had a very qualified doctor, Isabelle Wright. She brought a sense of calm to my worried mind. People were always dying from malaria. Remember, I was a survivor of malaria that I had contracted just before leaving El Salvador. She was excellent and once helped our daughter when she had tsetse fly bites. They can be very painful as the worm forms under the skin and has to be squeezed out. Later, we found out if Vaseline was put on the skin and a Band-Aid on top, the little bastard couldn't breathe, and he would come out and get stuck to the Band-Aid.

There are so many good stories of interesting happenings from our time in Malabo. We had a catalog from a northern European company, Peter Justesen, from which the embassy ordered two movie projectors to play movies we received periodically from the US Navy. Once a week, we had movie nights at the embassy. These were a big hit and a great morale booster. If people were approved by the administrative officer and the ambassador, all English speakers and guests from other embassies and international organizations could attend movie night. We had an average of twenty-five people once a week, and everyone would bring snacks and popcorn to share. However, if anyone fell into disfavor with Ambassador Ruddy, he took them off the guest list. This was great leverage, but I don't remember anyone being permanently removed.

On one occasion when the ambassador was away, we were invited to a Russian embassy national day reception. When we pulled into the driveway, a Russian employee used a flashlight and guided us around the side of the building to take our seats. We had to watch a movie using the side of the building as a screen to view a documentary about the Russian space program. I think Yuri Gagarin would have been in the documentary. Years later, on a private visit to Russia, I had my photo taken by his tomb in a cemetery in Moscow. People think I'm a little crazy, but when I travel, I like to visit cemeteries. They are often sculpture gardens honoring famous people. Take my word on this. When traveling to other major cities, take a city tour that includes the famous cemeteries.

At the Russian reception, dinner was served, and thank God, George and I were inside. Most of the people were on the patio and down on the lawn. I would not have wanted to be there, as everyone was fully exposed to malaria-carrying mosquitoes. I assumed we were invited inside because of rank. I met my first Russian, the ambassador everyone knew as just Boris. Everyone important was there, including members of the French, Spanish, and Chinese embassies, the German Technical Assistance Group (equivalent to our USAID), local government officials, and other members of the diplomatic corps. In Malabo, I had my first experience meeting a wide range of people from other countries, especially Eastern Europe and China.

When I remember the Chinese who were developing water projects and building roads, a special evening stands out. The Chinese ambassador invited us to his residence for dinner, and it was a special treat. We were served a great meal, with many courses on a huge carousel. A waiter asked what we wanted and served our plate. The ambassador was an excellent host, and of course, we welcomed any chance to have a good meal. When the meal ended, I waited expectantly, but when it was clear that the meal was over, I asked the ambassador, "Where's my fortune cookie?"

There was an awkward moment until a member of his staff explained to him what I meant, and then he politely told me, "In China, there is no such thing. It is only an American invention." George acted as if I had committed a major breach of diplomatic etiquette. I told him later that he didn't know either, and he agreed. For years afterwards, we had a good laugh recalling how that dinner ended.

We had to have temporary quarters in Malabo for embassy visitors. The accommodations at the two hotels there were very substandard. I got approval to go to Douala and check out the consulate's warehouse. I knew we could lease the fourth floor of the Hotel Impala, and I could make four ensuite accommodations. When I went to the warehouse, I found a treasure trove of furniture. White Craft furniture was outdated or not desirable, but I could make two apartments out of it that worked in this tropical environment. I found used Drexel furniture that, with cleaning and polishing, would work to make a third apartment. I had used Drexel in El Salvador, Uruguay, and now in Malabo. For the fourth unit, I got enough Ethan Allen furniture together to make my luxury suite. Remember, lots of things are relative. Everything was shipped by boat to Malabo.

I was very proud of my work, and I had embassy personnel to help. Our embassy cleaning people helped with moving and cleaning of the furniture, lamps, and so on. When everything was ready, Ambassador Ruddy arrived for the walk-through. Somewhere in my files is a copy of his letter of appreciation to me. Today, I found a long-lost memo from the Malabo Ritz. It reads as follows:

"*We hope you will enjoy your stay here. You are using US Government Temporary Quarters. A lot of time, thought and energy went into making these apartments as comfortable as possible. Our objective has been achieved considering our remoteness and lack of local resources.*"

There were eight rules, with the last one being, "*We hope you enjoy your stay in Malabo with its natural beauty and friendly people. Thank you, [signed] Jo Ann Staples.*" President Obiang's staff heard about these apartments and wanted to use them. I can't remember how this worked, but I think our ambassador handled the turndown with aplomb.

We had information there would be a US Navy show band coming to Malabo. Getting ready for such a visit would be a herculean effort for everyone. A local theater had been a nice facility during Spanish colonial times, but it was now a shell of its bygone years. It would have to be the site for a performance, but birds were roosting in the ceiling, and the roof had holes. We had to scrub bird shit from the walls, repair seats, and use a lot of paint. The plane landed, and I went on board to meet everyone and give them their itineraries. The hotel where they stayed had no air conditioning. We had to take air conditioners from the warehouse and install them. We made it happen. Hip-hip hooray!

The US Navy was wonderful. We might have starved without them . . . maybe a little exaggerated but true. We placed an order for frozen foods, and when they arrived, our freezers filled up. We had tropical fruit in abundance. My Catherine loved the little bananas.

Thank God, I was born in the hills of Kentucky and knew hardship. After a couple of months in Malabo, some of my city-born lady friends would have, I think, asked for separate maintenance, which is the State Department policy allowing a spouse to leave a hardship post, return to the US, and receive financial assistance. I must say it crossed my mind because I had a five-year-old baby girl and we were very isolated. For example, George has always been a sports fan, sometimes to the extreme. But in Malabo, where at the time there was no cable television and only a government-run radio station, he depended on his shortwave radio for news and sports. I remember once he tried to tweak the dials to listen to the Super Bowl at 3:00 a.m.

Our sense of isolation was even more evident when we wanted to make a phone call home to check on family. George would have to go downtown to the local telephone office and ask an attendant to place the call. Then he had to stay there to accept the call when it was finally connected. That might be in thirty minutes or three or four hours. George would leave home with a book and something to eat and drink in case he had to spend a long time waiting for the call. This is hard to imagine today with the internet, email, and mobile phones.

Chapter 29

In November 1986, we visited the island of Annobón, another part of Equatorial Guinea located in the South Atlantic Ocean. Part of what I'm about to tell was taken from a document put together by six members of the team going to Annobón. The purpose of this trip was to deliver Project Handclasp gifts that had been donated to the people of Equatorial Guinea by the US Navy on their 1986 West Africa Training Cruise. We were taking their donations of two cases of Tylenol, three cases of toys, notebooks, pencils, and nine hundred pounds of rice.

The island was about a forty-hour journey away on a small Dutch-owned freighter called the *Truman*. I thought if the ship could handle storms in the North Sea, we would be safe. We were a group of six passengers from the embassy and about thirty Annobónese. Many hadn't returned to their little island in five years. They traveled on the top deck. We had babies, grandmothers, men, and women. We had luggage, a duck, two trees, a bed frame, food, and personal bundles aboard.

Very special people were on board. Yes, Catherine was with me. I always tried to take her with me when I traveled. First, I didn't want to be separated from her, and second, I wanted her to experience everything. What does a five-year-old remember? I took my cook, Eustachio, with me because he was from Annobón. He had not seen his family in nine years. Everyone was enamored with Catherine. The ship's captain's wife, Ambassador Ruddy's wife Teri, her son Neil, and Sally Nist were on board and helped watch out for her. Sally loved Catherine and always paid special attention to her. Don't forget, Catherine was the only American child at the embassy. Eustachio was vigilant that Catherine didn't get near the ship's railing. He was very helpful to both of us. He also assisted in the kitchen. A friend who had married a Salvadoran told me, "Always be good to your staff, especially the residential staff. If a coup happens, your employees might be the people who save you. The marines or other help flying in might be too late." It was good advice, and it has always been my nature to be especially good to people in general. I have been accused of being too good to my staff. Some very special memories came from time spent with them just talking and listening to music.

I knew nothing about navigation. The water was rough and choppy, but I had to trust our captain. Catherine and I had a small room below deck, near the engine. Big mistake! It was hot and noisy. There was a constant *chuck! chuck!* sound, like the engine was laboring. Catherine started vomiting from the heat and rough seas. We went up on the deck where it was cooler and slept with everyone else.

During the night, I heard loud sounds from something beating on the hull of the freighter. When I asked the captain what was happening, he turned on the searchlight and said, "Come take a look." We went to the railing and saw thousands of flying fish that had surrounded us and were banging against our ship as we traveled through the night. It was one of those magical times that I will never forget.

Annobón was a lovely small island of volcanic origin. We were happy to be on deck because we were anxious to see our destination. There was an early morning haze, but it lifted and we could see the island, full of tropical vegetation. As we dropped anchor, I saw a white sand beach. I also saw a beautiful church sitting above the other buildings. First, we had to be social and meet officials who came on board and greeted us. A dugout canoe with an outboard motor met us with a delegation of Annobónese who handled the port formalities. A tree was cut in half and dug out to make these canoes, called *cayucos*. I think I saw this done in an old movie. *Cayucos* were the villagers' only means of traveling. I have a small miniature *cayuco* on my desk as I write about our arrival. We were surprised by the number of men and boys in *cayucos* surrounding our ship.

I was at the railing with Catherine and Eustachio. I could tell the people were poor, and most were clothed in tattered rags. An old man came up close. He was looking for his son. Eustachio said, "There's my father." As they waved to each other, I couldn't stop the tears. I learned that every time a ship had visited for the last nine years, the old man had looked for his son. I was very proud to have made this reunion possible. The *Truman* was the only ship to visit in more than a year.

Everyone went down a rope ladder to the bouncing *cayucos* to get ashore. The Americans were pampered, as we were able to use the ship's motor-powered Zodiac inflatable dingy to go back and forth between ship and shore. I told the captain, "Catherine is in pain. Could we go ashore first?" There was a doctor on the island. Catherine had three mango worms under her skin.

The island population was 2,006, consisting of 1,228 females and 778 males, about 900 of them children. These figures are taken from a 1983 census. For me, being on Annobón was almost like arriving in a lost paradise. Fish were plentiful, and wonderful tropical fruits could be found throughout the island. Clothing was a problem, and the people had very few material possessions. Clothing and soap were sent by relatives from Malabo or Bata on the mainland. The island had no stores. It was a trade-and-barter society.

There was no electricity on the island. The Spanish priest had three solar panels with batteries that supplied light to the church. The Spanish doctor had one solar panel that supplied energy for two light bulbs in his house. Travel was by foot and *cayuco*, and there was not a single bicycle on the island. A plane came every six weeks with supplies from the Spanish embassy in Malabo. The Spanish doctor had a radio in case of an emergency.

The distribution of the Handclasp gifts got complicated. As soon as we reached shore, we climbed the hill to the church. The Tylenol went to the doctor, the toys to the school, and the rice to the *padre* for distribution to the poorest. He agreed but said with some reservation, "We have to be cautious. Local officials prefer to handle the distribution of items brought to the island." After three meetings, he knew we were not giving in to his ideas.

Sally Nist or Teri Ruddy came up with the idea to distribute the rice in a plaza-like setting. One problem was with the men who refused to carry the rice but wanted to get in line to receive some. We came up with a plan to distribute the rice through the Women's Association, with the idea that the rice was from the American women to the women of Annobón. Neil helped with crowd control. I don't know where the stamp came from, but Sally stamped each person's hand who get rice so no one could double back for a second handout.

At an appointed time, the governor gave a speech explaining how the rice was to be distributed. Mrs. Ruddy said a few words, and the distribution began for women only, that is, each female head of a household. We had over three hundred women in line. It turned into a mob scene but an unknown man got things under control. He must have been an official and spoke sternly and in a loud voice that immediately calmed the situation. I felt wonderful because we gave out nine hundred pounds of rice, about two and a half pounds per head of household. Some was cooked that night. I know for sure we were successful.

We had brought the rice in diplomatic pouches. One of my very special photos is of a little girl leaning on a diplomatic pouch as things were unloaded. That little girl was my daughter, Catherine. We went to meet Eustachio's family and had a photo opportunity. The family, especially his mother, was overwhelmed with joy to see him again. The little village was clean, with no garbage. People used one area of the island as a toilet, and everything was washed out to the ocean.

On Sunday, our entire embassy group attended Mass, with a standing-room-only crowd of over six hundred, again mostly women and children. The singing was wonderful. After that, we trekked up to a crater lake and discovered many enchanted views of the island. The hike was demanding, but I had Eustachio to help carry Catherine. We could see the *Truman* docked below. It looked very small, but it had gotten us there, and it would see us safely back to Malabo. We had a good long rest and snacks in a grassy area. I have photos of this whole experience. We enjoyed mangoes, and Catherine ate her little bananas. The walk was very enjoyable, with a nice breeze and very pleasant weather.

The next morning, we visited the school. The priest had prearranged our visit, and we met the Spanish teacher at her house. There were about 650 morning students, ranging from ages six to twelve. We marched into the schoolyard, where the children stood in orderly lines. I was so proud of my five-year-old; Catherine helped with the distribution of books, writing materials, and toys. We explained how to use the toys. I even got excited about the Slinkys. The very disciplined and orderly children got very excited. It was another magical and unforgettable experience.

That evening, because the Spanish had been so hospitable, we invited all of them on board the *Truman* for dinner. How we pulled that off, I can't remember, but we were diplomats and used to making things happen with not a lot of resources, especially in Malabo. The following day, we invited the Annobónese officials. We had a luncheon for all of them and their wives on the deck. It couldn't have been more than twenty people. Mrs. Ruddy gave dress material to the women and bottles of whiskey to the men. We had a very good experience and knew our time would be over too soon.

The next day, we left for Malabo. For some, it had been an island paradise, and it reminded me of James Michener's novel *Hawaii*. All the Americans thought we had been successful and had generated good relations on behalf of our country.

Chapter 30

Our trip back to Malabo provided quiet time to reflect on life. One of my favorite songs is "Alfie" sung by Dionne Warwick. I love every word of the song. Indeed, "what's it all about?" I was in the past, present, and future. My mind was all over the place; it happens often. My Catherine was such a little diplomat. I have written in my journal about her beginning of life. One day, I would have to tell her more, but now it was too soon, and the time would come. What would I say, knowing myself as I do and never liking to lie? As I have gotten older, people will say to me, "I'm going to tell you something, but you can't tell anyone." I tell them not to do that to me, and I laugh and tell them that I might forget. I don't want the responsibility of keeping secrets. Of course, this isn't written in stone. There have been exceptions.

The return trip to Malabo was uneventful. Dolphins were on both sides of the *Truman*, keeping pace with our speed. How exciting for Catherine and me. We passed two islands on our way back to Malabo, the islands of São Tomé and Príncipe. My thoughts settled on the people of Annobón. Had I experienced paradise in 1986? Were their lives not so complex? What happened with so-called development and goodwill of Europeans who wanted to colonize Africa? King Leopold of Belgium was the worst. Over nine million died in the Belgian Congo, forced to work in inhumane conditions on rubber plantations. I didn't know about these atrocities until someone suggested I read a book titled *King Leopold's Ghost* by Adam Hochschild. We know about Hitler and the German atrocities in WWII and the murder of millions—how about Belgium in the Congo?

My mind returned to our trip back to Malabo. There wasn't the noise and excitement as before. Eustachio was missing his family, but I was so pleased I had made this trip possible for him. I wondered what the Annobónese who had made the journey with us were thinking.

The captain announced we were minutes out, and I knew George would be waiting on the dock. All the Americans were happy to be back in Malabo. It was our home until the next assignment. Catherine and I wanted a bath, our beds, and maybe a tuna sandwich.

Chapter 31

When we first arrived in Malabo, I heard about a village in the mountains called Moka. The Spanish had developed it but had abandoned their houses after the time of Macías. There was evidence of Spanish rule in the colonial era in a very positive way. The Spanish liked summer homes in Moka. It was cool and above the mosquito and tsetse fly problems. There wasn't malaria as in Malabo. I liked to go there and take Catherine to spend time with my South African friends.

Soon, it was time to get away from embassy life once again. I liked my job, but this was my first time living on an island. I needed to take advantage of a trip with my South African friends who were operating a cattle project. They had told me about a trip they were planning to take food supplies to a poor, isolated village on the other end of the island. They asked if I would like to go. I said, "Yes, sounds like it would be an adventure." I was geared up for a hike through dense jungle to take these supplies to a remote village that was cut off from the coastal waters about five months out of the year.

I was excited about being with my friends and traveling companions. I was the only American to go on the trip. Catherine and I had stayed before with the South Africans at their compound before, and they were good cooks with great hospitality. The French ambassador's secretary would be a nice person to make this journey with, and we were the only two women. The teacher from Moka was a special person. I had visited his school and was shocked to see him trying to teach world geography without a map. The students sat on a dirt floor. I went back to the embassy to get a map and wood to make benches. The husband of a lady from Moka also went on the trip with us. I had gotten to know him and felt good that we had him with us. There were also men the South Africans had hired to carry supplies.

We all gathered at the work building and did a last-minute check. My backpack was oversized and too heavy. I had too much water. I had never been in a jungle like this one. It was a very hard hike and too long. The jungle was very dense and, in some areas, required the use of machete. This wasn't a well-worn path. I put my leg up to cross over a fallen tree and fell backward. I had to have help to get back onto my feet. The sounds were incredible from all the insects, birds, and monkeys. The green, dense vegetation was incredible and a bit intimidating. Thank God, I didn't see any snakes. The sounds monkeys and baboons make can be very scary. I will always say, "I miss the sights and sounds of Africa."

We camped by a magnificent cascading waterfall that made a beautiful natural pond. The sound of falling water was incredible. It must have fallen hundreds of feet to the water. Over time, the waterfall had created a big pool of water. We slept the night in the jungle. I brought my hammock because I wasn't going to sleep on the ground. The men found a perfect place to string it up between two trees.

The next morning, we started early because we needed to get down to ocean level and hike to our destination. We had to climb to our destination mountain village before the tide came in. When I saw the beach, I was elated. As we walked down the beach, I looked back and saw our footprints in the sand. I thought about a movie I had seen years before called *Journey to the Center of the Earth*. The ocean air and wind felt great and renewed my aching body.

We were ready to climb to the village. I don't think it was a long climb, but it was steep. The greetings from the people were very touching. We socialized for a short time and then started setting up camp. I was fascinated by what was happening. People started dropping pieces of wood. I asked, "Why are you bringing us wood?" I was told it was a custom to bring wood to help with build a fire for visitors in the village. What a nice way to treat their guests.

The next day, I took my camera and got some beautiful photos that were Kodak moments. I asked a man leaning out a window to let me take his photo. He said, "I will never have a copy." I promised I would get the photo to him. I know he didn't believe me. I gave the schoolteacher a copy, and on his next trip, he gave it to the nice man. I'm sure he didn't see it for months. I have a copy at home in my photo album. I always feel good when I keep my promise. I'm sure the South Africans took gifts for the village. It feels nice when someone else is in charge. I was just along for the experience.

Our return trip was uneventful. Now we were going from sea level up a hill into the dense jungle again. I was nervous, but we were a group of about twenty-five. Some of the Guinean children stayed because they were on school break, and it would be months before someone returned for them. During the trek back to the South African compound, I chewed on too much sugar cane and it made me sick. You have to remember that in life, "high risk, high rewards."

After returning from the village, we rested for a day before returning to Malabo. I was happy to be back in my beautiful, clean house with the staff to take care of me. I was sick and stayed in the recliner for a week. Dr. Isabelle Wright gave me some medicine to take care of any parasites. The embassy did what we could to help her. We didn't have an American embassy doctor, but Dr. Wright was very good. I think that beautiful waterfall got me when I filled up my water bottles. I was a dummy and didn't remember to take iodine tablets with me.

One evening a few weeks later, I hosted a chess night at my residence. I set up tables for twelve people. One very memorable player was Boris, the Russian ambassador, who was a good chess player. He would make his move, check out the other tables, and then return to his table and make his next move. I don't remember how this happened, but I must have asked him about Russian vodka. I told him about Kentucky moonshine. We went to my pantry together. I had a jar of moonshine, and we had a drink together. No one else knew what we were doing. Maybe they were concentrating on their games. I love this story, which has always remained a big secret.

While reviewing our budget, I discovered we had a thief stealing fuel from our embassy generators. This was a very serious problem. I think of many things when I remember Malabo. The hum and smell of generators were very difficult to live with. We had a generator and a backup when we didn't have city power, which was almost nonexistent. I had our guards watch our fuel tanks, and the thieves were apprehended. I was given the name "Broderick Crawford," who played a famous police chief in the early years of television. I can remember a time when no one had city power for twenty-eight days. If the government couldn't pay the French energy company, they didn't deliver. I bet President Obiang had the last laugh when oil was discovered years later in Equatorial Guinea.

I always wondered why many so countries were interested in Equatorial Guinea. I met French, Spanish, Chinese, and Russian diplomats as well as an Indian merchant I liked very much. His name was Ram, and we accepted his invitations to dinner, along with businessmen from Spain and others. The Lebanese brother and sister who owned the mini-mart convenience store also operated the Beirut Restaurant. It was a place to watch people, which I like to do. It was like Rick's Café right out of the movie Casablanca. It was a place where diplomats, a few local officials, strangers assumed to be mercenaries, newcomers arriving on unmarked aircraft, and mysterious others showed up at any time.

I loved my trips to visit the South African compound. On one of these trips, I saw the roof of an abandoned house. I was told it had been a retreat for the Spanish prior to Equatorial Guinea's independence. I could tell it had been abandoned. I asked some villagers to bring their machetes and cut a path for me. I could tell this could be an interesting place. I left some money with a woman I trusted to have it cleared for me. I've always liked a project right up to the present time.

When I returned, Sally was interested in learning more about the mountain house. We decided it would be our weekend place where we could get out of town and up to a higher, healthier altitude. In Moka, it was sunny during the day and chilly during the night. As well, here I was living near the equator, and I had problems with insects and rashes. What a turn of fate.

Some extra furniture was available for the house from my decorating the temporary quarters for our visitors. The furniture was basic, with mattresses, chairs, and a patio table for the small porch. Remember, there was no electricity or running water. It wasn't for the people I was used to dealing with but was just right for me and Sally.

In Moka, the South Africans were just down the road, and with the house, I didn't have to take advantage of their hospitality. The North Koreans had a project down the road, and they grew lovely vegetables. I made the mistake previously of visiting them and asking to buy vegetables. They saw the diplomatic license plate on the car and knew I was American. They would not sell to me. In the future, I would go with my South African friends, and they would sell to me.

Life was good in paradise. Catherine had made a friend in Moka. His name was Esteban, and his mother brought other women with machetes to help me clean the place. She was a great help and watched out for our interests. Her husband had been on the famous jungle hiking trip, and her mother was still living. She and her mother planted in a small garden beside the house in Moka, and we had wonderful tropical fruit. Catherine, now about five, and I would take a blanket, put it on the ground, and watch the stars. I felt like the sky was so close. I had never seen so many night stars. No artificial light or pollution. We were close to heaven.

Sally and Ted were happy for the embassy to have our little hideaway. George wasn't that interested in my adventures but was supportive. He liked his work, his recliner, a good book, and his music. In hindsight, he never got malaria or was never put on a drip because of unknown infections and itching. But oh, what a life I have lived, and the memories are "too good," as Tomas, my helper at the embassy, would say.

I have a very good story to tell. How do I do it justice? On one of my trips to Moka, a policeman came by the house and wanted a ride to Malabo. I reluctantly agreed, even though I was driving an embassy vehicle. We agreed on a time and place to meet. When I arrived to pick him up, he had two females with him! I said, "Who are these women?"

He said, "They are my wives."

They got in the back seat. He asked to open the back door so he could put a burlap sack in the back. He rode up front with me. I said I would take him because he was a policeman in Malabo. The wives were so loving to each other and held hands. I know an extra wife can help with the hard work African women have to do.

As we drove down the mountain, I smelled this foul odor. I knew what it was immediately. I grew up around men who hunted. He had a sack full of dead monkeys. I pulled over, opened the back door, and made him take them out. I think he was ready to cry. I said, "Put them out, and I mean now." As the road got steeper, I felt something sticky under my feet. It was blood from the monkeys. God help me out of this one! When we got down the mountain, we stopped, and I treated everyone to soft drinks and banana chips. What I needed was a Jim Beam and Coke. The wives were still holding hands. We had to drive some distance by the ocean before we got back to town. I rolled down the window to feel the wind, smell the ocean air, and calm down. Would I be in trouble for giving them a ride in an official vehicle?

When I got to the embassy, the guards opened the gate for me. I told them I needed some help. Would they please clean the vehicle? Of course, they would help me. No one would know about the monkeys because the smell would be gone by morning. The guards liked me because I had asked for an on-premises washer and dryer for them and cleaning women to wash their clothes. I asked for uniforms to be made and a place to shower. I use the word "I" often, but I couldn't have done some of these things without authorization from Ted, George, or sometimes the ambassador. No one ever mentioned the monkey incident. I got a pass on that one!

Equatorial Guinea was one of the poorest countries in Africa. Ramona, who owned the beauty shop, was a very enterprising woman who had lived for a while in Spain. She and her daughters had returned home to Equatorial Guinea just before we arrived in 1985. She reunited with an earlier love in her life, they married, and she seemed to be happy. She was a wonderful lady friend for me. Her two girls were about Catherine's age.

We had a big swing set delivered in our surface shipment. It might have been the only one on the island. It had slides, gymnastic rings, monkey bars, and swings. Ramona's girls came to play as well as many other children from Catherine's Spanish school. There were lots of children for Catherine's birthday party. George met some government officials he wanted to get to know, but it wasn't possible because of how closely the government controlled its officials. When they'd come to pick up their kids from our home, George could have unsupervised time with them to discuss issues. A swing set can be a diplomatic tool!

After two years, it was time to leave Equatorial Guinea, and saying goodbye to our staff was hard. The people who worked at the embassy were very special. An embassy needs local employees, who would remain there after we left. I would miss dear, sweet Trudy and Tomas Dickens. Down the dirt road by my house came Ramona and the girls to say goodbye. I had a pantry with lots of leftover food supplies. I had shared some food with Ramona earlier, and this time, I gave her jars of peanut butter, plus pasta, spaghetti sauce, and an assortment of other items. I hated to leave Romano. When she left, I watched her walk down the dirt road with dense jungle to her right, the same road I had seen on my arrival two years before. Nothing had changed. Tears came to my eyes.

I saw Ramona fifteen years later when we returned to Malabo, this time when George was the ambassador. Equatorial Guinea had become a wealthy oil state, but Ramona still had her beauty shop! Time had changed things for her in a very good way. Ramona had become a wealthy woman with eighteen houses she leased to people working for the oil companies, then operating in the country. She also had a house in Spain and a condo in Texas for her girls, who were in college. I didn't have to worry about her anymore.

Loving my baby girl, in the backyard of our
home in El Salvador.

Catherine in her new jumpsuit.

Catherines' first tricycle ride on the Rambla
in Montevideo, Uruguay. In the distance lay
the remains of the WWII German Battleship,
The Graf Spee, scuttled after a battle with
British warships in December 1939.

Playing with Catherine at a park near our
residence in Montevideo.

Our housekeeper, Mirta, with baby doll Catherine.

Mirta's brother in his traditional gaucho clothing.

Our close friends Larry and Lucille Palmer. Larry later in his career became a U.S. Ambassador to two countries.

Cayucos meeting us on arrival in Annobon. What a beginning to a great visit to a small island in the South Atlantic.

Catherine's first official diplomatic responsibility. Standing with a diplomatic pouch in Annobon containing Project Handclasp gifts.

The American Ambassador's wife, Terry Ruddy, presenting the gifts to the people of Annabon.

Catherine and friends having fun on her swing set.

Having fun with my daughter, despite the hardships of living in one of Africa's poorest countries.

Chapter 32

Being in Equatorial Guinea made me often think of my family back home. There was an ocean between us. Africa was a long way from Kentucky, but my memories always brought me close to home. I could look at the calendar and know what special times I was missing.

Because of my father's death when I was seven, I had no strong male influence. My uncle Joe was who I wanted my friends to meet, and I knew he would make me proud. He was a gentleman when he was sober, and even when he drank too much, he never changed. So many people get drunk and want to fight. Their personalities change, and they want to prove how mean they are. Not my uncle Joe.

Uncle Joe was in the first draft prior to the outbreak of WWII and went to Fort Ord, California, for infantry training. This twenty-one-year-old man from the woods of Kentucky, now a soldier for his country, sailed the Pacific under the Golden Gate Bridge on April 8, 1942, his birthday. The Japanese had bombed Pearl Harbor on December 7, 1941. Uncle Joe was first stationed in Hawaii and helped remove bodies from the USS *Arizona*. When he left Pearl Harbor, he, like many others, fought in the terrible battles against the Japanese in the South Pacific. He would often say, "Boys, I got some good training at Fort Ord." He attributed his survival to the training. It helped that he had hunted squirrels in the mountains of Kentucky.

Uncle Joe sometimes told me about the terrible things he had seen in the war, in particular the liberation of Manila and the rescue of our nurses who had been tortured and brutalized. It left a lasting impression on his mind. He was traumatized and had very bad dreams the rest of his life. One day, many years later while I was visiting, he said, "Jo, the Japs got me last night." He never said "Japanese," and he wanted us all to buy American products.

My grandmother liked to tell the story of Uncle Joe's return from the war. It was late at night and pitch dark. There were no streetlights in the hollow. Mammie heard footsteps on the front porch. She said to her husband, "Ike, get up. Joe is home." Every time Uncle AY would make a run of moonshine, usually sixteen jars, he would keep one jar and hide one in the barn floor. When Uncle Joe came home, Uncle AY had put away eighteen jars. They told me Uncle Joe was hooked on quinine, which he had taken to prevent malaria. He slept in the barn loft for six months.

Uncle AY decided he had to do something to help his brother start to get over the trauma from the war. He quit his job in the coal mines. They drank up the 'shine, hit the honky-tonks, and chased women. Six months later, they had spent their savings and had to go back to work. That was PTSD therapy back then for Uncle Joe, my hero. He never talked much about the war until he was older.

At the age of eighty-six, he had a heart attack. I spent sixteen days with him at Baptist Hospital in Knoxville, Tennessee. We had good talks during those days. He asked me, "Jo, why have I lived so long?"

I said, "Because you are a good man."

Uncle Joe died at age ninety-two, six years later, and believed he was going to hell because of the killing he had done in the war. I wrote a letter to President Obama asking for help for veterans, especially WWII vets, but never got an answer.

Uncle Joe and his mother were very close. She was born October 9, 1892, and was the matriarch of her family. She was very outspoken. I can remember one time when we were enjoying some porch time. A man walked down the road past her house and didn't speak. She would give people time to pass her barn. People were supposed to say, "Good morning, Aunt Mary," or "Good morning, Mrs. North." She would give them time to pass her barn; then she would say in a very loud voice, "Speak ass if your mouth can't!"

I adored my grandmother. She had no formal education, but she could deliver babies, make medicine from digging up roots and tree bark, and make lots of teas for healing different problems. I remember willow, ginseng, sassafras, and ginger. She delivered her last baby at age seventy-six in an emergency. She delivered me before the doctor arrived. Uncle Joe, my hero, went by horseback to get the doctor, but they were too late. As you know by now, I was named after Uncle Joe. I was a baby-boom baby, born April 8, 1947. I came into this world six years after Uncle Joe went under the Golden Gate Bridge. We share the same birthday.

All Uncle Joe's nieces and nephews loved his 1949 red Studebaker truck. The shell of the old truck is now sitting in the brush down from my house. We could ride in the back of it and even put the tailgate down. What a life!

My uncle Porter, Aunt Della's husband, was a well-known seller of good whiskey. He made it in the beginning but had other people make it for him later. Are you ready for another good story? My dad and Uncle AY had a moonshine still hidden in the mountains. Once, Uncle Joe went to watch them make a run of moonshine. Much to their surprise, the lawmen found their site. Uncle AY and my dad got away. Uncle Joe got arrested and taken to jail. He said it was his still because he couldn't tell on his brother and brother-in-law. He was bound over to Frankfort, the state capital, because it was a federal offense. He was given a one-year probation. Maybe a factor was that he was a decorated WWII veteran who had seen four years of hard fighting in the South Pacific without taking leave.

After the war, Uncle Joe returned a troubled man but tried to live a peaceful life and be a good husband and a good father to my cousin Carson. Aunt Ruby, his wife, went to Detroit with her sister. She was a 'Rosie the Riveter' and helped make aircraft for the war effort.

Uncle Joe would go off in the woods to hunt. When he was young, he hunted to help with food for the table. Later in his life, the woods were out his back door. He didn't hunt then, and I think he enjoyed the solitude. He was a great host, and Aunt Ruby always had a pot of hot coffee and a cake under the cake stand.

Before our next post, Catherine and I went home to Pineville. George was in Washington for briefings. I had no seminars or language training to attend at the Overseas Briefing Center. Our next post was the Bahamas. Nassau, here we come. We're going to the beach!

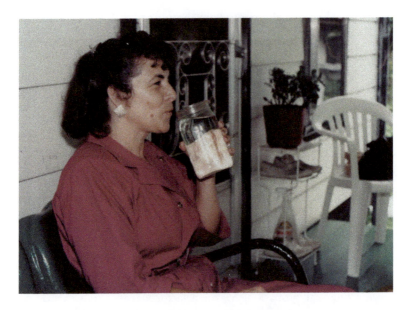

Sipping moonshine on Uncle Joe's porch.

Presenting to my Uncle Joe North, a display box of his medals and awards
for his heroism in the Pacific in World War Two.

Chapter 33

We arrived in the Bahamas in 1987. What a beautiful country with its tropical look and feel. What a difference from our arrival in Equatorial Guinea. We were taken to temporary quarters. I had to put people in temporary quarters only a few times—no more than two weeks, if possible. I had flowers, wine, cheese, and normal staples until I could take them shopping. In Nassau, I would not be so lucky. We stayed in temporary quarters for five months. I was livid at the embassy. We got our air shipment, and that was helpful. My surface shipment arrived but went to a warehouse. It was five months before our house was ready.

We had a nice school for Catherine, the Tamberly School, and she made several friends. Two of them, Juliette and Sharon, remain friends even today. That would be about thirty-four years. They were bridesmaids in Catherine's wedding. As it turned out, I met the mothers, Kathleen and Denise, and they became friends of mine. All have been to Kentucky.

During our time in Nassau, I started, in 1988, the construction of our permanent home in Pineville and finished it in 1989. I had always wanted the security of having a permanent home near my family. I had worked on the plan for about ten years. I bought an accordion file and took pages from magazines to help me with planning and decorating. George wasn't interested and left everything to me. He felt that from past work in California and at the embassy, I was prepared. He was tied to his work, but being so close to the US, I could travel to Kentucky when needed. My brother Jim and Uncle Joe were down the hill from me. Jim was on the job site and working as a carpenter. This should have been a happy time. Wrong! It was pure pleasure and pure hell. The house was finished, but it was over budget. I had to fire the contractor. After that, I finished with subcontractors. George was smart when he had left everything to me. He wanted to sit in a wing chair and read a book. He got his dream.

The home is up the hill from where I was born on the same mountainside. My sister, Pauline, and I were born in a house behind Uncle Joe's. From every room, I can see the oak tree. It is over two hundred years old, I think? I am a dreamer and have always been so. I thought all my friends and family would be there for years. My dream had some flaws. Uncle Bill died first, but at least Uncle AY did live to see my new home. Catherine got to spend some time with him. Mammie had been gone for ten years before I had a home back on the mountain.

Dear friend Judy didn't get to have a formal dinner in my dining room with a nice bottle of wine. I loved her so very much. Life isn't for the weak. Eva, Judy, and I were three friends from Pineville. We loved each other and had talked about who would be last to die. With Judy's death, we were now two. Eva and I were with Judy until the last breath. It has been my observation that some people don't love as deeply as I do. I hate death, and it hurts me too much. I am afraid to count the losses I have suffered.

Chapter 34

Back to the beach in Nassau and happier times. On Saturdays, Catherine and I would go to downtown Nassau. From there, we would take a boat over to the yoga retreat. We loved the atmosphere. We had vegetarian food, but Catherine was not familiar with it. I had been a vegetarian, but it was difficult in the Foreign Service. There was a platform at the retreat built to face the ocean. It was a great place to meditate. One time, as we were meditating with a group, Catherine asked me what everyone was saying—was it "home"? No, it was "Ommmmm," but we were saying, "Home! Home! Home!" I never made that mistake again.

My daughter and I were together a lot in Nassau. She was there for embassy special events. We loved to dance, and I started early with Catherine. Our all-time favorite dance was to "Graceland" by Paul Simon. When my friends Kathleen and Juliette got together with Catherine and me, we four danced to "Graceland." We would sing, "Graceland, Graceland, Memphis, Tennessee." I also liked his song "Diamonds on the Soles of Her Shoes."

The Bahamas were different for me. It wasn't the typical Foreign Service post, but one special thing happened: I made five lifelong friends. Kathleen McCormick, from Canada, married a handsome Bahamian, who was sweet Juliette's father. Denise Israel was from Israel and other parts of the world. Her husband, Giora Israel, was manager of the Coral World tourist site. This was one of our favorite places to see in Nassau. Carol Chaney from Arkansas was our embassy doctor. She was married to the minister of Health. Another lady was a friend of Carol named Rosa Sweeting. Rosa was Peruvian and had married a Bahamian named Kevin. I felt Rosa was a friend, and I told her I needed someone who spoke Spanish to live with us. She told me about a lady in Peru who had a nursing background and would be a great nanny for

Catherine. Her name was Ana Maria Aranda. We sent her a ticket and brought her to Nassau. She looked after Catherine for almost five years, and we are still friends. She was loved by all my family in Pineville. Years later, I went with her to her home in Peru. That's for another chapter, maybe two or three. I'll keep you waiting. As Tomas Dickens would say, "Mrs. Staples, it was too good."

Marian came to Nassau from Cincinnati to celebrate Catherine's seventh birthday. Eva came with my aunt Della but at a different time. My beautiful aunt had never flown. Lloyal, her son, didn't want her to go to Nassau, especially when he found out she would be flying. He threatened me if something happened to his mother. Aunt Della said, "Lloyal, just be quiet. I'm going, and if something happens, it is my time." She had raised seven children and had helped with her grandchildren and some of her great grandchildren. George's enduring memory is of Aunt Della sitting by the pool at our home with her coffee and a newspaper, relaxed and completely enjoying herself. She was always able to relax and have fun whenever she was with us.

Aunt Della had her country store for forty-five years. One of my favorite characters who traded with her was Johnny Bull. He looked like he came from another century. I will write more about him later. My aunt had worked in the local elections for thirty-nine years. She missed one because of my mom's death. She was a Republican to the bone. I was a registered Republican for years, and my family were all the same, except Uncle Ned. He was the only Democrat. Even so, I just voted for whom I thought was the best person. People would come by to talk to my mom and family. Of course, everyone talked about Franklin Roosevelt. He was a Democrat, and because of WWII, he was loved and respected.

I liked watching the news with my uncle AY, and that's where my interest in politics began. I didn't think of a political party. I thought about the person: the person who would fix the roads or the sheriff who would protect us and get help when a road was impassable. I never changed until this nonsense from Sarah Palin and the Tea Party came along. The county court clerk was a Republican. I told her how I felt and changed my registration to Democrat.

Back to the problems I was having with the embassy's General Services Section. After the five months in temporary quarters, I was mad and ready to talk with Ambassador Carol Hallett. I wanted to have my paintings, sculptures, carvings, and handmade rugs. The house the embassy had signed a lease for me to live in needed work, including installation of five air conditioners. When I worked in General Services, I don't remember a family ever waiting over two weeks to move into their assigned housing. I cared about making people happy. They are away from home and sometimes at a great distance. Your home is your retreat and your safe haven. First impressions are important and how embassy families are treated. I had people helping me, and work requests were taken care of immediately. If you have a family and babies, you need your washer and dryer taken care of as soon as possible. I liked making people happy, and not just in the Foreign Service. John Collins taught me that years ago in El Salvador.

Our time in the Bahamas was filled with a lot of new experiences. My family and friends could come to visit because the flight from and to Miami was about half an hour. Marian and I had a great time. Once, we went to the dock and boarded a beautiful sailboat called the *Wild Harp*. A very nice couple from New York accompanied us on this voyage. The Bahamian music was great. We started drinking Bahama Mamas. I think we had only two or three drinks, but Elvis, a crew member, must have used too much rum. Yes, that was his name! I have been an Elvis fan since I was twelve years old. Eva and I collected Elvis memorabilia, and Eva, sister Pauline, and I went to Graceland.

I'm not a very good swimmer, but the turquoise water was too enticing. Marian and I jumped off the side of the boat and got washed up on a coral reef. We were really scratched up, and we had to remove pieces of coral from our hips and legs. Elvis had to help us off the reef. This story has been told and laughed about for years.

Kathleen and I would go to a section of Nassau called "Over the Hill." It was an area not visited by tourists, where the locals would go to eat and drink. I loved the stewed fish, and the johnnycake tasted like Jiffy cornbread. We went by bicycle to the places we liked, such as our favorite swim area. It was our secret. We took our clothes off and went skinny-dipping. Oh, those were the good ol' days!

After our assignment ended, Denise came with her girls to see me in Kentucky. Sharon was about eight, and Michelle was about four years old. Years later, George and I went to Sharon's wedding in Miami. George is still talking about the Latin band at the wedding. Michelle is married now. Denise is a great photographer and came to Kentucky with Sharon, where she took photos of Catherine's wedding. As noted before, Sharon and Juliette were maids of honor in my Catherine's wedding. Carol had gone to Brazil and adopted a baby boy she named Seth. She eventually took her son back to Arkansas and now is a very happy grandmother.

Maybe what I've told you has been too much, but I'm happy to say I remain friends with all the women I met in Nassau. I have friends from most of our embassy assignments.

Chapter 35

After many weeks in temporary quarters, the day arrived when our Nassau house was ready, but it would take my talents to make it a home. The books were in the bookcases, and Doris's sculptures were unpacked and put on the pedestals. My two paintings from El Salvador found a home. I loved my Mario Escobars and my other treasures from El Salvador. I had a beautiful oil painting of fishermen going out to fish in the morning. My country scene of an asado with gauchos wearing flat-top hats like Mirta's father wore in Uruguay, dogs, and meat on skewers was a welcome reminder of a very happy time for us. I had been too long without my treasures. Oh! I can't forget George's painting from Montevideo of his sugar cubes that went with afternoon coffee.

George wanted a dog, and here came a black Labrador into the family. We named him Tag, after the dog my father gave me when I was two years old. Tag was a large Labrador. The breeder decided we would have the first pick of the litter when the puppies were born. We had to pay three hundred dollars to a lovely lady named Corine, who lived on the other side of the island. Tag would become George's dog.

While we were there, not too much was going on in the Bahamas. George was in the Political Section—no radical students, communist parties, or labor problems to report about to Washington. The Drug Enforcement Agency took care of drug issues.

We were not allocated very much in representational funds—the US government funds allocated to spend on dinners, lunches, and receptions. The embassy's representational funding for official entertainment expenses goes first to the ambassador, who decides how to distribute the funds. Our ambassador, Carol Hallett, was a former California legislator and a political appointee, not a career Foreign Service officer. We liked her very much, but there are always some things only a career ambassador would know. If I entertained, we had to pay for almost everything. I got very mad about the situation. The last cocktail party we paid for was about seven hundred dollars. I told George no more money was coming out of our savings account. I was going back and forth from Nassau to Kentucky, trying to build a house, and it had gone over budget.

A very nice thing happened in Nassau. The ambassador asked a friend from California to display her art in the ambassador's residence. The art was on loan for the length of the ambassador's assignment. Years later, when I was an ambassador's wife, I asked a Kentucky artist to loan some of his paintings to me, and he said no. He didn't want to be part of the Art in Embassies program. Ambassador Hallett's friend had said yes. Her name was Vel Miller, and she was a great painter and sculptor. She let Ambassador Hallett display a beautiful life-size bronze Native American woman and other paintings. I remember there was a bronze of a little boy riding on a stick pony. I fell in love with the eighteen-inch sculpture. I had ridden a stick pony when I was young with friends. My stick pony was just a stick between my legs. I wonder who bought it from Vel.

I have seen Vel and her wonderful husband, Warren, through the years. She lives in Central California about half an hour from Hearst Castle, a favorite place of mine. Inside Vel's home are many oil paintings. She has a most unusual home. I don't know how to describe what it is like to be there. Her home is part western ranch with a big barn, and there is enough art to fill a gallery, with a collection of hundreds of interesting things from Native American reservations, where she has spent time throughout many years. It would take many visits to see everything. I adore Vel, and her touch is so gentle. And she makes a great tuna sandwich.

Warren and Vel raised longhorn cattle. Once, Vel took me for a ride up the hill to see their cattle. She opened the fence and invited me to walk through. We were right in the middle of the cattle, who were raised for show and were award winners. I was a little nervous, but Vel knew all their names and even their mothers' names. Years later, during our assignment in Rwanda, I bought George a set of longhorn cattle horns for his birthday. We were then living in Kigali, Rwanda, where George was ambassador. I asked Mrs. Ergibe Boyd, his public affairs officer, to locate them for me. These horns, however, were from the famous Rwandan longhorn cattle. These cattle, from my understanding, originated in Rwanda, then were shipped to Spain, then to Texas, and eventually dispersed throughout the US, where Vel and Warren's could now be found. The horns were a big surprise for George and are proudly displayed in our residence in Kentucky.

While assigned to Nassau, I was very involved in a traveling Smithsonian Institution exhibit honoring Native Americans. A generous Bahamian man let us use the left side of his antique store, which I believe was called Marlborough Antiques on Bay Street. He was a great help with making the displays work right. We brought in heavy black plastic to protect his floors. Wooden poles were used to hold back the sand. We used small trees to display some of the artifacts. I can remember a very big Native American chief's traditional headdress, lots of turquoise jewelry, clothing, and beautiful blankets from different American tribes. Vel and Warren were a great addition to our effort. She had a Crow Native American woman with her who demonstrated weaving techniques. Vel had put up an easel to do drawings. I'm very happy my Catherine sat for Vel to do a sketch. Vel brought some things to share from her exhibit that were on display at Ambassador Hallett's residence.

The exhibit was a great success. If I remember correctly, about eight hundred children came to see the exhibit. I loved volunteering for this event. I enjoyed seeing everything. We tried to display different themes highlighting Native American life from the desert and the mountains. Afterwards, I helped take down the exhibit, and we moved it to Freeport, the second-largest city in the Bahamas. We again had great attendance. Adults enjoyed the event, but as in Nassau, it was really for the children.

I was happy being in Nassau after Malabo. George had to be challenged with dealing with major policy issues, not tourism concerns. I thought in Nassau, he could play tennis, make friends to play golf with, and go to a casino to play blackjack. Wrong! He was bored and wanted to curtail the assignment. An island five miles wide and twenty miles long can feel closed in.

However, I could easily fly over to Miami with Denise and go to an open-air art exhibit. I bought a painting in Miami that I love to this day, *Paths I Have Walked*. It reminds me of a girl walking up my driveway in Kentucky. The artist painted her from the back, with overgrown trees hanging over both sides of the road. I decided several years ago if I ever got my notes together and wrote this book, the title would be *Paths I Have Walked*. God let me live to be healthy enough to finish my book. Hip-hip hooray.

Our assignment in Nassau was over, and Catherine; her nanny, Ana Maria; our dog, Tag; Don Quixote, my black cat; and I were heading home to Kentucky.

Chapter 36

When we returned to Kentucky in the fall of 1989, one member of the family was not present. George was back in Washington, DC, at the State Department for a year as senior watch officer in the Operations Center. He loved the assignment. George is a news person. Once, I went to visit him at work. TV screens were monitoring events in real time from around the world. For example, if there was, let's say, a coup attempt in Egypt, then it was George's job to decide what senior officials to immediately notify and if he should awaken the secretary of state. Then the secretary of state would decide to brief the president or not. It was a very challenging and exciting time for George.

Meanwhile, back in Kentucky, we were settling in, and the house was starting to come together. It was nice to be back home and not in a foreign country. It was wonderful to have Uncle Joe and Aunt Ruby down the hill, and below them were my brother Jim; his wife, Tina; and daughter, Tressie. Across the field was my uncle AY, and around the mountain in Big Clear Creek were Aunt Della and family and her store that I loved. Uncle Clyde and his beautiful wife Evelyn's home was in Little Clear Creek. I loved Evelyn, an artist and social worker. We talked and dreamed of places I had been, and hoped we would return to together.

Back home in the mountains, I got to hear whip-poor-wills again. Uncle Joe, my beloved uncle, would call and say, "Jo, go out on the porch and look at the full moon tonight." No one loved nature more than my uncle Joe. I built our home near a large oak tree, and from inside almost every room, I had a view of the tree. It must have been two hundred years old.

One windy day, I was sitting in my wing chair reading my *Art & Antiques* magazine when I heard a loud crash. I grew up in the mountains, so I knew what it sounds like when a tree falls. I went to the front porch and saw nothing, but there was more light than before. I looked all around the house and saw no fallen trees. I went back to my reading. Moments later, something terrible came to my mind. I said, "Oh no." I ran to the front porch, went maybe twenty feet to where the yard slopes down the hillside, and started crying at the sight of my fallen beloved oak. I called my uncle Joe and cried like a baby. The old oak had also meant a lot to him. He said, "Jo, everything dies." The house I grew up in down in the hollow had a view of the mountain, and we could pick out the old oak from a distance.

I loved my uncle AY. He never married but had had his share of women. I think my grandfather asked him to take care of my grandmother; this was a deathbed wish and a mistake. Uncle AY knew my grandmother was too difficult to share her home with another woman. I have heard people say, "Two dishrags don't belong in one kitchen." It is true that most women don't want another woman trying to run their kitchen. All his life, Uncle AY had a terrible complex about not serving in WWII. He had been given a medical deferment. AY would joke, "Someone had to stay home and take care of the women." All his cousins and neighbors had left for the South Pacific, the Panama Canal, and the European Theater. That's how the government works. Men who were poor with not much education went into the infantry. The well-off who didn't want to serve had fathers who got them a deferment. That's not fair but is the way of life. I'm not saying the well-to-do and better educated didn't go to war, but most often the poor guys went into the infantry. I saw this firsthand among those who served in Vietnam.

Uncle AY didn't have biological children, but he had us. After my father's death, we moved back to be near him and Mammie. He was a bit hard on us, and he drank too much. He had a nice new car, or so the story goes, but I never saw it. He was about twenty-five years old when he was told to give up either drinking or driving. He never drove again! Uncle AY lived to be sixty-two years old. He was a character and well loved, but he was a pest when he was drunk.

What great memories were made during those days. As you know from previous chapters, Mammie left us when I lived in California. She never got to see my home or sleep with me there.

When my grandmother was alive, big family get-togethers happened at her home. Uncle Ned; his wife, my aunt Addie; and my cousins came to those get-togethers. I still think of Aunt Addie. When I came through the door, she would always greet me with a "Come in here; where have you been?" and give me a hug. My mother's younger brother, Uncle Bill; his wife, Aunt May; and my cousins would also come. They lived down the hollow from us. I loved him so very much. He was good to me. I would drive our car to Uncle Bill's. I started driving when I was thirteen but not out on the big road. Uncle Bill would drive us to the drive-in movie theater. Those were such good days. I feel sorry for those of you who didn't have those drive-in movie experiences.

Catherine and I were home from the Bahamas, and we had good times together. My family loved my Catherine, and they loved her in return. She for the first time had her own bedroom in her permanent home, and she has it even today.

I remember seeing my two uncles dance for the first time at a party I had. When the party was over, Uncle Joe said, "Boys, we will never have another time like this one"—and we didn't.

While we were home, Uncle AY was diagnosed with inoperable lung cancer. Thank God, I was home to help him. I was there when his doctor said, not so gently, "AY, get your affairs in order." He had about six months.

I put my arm through his when we got to the street. I said, "Don't worry. We'll go to Knoxville or Lexington to get the best help."

He said, "Oh hell, you can't worry about something when you have no control of it."

I wanted to know if he'd had good preventative care so I asked the nurse when he'd had his last lung X-ray, bloodwork, and so on. I found out later there were no lung X-rays at the doctor's office. They said they kept only up to seven years' worth at the office. They told me to check at the hospital: no records there.

Uncle AY was a real stickler for time. Once, the road was blocked because some trees had fallen and grading was in progress. It looked like Uncle AY might be late for his radiation treatment. I was driving him and said, "We won't be late. Hold on!" I put my old fateful Bronco truck in four-wheel drive, went up on a hillside, cut through the trees, and could see where we could get down and connect with the main highway. Uncle AY said, "That was one hell of a ride." And we were not late for his appointment.

Once again, there was no preventive care for the poor. Uncle AY was a coal miner for years and later worked with Uncle Joe at the sawmill. He was a smoker. One would think with his medical history that he would have had X-rays. Nope! I was livid. A lot of dust was inhaled with the work he did and no mask. Uncle AY was a great lumber grader and, which I understood, entailed the following: Wood was cut with big saws when it came into the lumberyard. Then it was sent down rollers, maybe thirty feet long, to be evaluated by type of wood and quality. Uncle AY had to do the math to determine the board footage, and each board had to be flipped over to look at the other side. The lumber kept coming at a fast pace. Men working in the yard determined by my uncle's marks where it would be stacked. The wood was then sold and put on trucks to be hauled away. This was very hard manual work for my grandfather and, later, for my uncle AY and my uncle Joe. Their cousins Murphy, DC, Jim Frank, and Casey also worked at the sawmill. They made the owner rich while they stayed poor.

Off I went with Uncle AY, like sheep, to thirty-six radiation treatments on his lung area, for what purpose except to burn him up, I don't know. I put lotion on his back because it was black. He was burned from the front of his chest through to his back. Can someone tell me when one lung was inoperable and the other had only thirty-percent function, why was it necessary to do radiation and put him through all of that? He ended up on oxygen full time, and the cancer wasn't stopped. Yes, I knew Uncle AY would die, but he would have had a few more months. His quality of life would have been better without the radiation.

One day, I went to make breakfast for him, but he couldn't get out of bed to let me in the door. I managed to get inside quickly and went to help him. He was sliding off the side of the bed, and I couldn't hold him much longer. Thank God, Uncle Joe was coming through the bottom field, and he helped me. I put Uncle AY's oxygen tube in water and saw bubbles which meant the oxygen was working, but he couldn't breathe properly. Uncle AY didn't have a phone, so Uncle Joe hollered to my brother Jim to call the ambulance. Then Jim rushed to see if he could help. The ambulance arrived, and we went at a very high speed. The emergency personnel thought he wouldn't make it to the hospital.

Dr. Cabway was in the emergency room. They worked to stabilize Uncle AY. At a certain point, he opened his eyes, looked at the clock, and said, "Boys, is it twelve o'clock?" We all went wild because he could speak. There were shouts. Dr. Cabway was praying and thanking God. A nurse and I were crying. In a big city, I could not have ridden in the ambulance and stayed with my uncle in the emergency room.

Uncle AY was given a room. He rallied for three days. I had heard people can get better for about three days. He said, "I'm not leaving my money to anyone. I'm going to use up my money-making moonshine." The man from the lab knew Uncle AY. His father, my dad, and my uncle went to live chicken-shooting matches together. Uncle AY had a good time visiting with people who knew him. But then he worsened. I got him in a sitting position to hit him on the back, but he was gone in about an hour. The nurses couldn't help. Doctor Hays, my doctor, was on call, and he pronounced him dead. They reclined the bed flat.

A lot of families had started to gather at the end of the hall. I know Aunt Della was there. She was the matriarch of the family and a good one all her life. She loved all of us with unconditional love and would kill if anyone hurt us. She and other family members had been on their way to what they thought would be a visit. Dr. Hays asked me if I would like to have a few minutes with AY. I said, "Yes, I'd like some private time with my uncle." I just sat there and looked at him. The soul was gone; there was no life left. Would I see him again?

A couple of months before he died, Uncle AY asked me to go to his doctor's office to see if he owed anything and to the pharmacy to see if there were any bills outstanding. He never wanted to get "dun." That's country talk for a late bill. He didn't want to leave this life owing anything. He died with twenty thousand dollars in the bank. The money went to his brothers and sister. Uncle Joe had money for his burial. What a man! What an uncle!

Uncle AY never made above minimum wage, which then was about $3.50 an hour. When he retired, his Social Security check was less than four hundred dollars a month. Never one dun came. He didn't respect anyone who didn't work hard. AY called people in the neighborhood who had more money but who had never worked "sorry." He told me, "Jo, if you can't pay your way, you stay at home." He never had central heat or air-conditioning. He cut trees and split them with a wedge for wood to heat his house in the winter to keep his utility bill small. He canned and preserved food in the summer to have for the winter.

At the time Uncle Ay was going for those damn radiation treatments, George visited Pineville after taking a short leave from the State Department. George asked if he could drive Uncle AY to his treatment, and my uncle agreed but insisted on paying for the gas. George thought he had gotten one over on him because he said, "AY, I filled the gas tank earlier." My uncle told him to pull over and he would buy lunch. George was getting a taste of what we call "poor and proud."

Chapter 37

During our time at home in Pineville, Catherine began attending public school for the first time. She had to adjust to being with American kids and got to know her cousins and extended family. We made friends with a lovely family: Larry Edmonson; his wife, Laurie; and their children, Brandy and Chandler. Catherine and Brandy became acquainted in third grade. Laurie and I worked out at the same gym. Laurie was serious about her weight training. I didn't own a weight-training belt. That changed because I had to look the part. Laurie and I became very close. Later, when we were on a Washington assignment, the family came to see us and to take Chandler to get to know his country's capital city. Laurie and Brandy also visited us when we were in Cameroon.

Larry was Laurie's dream man, a former marine and a hard worker. Laurie was a worldly woman, having grown up in Florida with her father, who owned three Suzuki motorcycle dealerships. She was going to teach me how to ride a small Harley-Davidson. Larry was from Pineville. Such different worlds the two came from, but Laurie made a home for them all in the mountains. I loved seeing her coming around my back walkway with a bright-colored dress, bottle of wine, a smoke to share, and a big smile. We became friends for life. She was a great mother to Chandler and Brandy. She told Larry, "I will have you a son if you pay for a tummy tuck!"

During this time at home, besides enjoying being with family and friends such as Laurie, I had time to read. I have read many, many books and like authors of mystery and adventures, such as Ken Follett, Nelson DeMille, Lee Child, and Greg Isles, and lots of books on the evolution of man. Authors Saraban, Gear and O'Neal, and Jean Auel have stories that intrigue me about human development. Beatrice Small, who wrote historical romance novels that always thrilled my soul, is another favorite. I especially love time travel stories by Michael Crichton. My latest discovery is the *Outlander* series.

I recently read *Hillbilly Elegy* by J. D. Vance. His family moved from Jackson, Kentucky, to Middletown, Ohio. I waited until my memoir was in the final draft stage before reading his book. I thought our locations and culture would be very similar with our Scots/Irish backgrounds. I didn't want to write about a lot of similarities in our lives. In the sixties, I myself went from Pineville, Kentucky, to Norwood, Ohio.

Chapter 38

Eva Taylor, my BFF, was always my greatest cheerleader, and she continued to be when I returned home from the Bahamas. She would say, "You are the prettiest of the three of us" (Judy, Eva, and me). Of course, I would disagree. She told me that people should remember that I was very smart long before meeting George Staples. She made me believe in myself and that I was the greatest mom, who could always beautifully decorate apartments and homes.

Catherine and I got to spend time with Eva; her husband, Jack; son Jackie; and daughter Christy on what Eva called "Taylors' Mountain." Eva was a very good cook, and she was also a quilter. She was slender and beautiful. She went to the beauty shop often and always wanted her hair to look nice. She used to tell me that if she didn't have money for the hairdresser, she would pick up aluminum cans for recycling.

I got interested in collecting Depression glass and got carried away with Sharon or Cabbage Rose, as the pattern was known by two names. Whenever I left the country on a new assignment and could no longer visit antique stores, Eva would carry a list in her wallet of the pieces I was missing. There will never be another Eva. She loved my whole family: Aunt Della, my grandmother, sister Pauline, and brothers Jim, Alvie, and Bill. She was so happy I had a home here in Pineville on the mountain. She was the life of the party and could always tell a good joke.

Eva and I both had other friends. There was never jealousy on my part because my friends became her friends, especially Marian. A woman is never jealous of another woman when she knows who she is. If I could teach women one lesson, it would be to believe in yourself. George has always said, "Jealousy is an unworthy emotion." I've always agreed with him about that.

Eva and I had difficult childhoods, but nothing compared to my father's mother, who had to send five of her seven children to an orphanage. My dad and his sister Pauline were too old to go to an orphanage. I know my aunt Pauline died while riding in the back of a truck that turned over going around a steep curve. When I spent time with my grandma on my father's side, we didn't talk about what happened. A man had shot and killed my grandfather while he was riding on horseback. My dad lived with different families until he served in WWII. I know his mother didn't want to give up her children, but there was no financial help for women in those days.

During this time between overseas assignments, I was home for the Fuson family reunion. It happened every Labor Day weekend. Our Pine Mountain State Resort Park is beautiful and the oldest in Kentucky. A very special event happened during my time at home. A cousin, Mary Dean, from Shelbyville knew her father had been adopted from Pineville. She told me she felt he was missing something in his life. She did the research and came up Route 92, looking for Ben Fuson's children. She stopped at a store, and my cousin Dessie was working there. Mary Dean told my cousin about her quest, and Dessie said, "I can take you to their house."

Brother Jim was in his yard when Uncle Robert entered and introduced himself. Jim told him, "What took you so long? I knew you would come someday." Tears were shed by both men. Wonderful, sweet Aunt Dorothy, his wife, was with him. My brother Alvie made an entrance. Alvie looked like their only son, who had died in a motorcycle accident. More crying.

I loved them so very much it hurts me to write about my wonderful aunt Dorothy and uncle Robert. They came late into our lives, but we made up for lost years and lived our time together to the fullest. My house was just about finished, and whenever they visited, they had a home with us. They loved Catherine so very much. She went to spend some time with them in Shelbyville. Uncle Robert's nickname for Catherine was Petunia.

When Uncle Robert and Aunt Dorothy visited Pineville, it would touch my heart to see Uncle Robert and Uncle Porter in the swing on the back porch at aunt Della's house. Uncle Porter was a farmer and moonshiner. Uncle Robert had been adopted by a doctor and his wife. Both were intelligent, and life took them in different directions. Both were very good men and first cousins. Their mothers were sisters. Uncle Robert served in WWII, and after returning home, he worked for and retired from General Electric.

My dad and Uncle Robert were brothers. My dad had died many years before, and they had never met each other. I gave Uncle Robert a picture of my dad in his WWII uniform, and Uncle Robert had a WWII photo of him in uniform as well. I was in my uncle's bedroom and saw their photos on a corner shelf side by side. They looked a lot alike.

Soon, it was time to make a pilgrimage to visit Elvis the King. Eva, sister Pauline, and I were on our way to Graceland. We were "going to Graceland, Graceland, Memphis, Tennessee," a verse from Paul Simon's song. A friend loaned me a light-blue Cadillac. We had to arrive in style to see the King. When we checked into the hotel, I asked the desk clerk what three women who had never been to Memphis could do for the evening. He said, "Give me fifty-two dollars and fifty cents each to do the night tour of Memphis." The first stop was B. B. King's for blues music and ribs. I saw B. B.'s original guitar, named Lucille, displayed on the wall. On to other nightspots for more music and entertainment.

We met two ladies from California who were in the entertainment business. The five of us had a great time. They gave us a very big tip about visiting Elvis's home. They told us Elvis was still alive and really was upstairs! They had been on the day tour, had had a great visit, and got to go upstairs to see him. We thanked them for the big tip. We saw St. Jude Children's Research Hospital and Danny Thomas's burial site. We saw the pyramid built on the river, which had a Hard Luck Café in it.

The end of the night tour was to drive by Graceland. We got out and took photos of the famous gate with the musical notes. We went back to the hotel and went to sleep, wondering what tomorrow would bring.

The next day, we got dressed and took the bus to Graceland. I was very excited because I felt that Elvis was my kind. We were from the same culture, religion, music, and love of our mothers. I was a quiet fan, never a screamer. We saw everything at Graceland inside and out, and his grave, clothes, and record albums are still in my mind after all these years. Sis went back to Knoxville, and Eva to Taylors' Mountain, and I went home to my mountain. After a few days, I found a card from the two Elvis fans from California. I sent a card and thanked them for the big tip. I told them we sneaked up the steps, and sure enough the King was there. Such a memory! I loved all his songs. My favorites are "Always on My Mind," "Memories," "In the Ghetto," and "Farther Along" (an old southern Christian song from church).

Despite so much happening in Memphis, I missed my baby girl. It wasn't a long trip, but I never liked to be away from Catherine. That's still true today. I went back to work when she was four but only for half a day, and she was five minutes from the embassy. In Malabo, I left her for a trip to Germany to see my "little sister" Claudia Meier when Catherine was five. Claudia had dated my brother Alvie when he was in the army and stationed in Germany. Catherine and I have never liked being away from each other. George was more practical. He wanted to send Catherine to a Swiss boarding school when she was about twelve. He loved her, but a better education was more important to him than being emotional. I stood my ground and said, "No way. She stays near her mother."

Our Ambassador to The Bahamas, Carol Hallett, and her husband Jim. A wonderful and effective team, and a great example to emulate.

Aunt Della and Eva, my BFF, arriving in Nassau for a visit.

Vel Miller at her ranch in California. A wonderful artist and friend who I first met in Nassau during her participation in the Smithsonian Institution's exhibit honoring Native Americans.

Warren Miller, Vel's husband, a rancher and lover of the outdoors.

Kathleen McCormack and her daughter Juliette Diehl. Juliette and Catherine attended the same girl's school in Nassau. Kathleen and I met at the school and have remained lifelong friends ever since.

With Kathleen in The Bahamas, where true love and friendship shines.

With my one and only sister, Pauline, on a visit to Graceland.

Our home in the Kentucky mountains, built during our assignment to The Bahamas.

My brother Alvie and our love for each other.

Ana Maria Aranda who joined our family in Nassau. She became Catherine's nanny and has remained a close family friend ever since.

Years later, I had the pleasure of traveling with Ana Maria to Peru, meeting her family, and visiting Machu Picchu.

Chapter 39

Our next assignment would be Zimbabwe, and Uncle Robert and Aunt Dorothy were our first guests. They met George for the first time on their arrival in Harare. George loved them from the first week. It would take another book to write about our adventures in Zimbabwe, but I'll share some highlights.

We transferred to Zimbabwe through London, and while George had meetings, Catherine and I toured Windsor Castle. My baby girl has always been a trouper. She indulges me when I want to stay too long in an art museum. Later in life, she came to appreciate the education I had given her. Catherine is mad with herself when she sees a painting and recognizes the artist without reading the name.

When we checked in at Heathrow Airport, George, Catherine, and I were nervous with seventeen pieces of luggage. We had an extra weight allowance but for a few pieces, not seventeen. We put our diplomatic passports on the counter. George had the old faithful American Express ready. We told the lady we were going to Zimbabwe for a three-year assignment at the American Embassy. She gave us our tickets without any extra charges. We took a deep breath, and I said, "Let's go to the bar." Since Catherine was small, it was her job to be in charge of the boarding tickets, which she guarded carefully, and we flew to Zimbabwe without incident.

When we arrived, we were met by the ambassador and other embassy personnel. George told Al Marquis, the administrative officer, that we would need a van for all our luggage. They came with two cars and had to return with another from the motor pool. Thank God, there was a residence to go to from the airport and no temporary quarters.

The residence was very nice, with lots of possibilities. I would be working at the embassy and decorating our new home. The residence needed lots of gardening changes. The staff had worked for some time at our new home, and I always like to give everyone the benefit of the doubt. Since we had to pay their salaries, it was my decision whether or not to continue to employ them. George wanted nothing to do with managing the staff. That was for me to decide because I trained them to do things my way. Ronia was the cook; Krecencia was the housekeeper; and Ben, Linus, and Killian were the gardeners. We were pleased and never made a change in three years.

Ronia was a good cook. She made my recipes even better. We worked well together. Krecencia got to be great with training. When I left Zimbabwe, she said, "Mrs. Staples, you have taught me well. I could go to work at the presidency." With the help of my three gardeners, we ripped out about seventy-five percent of the garden. Killian was a true gardener. I learned so much from him. I went with him to the nurseries, and we made some great decisions on what to buy and plant. When Uncle Robert and Aunt Dorothy arrived, they loved the gardens and landscaping because they were avid gardeners back in Kentucky. I saw them often in the garden.

While I was in Zimbabwe, I was looking for a jogging partner. Embassy personnel never would commit to a schedule and didn't show up. Ronia and Krecencia jogged with me. Ronia would knock on my bedroom window at 5:00 a.m. Ronia and I were evenly matched, and Krecencia, who was bringing up the rear, always finished. We eventually got up to three miles. After our jog, I had to shower and get ready for work.

Uncle Robert could often be seen down in the garden near a tree checking out the weaver birds. He got me so interested in birds; I took a birding class. He taught me about telling the direction from east to west if I was ever lost in the bush by checking out weaver birds' nests. When the sun comes up in the east, their nests will be built on the west side of a tree to avoid the hot morning sun.

He was a quiet, strong man. Like me, his niece, he could never be found without a book in his hand or close by. One of his favorite authors was W. E. B. Griffin. George is also an avid reader.

In Zimbabwe, Aunt Dorothy made many friends. She had been in the antique business for forty-five years. She taught me that people want a story about a purchase. If you don't have a story, make one up. People also expect you to bargain. Gib Lanpher was our ambassador. Aunt Dorothy was making fashion statements at events. She arrived with some of her collection of antique bracelets, necklaces, earrings, and gorgeous broaches. Gib's wife, June, would say to me, "I wonder what Dorothy will be wearing tonight." I was so proud of my Kentucky visitors.

How did my aunt and uncle and I do so much in one month? We went to villages, to sculpture parks, and on game drives. We stayed at the Elephant Hills Hotel in Victoria Falls. Uncle Robert liked to see the warthogs on the golf course. On one of the game drives, we saw a lot of animals. Other viewing tour groups sped by trying to get to the watering holes first.

Because we slowed down to watch for birds thanks to Uncle Robert's interest in them, we saw more animals than we expected. Normally, the Jeep driver would slowly approach an area by cutting the engine and coasting to a stop in order not to frighten the animals. On one memorable occasion, I was sitting up high in the game drive vehicle with Uncle Robert and Catherine. We looked to the right side and there, stretched out in brown dry grass, was a lioness. I think the female does most of the hunting. She could have pounced and been with us in the Jeep in an instant. Uncle Robert gave a very serious instruction to the driver: "Don't cut the engine!"

We also went on a night game viewing in a tour Jeep with a spotlight. We saw very big eyes and all the nightlife. We also went on a dawn drive. Sometimes, there were impalas running beside us. We saw herds of Cape buffalo, and we might round a curve and see five or six giraffes. There are too many to mention. Oh, I can't forget Uncle Robert's wildebeest. He said that animal was so ugly, it took a committee to make it!

AIDS was out of control in Zimbabwe while we were posted there. We were also losing local Foreign Service National (FSN) staff members. They are very important people at an embassy. As I previously mentioned, they are vital to a well-run mission. We leave and they stay. One day, people went to the mailroom, and the attendant was there behind the counter. The next week, he died suddenly. We were fortunate we never lost any of our domestic staff. They were my helpers and felt like family. I liked to make an excellent presentation when we hosted dinners and receptions, but I couldn't have done it without my well-trained staff. I trained them, and they made me proud. They were so good that June, the ambassador's wife, asked for their help, as did other Americans. It was fine with me because I knew they could use the extra money.

Yes, I taught them about setting up new restaurant accounts; helping with the color scheme for tablecloths and napkins; training waiters to serve from right or left; how to take away dinner plates, wine, and water glasses; always serving food on a warm plate; how to set up a bar; how to make a beautiful buffet; and most importantly, not to overpour. I even taught my staff flower arranging. In Harare, I took a class myself on how to mix plants and silk flowers for hall and foyer statements. I never knew those long hours and tired feet would be valuable experiences later in life. I don't know if there are training programs now. I've offered to help junior Foreign Service people who are very insecure about formal dinners. My grandmother told me not to brag about myself, but on this occasion, I couldn't help myself. A couple asked me for help because growing up in their parents' homes, they used paper plates.

Chapter 40

Where to next on our great adventure? I took my aunt and uncle to meet Patrick Mavros, a famous silver jewelry maker. Aunt Dorothy left part of her traveling budget with him. George and Uncle Robert were interested in his collections, especially spears. I have beautiful jewelry made by Patrick and his staff, including silver earrings, necklaces, and bracelets. I also have the same but made from black buffalo horn. I still get Christmas cards with photos of Patrick's family. He and Catcha, his wife, have four good-looking sons.

In Harare, I had a small project to feed about thirty-five children one meal a day. I asked Uncle Robert and Aunt Dorothy if they would like to visit the feeding kitchen. Mrs. Hungue, the deputy minister for women's affairs, had asked for help with children's feeding kitchens. I met a nurse who had worked for years in the US but had returned to Zimbabwe. I can't remember all the details, but I know what I committed to do. The embassy wasn't involved and did not contribute a penny. I would buy food, and the former nurse would secure a place to safely keep the food. I bought dried fish, very small ones, and ground nuts that were made into a peanut sauce to mix with the fish. The mothers volunteered to prepare the food. We cooked a type of greens called rape, a staple throughout the country, to complement the meal. It was like our poke salad.

My uncle and aunt were happy to donate to the kitchen. I gave about a hundred dollars a month. Terry and Jill Robinson from Laguna Beach also helped me when they visited. I would go after work to check on my children for the day. I asked George for help with funds for the feeding kitchen, but he informed me he couldn't because it wasn't an embassy project. I was fortunate that the favorable exchange rate meant that a couple of hundred dollars went a long way.

My feel-good project had its downside, as some days, we encountered problems. For example, sometimes I learned we had lost a baby to AIDS. I went to a lecture where l met a woman at our health unit who was very knowledgeable about the spread of AIDS. She felt it got into the blood because of eating bush meat, like that from the colobus monkey.

One Saturday, George, Catherine, and I took our visiting Kentucky family to the racetrack. Of course, as Kentucky ladies, we had to wear our hats. Uncle Robert and Aunt Dorothy lived not too far from Churchill Downs Racetrack in Louisville. They were very interested to see that the horses in southern Africa ran counterclockwise. That was a surprise we hadn't told them about in advance. A great day was had at the track, but I don't think any of us won any money.

Speaking of horses, I had always ridden Western style when I had an opportunity, but in Zimbabwe, I took lessons to ride English style. I preferred the Western style saddle, which is bigger and more comfortable; English style is riding on a smaller saddle with stirrups more elevated, and riding was harder on my knees. I started having knee problems way back then.

After our racetrack outing, we went home to a fabulous meal by Ronia. George and the staff wanted very much to please our houseguests.

Uncle Robert wanted to try everything on a menu when we went to a local restaurant. He tried crocodile, impala, eland, and anything that was African. I was worried about him getting sick. But the irony was that after he returned home, he went to McDonald's, ate a burger, and came down with E. coli! Couldn't believe it!

Before Aunt Dorothy and Uncle Robert left, we went on a breakfast champagne cruise on the Zambezi River. We also went to Zimbabwe's Eastern Highlands and stayed at the Leopard Rock Hotel in the Vumba region to enjoy the mountains. The famous artist Irene Duggan and her husband, Bob, joined us for dinner. I had met her by accident as she was dropping off paintings at a gallery. I opened the door for her, and that was the beginning of our friendship. Aunt Dorothy liked her paintings and came home with some small ones she could put into her luggage. I bought a large one and shipped it home in my surface shipment.

We also went to the sculpture village in Harare, which had a big selection of stone and wood sculptures. Many different stones can be used for carving, and Zimbabwe may be the only place in Africa where you can find so many of them. My sculptures are black and green serpentine and opal. The wood items I purchased are called ironwood because they're so heavy. I don't remember the African name. Uncle Robert and Aunt Dorothy made a few sculpture purchases. I remember we laughed a lot because we made good bargains, and their bedroom was getting more crowded every time we went shopping.

In a village we visited near Victoria Falls, I saw words carved on a rock that said, "A pilgrim's reward is the memory of having been there." I photographed those words and told Catherine I might like that to be carved on my headstone. I put the photo in my copy of the *Meditations* by Marcus Aurelius. The book is worn, tattered, and stuffed after forty-three years. The book is always near me and is one of my treasures.

June, Ambassador Lanpher's wife, asked Uncle Robert to play Santa Claus at their residence for the embassy's Christmas party for American children and other invitees. I captured a Kodak moment with my Catherine in Uncle Robert's lap. During that holiday season, I needed a Christmas tree for my residence. The year before, I had asked for help with topping a large tree in the yard. It was a big production to get the top off and not damage the tree. Uncle Robert and Aunt Dorothy had chairs brought down in the yard. They took their seats, and Uncle Robert had his movie camera ready for the big event. Success! The top wasn't damaged in the fall.

About this time, I met a very interesting American woman, Diana Rambo, at the women's club monthly meeting. She and her husband, Loren, became great friends. I will write more about her later. When we first met, we went to their farm for Thanksgiving. We stayed a couple of days, and as usual, Aunt Dorothy and Uncle Robert loved being with them. Aunt Dorothy taught Diana to make turkey hash. Both were excellent cooks. Loren took us on a ride to see his farm. We were near the small town of Karoi. Loren had lived in Zimbabwe for years. Diana was his second wife. Loren had a few endangered black rhinos, and he was paying guards to protect them from poachers. Uncle Robert and Aunt Dorothy enjoyed being with the Rambos.

Soon, it was time for Uncle Robert and Aunt Dorothy to leave. I had a buffet for them in our lovely garden with tables nicely arranged with beautiful floral table cloths, china, and crystal. Nothing but the best for my aunt and uncle! The garden was spectacular thanks to Killian, Linus, and Ben. The front side of the swimming pool was planted with English lavender. The top of the garden was terraced into three levels. There were blue hydrangeas, calla lilies, azaleas, and bougainvillea in all shades, too many to write all of them down. When we walked outside the gate, we could see flamboyant and jacaranda. When the petals fell, the street would be covered in purple and red. I had poinsettia trees by Catherine's bedroom. They were the same as the potted plants we give at Christmas. We also had a rubber tree that was taller than the house.

I was so pleased my aunt and uncle had gotten passports and traveled to Africa. They were adventurous to travel outside the USA for the first time, and to Africa! They were pleased to meet George and spend time with me and Catherine (Petunia). I was in heaven on earth. I took my aunt and uncle to paradise when they visited Zimbabwe. I miss them so very much.

Chapter 41

An assignment to Zimbabwe was highly sought after at the State Department. The country was referred to at the time as the Pearl of Africa. When we got there in 1995, we thought President Mugabe would prove to be like Nelson Mandela in South Africa. Mugabe was Zimbabwe's first president after independence in 1980. The British had left an infrastructure that was better than most newly independent countries. People had been trained and could take over after the British gave up control. What Mugabe did by seizing land owned for generations by white farmers, the backbone of the economy, was violent and illegal.

In Zimbabwe, I was friends with Mary and Max Rosenfel and their son, Peter. I spent time at their farm, and I loved them. Mary came to Kentucky and spent time with me. She loved the thrift stores and bought gifts for people on the farm. She was a nurse by profession and would drive into Bulawayo, Zimbabwe's second-largest city, and work at the hospital. She was a serious bridge player and played duplicate bridge. She attributed keeping her mind so sharp to playing bridge. I have three watercolors and a carved elephant standing on one piece of wood that are beloved gifts from Mary and Max.

One of the highlights of my time in Zimbabwe was being invited to go on a ride in a wagon similar to those early settlers from South Africa used a century ago to trek north into Zimbabwe. They used these wagons with steel rims to make the trip from South Africa to what is today the Great Zimbabwe historical site. The wagons were very heavy with people and cargo. It took sixteen oxen to pull one wagon. The trick was to get all sixteen to pull together at the same time. It took a man with a whip and some time to get the oxen to pull in an S shape and then pull in a straight line. I know this is factual because I was on the wagon. I think this must have been more difficult than our settlers' western journey in a concord wagon. Participating in this hundred-year celebration of the original trek by settlers from the Cape Town area to Zimbabwe was a special honor.

While we were in Zimbabwe, life was getting very hard for the white farmers there. I can only write about my personal experience. The government was taking farms after independence in 1980, defying the agreement, not between all parties, to leave the land situation alone. The commercial farmers got together and did a survey of the farms. There were farms with absentee owners, underdeveloped farms, and developed farms that had been used to grow corn, tobacco, wheat, and other crops for generations. The government wanted to take the developed farms that had taken years and generations to make them productive rather than redistribute unused land. I can remember being at a farmer's auction, which I found to be very interesting. I'm from Kentucky, a tobacco-producing state. Representatives from different tobacco manufacturers came to bid on Zimbabwe's tobacco crop. The government wanted to seize these farms as well. At one time, Zimbabwe was known as the breadbasket of southern Africa, but not today. I heard stories, maybe one sided, but I felt it was the truth about the economic devastation that had befallen that beautiful country.

During our assignment, George and I visited a project to see how Black farmers who had been given land in a barren area of the country were doing. When we arrived, it was clear they didn't have a chance of being successful. They were young people and had no interest in being farmers. I think maybe they had been forced to be there, and they had no tools or equipment. A lizard was lucky to have lived there. Not everyone wants to get up at four in the morning. Farming required working long, hard hours. I know how hard my family worked doing subsistence farming in our mountains.

People were hoping President Mugabe would be a tolerant, open-minded leader. Instead, he turned into a dictator. Through the years, I stayed up on issues in Zimbabwe from afar. People I knew left the country, and not just farmers. My friends Bob and Irene moved to Durban, South Africa. Lauren and Diana relocated to Fresno, California. The Rosenfels stayed on until their farm was reduced to postage-stamp size, as their son, Peter, described it. They lived in Marula, and their farm was Sandown North. They had built a dam and named it Magaia. Drought was always a concern, so Mary took me to visit Bomboncito, the place of the rainmakers. People would call in a group to dance and pray for rain.

Mugabe's second wife, who was much younger than he, was a negative influence on the president. She played a big part in the corruption that occurred after we departed in 1995. Mugabe's first wife was well liked because she helped and cared about the people. The embassy had good information from a variety of sources. I got my information from staff gossip around the kitchen bar!

I know there are many aspects to the story of Zimbabwe. I can be very objective, and I try to look at both sides. When I would hear conversations about the size of some of these farms and land holdings, I couldn't grasp the magnitude. I would think, *Do the owners even know the borders of their property?* I could grasp how my staff lived in overcrowded conditions when I would drop them home. Krecencia would say, "Mrs. Staples, if I could only play my radio and no one would complain." Most Zimbabweans were very poor. There were lots of street children, and the public school system was poorly funded. President Mugabe had been a teacher and headmaster before becoming a leader of Zimbabwe's independence struggle, yet he did little to improve the educational system.

Everywhere we went in Africa, people would literally starve to get money for school fees and material to make school uniforms. Education was viewed as the only way to advance. What hurts me was what Mugabe did to one of the stars of Africa. The country was on its way to a great future. I wish there could have been more compromise on both sides.

Chapter 42

Famous actors Danny Glover and Morgan Freeman came to Harare to make a movie called *Bopha!* about a South African policeman working for the apartheid government and his conflict with his son, who was opposed to the system. Danny was a hit with the diplomatic community. We met him and invited him to dinner. I introduced him to our Italian and Spanish friends who joined us, and the man loved to eat. I remember my staff passed seconds. I was surprised when Danny went to the kitchen and got thirds on his own. Everyone liked Danny, and he often went to Marine House to watch sports with embassy marines.

Morgan Freeman was different. I introduced myself to him at the Sheraton Hotel, told him who we were, and asked him to come to dinner, but he declined. We were, however, invited to be guests at the film location. I met Alfre Woodard and liked her. I tried again to get Morgan Freeman to dinner. I promised him greens, pinto beans, and my special cornbread. I could never get him to accept, but I was told not to be offended because he wasn't accepting any invitations. This was his first time directing a movie, and his total focus was on the filmmaking.

During this time, we were invited to the opening of the movie *The Power of One*. I was happy to be seated next to Danny Glover. To stay in shape while making the movie, I was told he rode the Sheraton Hotel's stationary bike for one hour every morning. Maybe that was the reason he didn't have to worry about weight. I think he wore out the bike and should have replaced it at the hotel!

Danny was such a nice guy. He said to me, "Kids brag to other kids about whom they have met. Do you think your daughter would like me to visit her school?" I had George's driver pick me up at the residence, and then we went to pick up Danny. He was greeted by the kids and teachers. Catherine attended a British-style private girls' school whose students were from well-educated families and members of the diplomatic corps. I guess that was the reason the faculty and students knew about Danny Glover. The visit was a huge success, and Catherine loved the extra attention from her classmates.

In addition to having Danny Glover and Morgan Freeman with us, John and Philicia Collins, our dear Foreign Service friends from our El Salvador days, were assigned to the US Embassy in Pretoria, South Africa. They drove up to Zimbabwe to visit us. They had two friends visiting them from a previous assignment in Bogota, Colombia.

During their visit, Philicia said to me, "I would like to see the insides of a rondavel [an African village house]." I arranged with one of our drivers, Jeffery, to visit his village. We took off from Harare with lots food, ice, bottled water, beer, wine, bourbon, vodka, and blankets. To the present day, I never learned how to travel light. Jeffery had arranged a grand reception for us. The ladies from Colombia were well traveled. One was an attorney, and the other was a banker. We drove as far as we could and had too much to carry down a steep slope to the village. Jeffery sent for a wheelbarrow to help with my heavy cooler and everything we could pile on top of it. We finally arrived with lots of village help.

To my surprise, Jeffery was a chief or elder in his village. He was someone important in his world. There were traditional homes, but he had a concrete block home. I think there were four rooms. I can't remember the exact sleeping arrangements. We were okay as far as everyone in our group was concerned, except Philicia, who wasn't quick to adjust to African village-style living. There was lots of drum music and dancing. John was over on the side in a huddle with the village elders and having a great time. We ate the food we had brought. The evening entertainment was to begin with speeches and drinking. Philicia, her friends, and Jeffery's wife were sitting on a porch that looked down into the yard. More drummers were arriving, and the party was on. Philicia was looking miserable and fanning flies. John was dancing and kicking up dust! A woman suddenly went into a type of trance and was in a hypnotic state. She was rolling in the dirt in one corner of the house and making predictions about the future of the village.

Meanwhile back on the porch, I realized the men were drinking, but one woman told me they had no alcohol in what they were drinking. Surreptitiously, I opened my cooler and started giving them vodka, gin, and bourbon in their cups. Now the party was at full blast. The men started to wonder what was happening to the women. I never told Jeffery. The party lasted until about four o'clock in the morning.

We spent two nights in the village, but it was torture for my friend Philicia. Her friends were walking around the village talking to people and taking photos. I was holding a baby and enjoying myself. John had grown up in South Carolina under similar conditions as mine. Philicia was a city girl from DC. I knew others like her who had grown up with central heat and air. John and I were more flexible, and in the Foreign Service, it was necessary. Much later, Philicia told George to be careful what you asked Jo Ann for because she just wanted to see the inside of a traditional village hut. I took her to a village for two days! She was thinking about the poor conditions she witnessed. Philicia told George when we returned to Harare, "When the slave traders came, thank God, my ancestors couldn't run fast enough!" She eventually forgave me for taking her to the village, and she loves me . . . I think!

Chapter 43

I had another great adventure because of a National Park Service elephant relocation project. In 1992–1993, Zimbabwe was experiencing the worst drought in one hundred years. Areas overpopulated with elephants were a serious problem to people and other animals. Elephants can destroy a large area. They can move the jungle by taking every leaf off the trees and rubbing up against a tree until it falls. That's why select culling is important. We got to see the effects of too many elephants.

Because of the severe drought, there was funding for the relocation of seventy-five elephants to private farms and conservation sites. I had the good fortune to be a part of one such relocation. You, the reader, are maybe thinking that it wasn't such a big project. Wrong! Try moving just one elephant. The logistics for this big event took about twenty men, a helicopter and pilot, a very large truck with giant wheels and a lift on the back of the truck, one huge piece of thick leather, and a trained person with a dart gun.

I was in the Hughes 500 helicopter with the pilot. It felt good to be seeing some of the jungle from the air. The pilot had a rifle and dart gun. We could see the crew on the ground. He darted the elephant, and soon, it was down on the ground. The men were ready to place the elephant on the huge piece of leather. Then they pulled the animal to the lift and raised him up to put him in the truck. The timing was very critical to get the tailgate closed. It was life-threatening if the elephant fell on his trunk. Two men had to go inside the truck to check the elephant—a dangerous job—but he was still out from the injection. A man got on the top side of the truck bed and gave the elephant another injection to reverse the effect of the first. Soon, the animal was standing up and mad as hell.

The helicopter had landed not too far from the site. I got to see most of the procedure. It was a tense moment for everyone. I saw one relocation, but I couldn't stand the tension of seventy-four more. George was on the ground filming the operation. Thank God, it went as planned.

Chapter 44

B efore we left this incredible assignment, friends arrived from Laguna Beach, California. We welcomed Dr. Terry Robinson; his wife, Jill; and children, Ryan and Krista, who were about twelve and fourteen. A good time was had by everyone. We visited Victoria Falls, went whitewater rafting on the Zambezi, went to Mana Pools National Park, and did lots of shopping. If there was such a thing as a male soulmate in my life, it was Terry Robinson. We had met years ago in California before I was married, and he was a warm, kind, generous person who had a gift for getting the most out of life. If you were around him, his personality was contagious. We had some great times together and made some lifelong memories in Zimbabwe. Our trip to Victoria Falls, one of the most famous and historic natural wonders in the world, was very special, and we shopped at the Tengenenge Art Community and bought stone sculptures.

I can't remember the exact order of all the experiences we had with Terry, Jill, and family, but a highlight was visiting Victoria Falls. There's not one waterfall but several depending on the time of year. I also took them to meet Patrick Mavros, a very famous Zimbabwean jewelry maker, and they participated in an official reception we hosted at the residence.

First, let me tell you about whitewater rafting on the Zambezi River. I don't think Terry, Jill, and I realized how dangerous this experience would be. We had an orientation briefing before going to the raft and were told there were sinkholes under the water. People have gone into these holes, never to be found again. There are also crocodiles in the Zambezi. Our guide explained that if somebody got thrown from the raft, there were two types of swimmers: long and short. Long swimmers might be too far away to grab. Someone would go and rescue them on the riverbank. The short swimmers could be reached and pulled back into the raft and saved from drowning. The water was very swift, and I was not a good swimmer. I prayed that if I went out of the raft, I would be a short swimmer. My mind must have wandered because I missed the procedures to follow if someone went out of the raft.

We climbed down the riverbank to our raft. Before getting on the river, we had to pray to the Nyami Nyami River God. As part of our orientation, I got a necklace on a piece of leather with a circular wooden shell carving for good luck. I was toward the left side to the back of the raft. I think Terry and Jill were on the right. Everyone was wearing life vests. There must have been a couple more people, but that is a complete blank for me. Once again, I might have been in over my head, literally. Then we were off!

I was holding onto a rope that ran around the side of the raft. At first, the ride was mostly smooth. Then the water started to get rough, and then we heard the sound of the water going over the falls. The rapids on the Zambezi were categorized in different levels, with a six being the highest. The guide didn't tell us what level was coming up. Maybe it was three. We went over the first rapids. It was very scary. The second was even worse. The front of the raft was underwater. I couldn't see the person on the front, but the raft popped up. God, that was damn scary!

On one of the rapids, I went out of the raft. I never knew the classification number, but it was big. We entered a big gorge, and I was sitting in the bottom of the raft facing the water and holding on for dear life. I think I did a somersault out of the raft. This was the part of the training I didn't pay attention to. The guide was holding on to each side of my vest and trying to push me under. I didn't understand that it was necessary to do that for me to pop up so he could get me into the raft. I think Terry explained things to me later. I believe we went over a level five rapids. At one point, we were approaching a six. Everyone helped carry the raft around the category six rapids. We continued to another rapids, and I made it!

We had reached the end of our rafting experience on the Zambezi. Terry and Jill were in much better shape than I was mentally. I didn't realize what a deep gorge we were in until we had to climb up a steep hillside to get out of the river. As my grandmother would say, "Let's make two of this—our first and last!" I don't plan to go whitewater rafting again.

We spent the night and went game viewing the next day in Hwange National Park. We saw many, many herds of animals running in their natural environment. I'm sure before the visit was over, we saw the big five: Cape buffalo, elephant, lion, leopard, and rhino. Afterwards, we flew back to Harare and went back to the residence to recover with good wine and wonderful care from Ronia and Krecencia. George was happy I survived.

After a few days, Terry, Jill, Krista, and I prepared for the Mana Pool experience. Few tourists are allowed in this park. The park isn't developed as some others are. This park is unique because it is unfenced, and we lived among wild animals. George got special permission for us to go there. We planned to stay three days. Thank God, we had a rondavel made of mortar with a thatch roof. There were dirt roads in the park. We went through a security check and then signed a release form. I would understand later how dangerous this park could be. We were instructed to stay in our rondavel from sunset to sunrise because wild animals roamed through unfenced campsites during the night. It was a national park but very natural and undeveloped and few trees.

The park ranger took us to our site. We were traveling with everything we would need, including coolers with ice, drinks, and food. Knowing the Robinsons, I made sure we had some good wine. We got organized and made the place comfortable. Ronia had taken care of everything. She knew me well, and we had packed for many trips. In Africa, the critical thing to pack was toilet paper and bottled water.

After getting settled, we walked over to look at the river. We were just a few feet from the Zambezi. The bank was about a twenty-foot drop. The river was meandering down with some sharp turns. We could see quite a distance to the right. Wow! There were some hippos. A little disconcerting to me, but I guessed it was safe. Terry and Jill had the master suite. Krista and I shared a room with two beds with a window in between and mosquito netting. During the night, an elephant came near our window. He was standing on his back feet and eating pods from the tree. I heard this little voice saying, "Can I sleep with you?" I held back the blanket, and Krista got into bed with me.

The next day, we looked at our map to take a game viewing ride. We were on our own. I didn't have a rifle and felt that was a mistake. We didn't see much, but the landscape was different. We saw just a few animals.

The following morning, I took my coffee and went over to the riverbank. I thought we could view a few hippopotami in the Zambezi River. When I got back for my early morning coffee refill, I saw a leopard going to the river. He was maybe thirty feet over from where I had walked. The park rangers were looking for him. He had killed something during the night. Everyone was up and dressed now. The animals were always around us but, on that day, not in our area of the park.

On a game drive, someone got the idea to roll down the windows to look for animals. The land cruiser was swarmed with flies. I think they were tsetse flies. We used magazines to fight them off. We must have also had spray. What a damn ordeal. It seemed as if there were thousands inside the car. Terry was driving and not much help in getting rid of the flies. We had to be always on the lookout for animals. We returned to our campsite all beaten down. There was a saying we used often in Africa: "TAB," which means "That's Africa, baby."

After we ate, I started having issues with my finger. I had a bite above my ring, and my finger started to swell. We had no ice left, and it was now dark. We couldn't leave the camp until morning. I was in pain all night. I couldn't turn my wedding band around.

In the morning, we packed everything as fast as we could and left the park. We had no phone service, so we stopped at a roadside business and asked for help for my finger. We had friends in the nearby town of Karoi. They got Loren Rambo on the phone and explained my situation. Loren said he would meet us on the road to Harare. Loren and Diana had friends visiting from California, one of whom was a doctor. My finger was blue, and I'm sure Terry was thinking there was no blood circulation. Loren had something the doctor could use to cut my ring off. After that, I had some pain relief, but I was still suffering. We were 120 miles away from Harare. Upon arrival, I went to the embassy nurse, who followed up with medical assistance. Getting my ring off in time saved my finger. If I think too much about the painful experience of almost losing my finger, I'll go crazy.

Chapter 45

My visitors and I were back in Harare to rest and start another day. For Terry and Jill as well as me, Zimbabwe was a shopper's dream, especially for wood and stone sculptures. The exchange rate for the dollar was great. Peter Birch was a favorite local artist of mine, and I have some of his paintings. When my daughter, Catherine, was about five, I started buying nice works of art for her. When she was in college, I think she probably had the best-decorated apartment off campus. Jill carried a heavy Shona sculpture in a backpack when she returned to Laguna Beach. Later at their home, Jill had a nook built in the wall to display her treasure.

More good memories were made when we went to Victoria Falls. When we made the flight there, the whole gang was on board, except for George, who had to work. My job as warehouse supervisor was flexible, and I had a good crew working for me and had no new Americans arriving to help with their relocation to the embassy. George would later go with us on a houseboat trip on the Zambezi. We checked into the Old Victorian Hotel. It was very lavish with period decorations and great service. This made up for the rondavel in Mana Pools!

On the next part of the journey, George was with us. We went in our car to Lake Kariba. We had reservations to spend a few days on a big houseboat. I think this was the first adventure when all seven of us were together, along with Neville, the houseboat owner/captain, and the crew. This was a restful time on the water to sunbathe, drink, and nap. We could see animals on the shoreline. There was no swimming in the lake because this was crocodile-infested water. Maybe that is an exaggeration, but I had no doubt they were there.

Neville had a cage that could be cranked down into the water. It was too small to swim in but big enough to get into the water with a glass of wine and cool off. The food was great with wonderful fish dinners. There was lots of good-tasting fruit, and it was fresh. We had pineapple, mango, and papaya to eat with every meal. There was lots of fun and laughter.

One morning, Jill scanned the hills from the boat with her binoculars. She said, "Jodi, look up on the ridge. Is that a lion?" It was definitely a female lion. Down on the shore was a Cape buffalo. The chase was soon on, and the lion jumped on the right hip side of the buffalo. The other lions came down the hillside. The buffalo was smart enough to get to the lake and run in the water. We saw the male lion, "the Old Man," up on the ridge with his huge mane. He was waiting for the girls to get his breakfast. We saw all this happen in real time without binoculars. Neville said he'd been in Zimbabwe thirty years and had never seen a pride of lions carry out a hunt.

Neville told us there was an interesting Pygmy like village nearby if we would like to visit. We all agreed that it would be an interesting outing. It turned out to be a great idea. The main tribes in Zimbabwe are the Shona and Ndebele. President Mugabe was from the Shona tribe. George and Terry stayed on the boat. Jill was interested in everything. Cookware, racks for drying fish, chicken coops and other items were built on racks about three feet tall. We saw the tribe's version of how to dry dishes. They put them on racks to get the sun. They dried fish with the same method. We saw their version of a chicken house. The people were so hospitable to us. They had been relocated when a dam was built. Maybe there was hostility to the move, but they were moved to what was a better area. We took lots of photos. I got some good shots of Krista, Ryan, my Catherine, and Jill. We left with feelings of a good day and were glad that Neville had put this on our trip.

Meanwhile back on the boat, Terry and George were having a brandy bonding experience, smoking a cigar to celebrate George's first catch of a fish. It was about six inches long; I'm serious! He has never gone fishing again. I was feeling good because everyone was in a good mood. I love making people happy, especially my dear friends. There will be many stories to tell with Terry and Jill in the future with good wine and a sunset over Catalina Island. We photographed wonderful sunsets on Lake Kariba.

These were difficult times in Zimbabwe. We got there when drought was difficult and AIDS was part of daily life. The embassy was trying to keep five million people from starvation. USAID was very involved, and Ted Morse, the director, had lots of experience in dealing with humanitarian crises. The Zimbabwean government was overseeing the international relief operation. My guests knew there were serious problems but not the full extent. That's why George couldn't go with our guests on all the adventures. Our visitors were a great release from my worrying too much. Our many friends and family were with us a total of about three months. We were in Zimbabwe for three years.

Chapter 46

Claudia Meier, whom I call my little sister, came from Germany to visit us in Zimbabwe. I do love her and feel I made a small contribution to her success in life. She came with her friend, also named Claudia. We had a wonderful time and repeated some of the same trips as our other guests, including my Catherine. We took photos of the balancing rocks in Zimbabwe. These are giant rocks stacked on top of one another. I don't think there was a recorded history. I didn't take my other guests to meet Max, Mary, and Peter Rosenfel in Plumtree.

I drove our guests from Harare to Bulawayo. We went to the museum and saw the world's second-largest elephant on display. The largest is in the Smithsonian National Museum of Natural History in Washington, DC. We then continued to Plumtree. They enjoyed being on a working farm and meeting the Rosenfels. Mary was a great cook, and she taught me how to prepare chicken in a clay pot. Big things and small things are such treasured memories.

Of course, everyone went to Victoria Falls. There was a difference this time, as we saw the falls in the rainy season. The Zimbabweans call the falls "the smoke that thunders," and sure enough, water sounds like thunder as it crashes over the rocks. Remember, there are more than one falls depending on the season! We were wet even with raincoats. I have some great photos in our rain gear. There were no barriers except for branches from trees on the walking path. I hope it hasn't changed with time and has stayed natural.

Marian also came from Cincinnati to visit us. We took her to our favorite place in the Bvumba Mountains in Zimbabwe's Eastern Highlands. We stayed at a mini version of a castle, which must have been a private home at one time. Two great men had turned it into a bed and breakfast. Marian, Catherine, and her school friend Natalie were with me. This was the one place I would go every chance I got. George liked to go there also. The landscaping was beautiful with a hillside of lots of hydrangeas. My room had a great wall of glass with a wide piece of wood for the bottom at the floor level. I could sit on the board in the window. There was a balcony from which could see all the way to Mozambique. It might have been two hundred miles. There was one downside to being at the castle. Two damn big hornbills, a very special bird found in southern Africa and Asia, were in a tree beside the castle and would make a horrible sound early in the morning.

Chapter 47

So many things were happening in Zimbabwe. Maybe it should be a separate book. No! That's not a good idea because I would have to try to explain the impossible. I will let the historians explain what President Mugabe did to my beloved Zimbabwe and the wonderful people of the country.

Before I leave Zimbabwe, I must share two more events. One was our opportunity to represent our country at a state dinner, and the other was our safari trip.

The embassy received an invitation to a state dinner hosted by President Mugabe in honor of newly elected President Mandela of South Africa. The new US Ambassador, Johnnie Carson, wasn't in the country at the time so George and I got to go and represent the US. The day of the event, we had embassy employees polish the official old black Cadillac. We put on our best official clothing. When we arrived, I thought we would have a table up front. I don't know who handled protocol, but our up-front table ended up back near the press corps. President Mugabe was very particular about protocol. Weeks later, when Ambassador Carson arrived and presented his credentials, George and I had to practice curtsying before we could see him. It was comical, and we didn't do very well. At the dinner, I was very pleased that I got to see President Mandela. I felt I was in the presence of greatness. We didn't get to talk with him, but I was happy to have been there.

In Zimbabwe, I was working in the embassy's General Services Section, this time as the warehouse supervisor. At one point, I went to South Africa to learn the State Department's computer system to keep track of US government property inventory. I learned a lot, and it helped with training my warehouse crew. Traveling to South Africa was an opportunity to once again see John and Philicia Collins, who invited me to stay with them. Their residence was beautiful. John was in charge of the Administrative Section. They had worked hard as a couple. Their residence was the only house I've ever been in that had heated floor tiles.

I was in South Africa on its presidential election day. Everyone expected Nelson Mandela would win, but many were concerned about what would come next in a transition to black majority rule. I made my own prediction that the day after the election: if you were a housekeeper, bus driver, or banker, you would go back to work as normal. There was some unrest but nothing like what had been predicted. I was there at a historical time for South Africa; however, I felt uncomfortable going out in the street. I asked an embassy employee to get me three Mandela campaign posters. I have one in Kentucky. I gave one to a friend who now lives in Seattle and another to a friend in Cincinnati. If I ever get to Las Vegas, I might visit the Pawn Stars shop and ask Rick how much he would pay for my poster.

In South Africa, I saw a real fortified embassy for the first time. It had no windows to the outside except at the top level. It was built around a courtyard, with offices on several levels that had access to an inner balcony. I was taken to the top to see the deputy chief of mission's office and maybe the ambassador's office. The top floor had some windows, with a safety door like on a ship.

In South Africa, I went shopping and bought three Tonga baskets. They have the reputation of being the finest woven baskets in Africa. I saw Tonga baskets on display in Pretoria when I visited the national museum.

Chapter 48

In nearing the end about Zimbabwe, I have a lot more to write about! George and an embassy colleague named Bill bid on a bag, as it was called. The winner got to take part in an annual national park-sponsored hunt for a Cape buffalo and kudu. There were five animals in total that could be hunted, but I can't remember the others. I'm sure no elephant was allowed to be killed. There must have been twenty people in total on our safari. I paid for this experience for George with money that was burning a hole in my pocket. I went for the adventure, not the hunt. The safari included trucks and drivers, two professional hunters, trackers, and even a spore man, whose job was to put his finger in the dung to check the temperature. He could then tell how long it has been since a herd had been through. We had a full kitchen staff to cook and clean, plus people to set up camp, and so on. Hemingway had nothing on us.

We were in the bush for a week. The first day, no one saw anything but monkeys. I didn't want to get up early to go with the men. I was enjoying the camp. On one of those days, George spotted a kudu. He missed his opportunity. His rifle should have been up and ready. The kudu wasn't called the gray ghost for nothing. They blend into the natural setting. George never had another opportunity for a kudu. Bill got a kudu. Professional hunters pay the government to hunt trophy-sized animals. For example, I heard a trophy Cape buffalo had to be forty-eight inches from one horn tip to the other.

George did shoot a Cape buffalo. The rule was he could kill only a female. Everything you hope not to go wrong went wrong. He shot her, and she ran into tall grass. There was supposed to be a death bellow. It didn't happen! Two professional hunters were with George. They all had to walk into the tall grass and make sure she was dead. I wasn't thrilled about what had happened. I guess it's a man thing! It was a tense time because there was a story about one that circled around, came back, and disemboweled a professional hunter and his client, and both died.

I want people to understand that George and I had a great experience. When you kill an animal in Africa, the meat is usually given to nearby villagers. The cooks made jerky from the buffalo, and it was widely shared. That made me feel better. Bill had his heart set on a Cape buffalo but never had a chance to get near one. On the last night, after sunset when the hunt officially ended, a herd suddenly appeared and ran right by the camp! That's Africa, baby.

Chapter 49

Gold! Southern Africa is known for gold and diamond mining, and Zimbabwe had gold mines. I was asked if I might like to visit one of the mines, and being from Kentucky and a coal miner's daughter, I accepted and joined other diplomats for the visit. Upon arriving at the mine, our group was given white coveralls and hard hats. After a brief orientation, we entered a wooden elevator, which our host announced would be going down eighteen stories! And I have claustrophobia. What had I gotten myself into yet again?

When the elevator door opened, we exited and found ourselves in a chamber with timbers askew and water running down a small ditch by the wall. Small African men were running around doing their work. I asked, "Where is the gold?" Our guide said to look at the wall. I had my hard hat with a headlamp on and saw a seam of gold about the size of a pencil mark. I was expecting to see a seam like in a coal mine, but the pencil-sized seam was a complete surprise. Our guide said that tons of ore had to be mined and sifted to get just five grams of gold, which was the size of a button on a shirt. I was glad when the tour was over and we got back to the surface. This was one of those times to say, "Thank you, Jesus; Lord have mercy," and fall down on my knees!

Chapter 50

With the help of my staff, I organized some big events. The Fourth of July national day reception in Zimbabwe was always a big production. The American Women's Club was an organization of spouses that did charity work. All the work this organization did at many embassies made a huge impact.

I had a hundred women attend a Women's Club luncheon at my residence. Ronia and I used my chicken Marbella recipe. I had fifty chicken breasts cut in half and marinated for twelve hours in wine, prunes, olives, and so on. I had to have a podium and speaker system delivered from the warehouse and set up. These are just two examples. We made hundreds of hors d'oeuvres for cocktail parties. I had to set up two bars depending on the number of invitees. My old restaurant and bar knowledge came into play. I would rather host three hundred for a cocktail party than twelve to sixteen for a sit-down dinner. Keep in mind, I never got paid for any of these events. With diplomatic couples, the State Department gets two for one. Hopefully, there have been some changes since we retired.

Oh, I can't forget CODELS, short for congressional delegations. These people come into the country with great expectations. They are so damn demanding. "I'm a congressman or senator, and I need cars, appointments with government officials, and a motorcade." For a presidential, vice presidential, or secretary of state visit, people are jumping through hoops to please them. That work is important, especially since these are the people who, back in Washington, make funding decisions affecting the State Department. I liked Secretary of State James Baker, and also General Jim Jones when I met him in the Pentagon. I met all the secretaries of state, from George Schultz to Condoleezza Rice.

A few days after the luncheon, it was time to say goodbye to the staff. We thanked Ronia, Krecencia, Ben, Linus, and George's driver, William, for all their work in making our time so enjoyable and effective. We had pulled off some wonderful receptions and dinners with aplomb. I know the Staples family made a very positive impression on everybody. And we had fun when I took our household staff to a movie theater for the first time, to see *What's Love Got to Do with It*, the Tina Turner story, on the big screen. I was the only White person in the theater, and it didn't bother me at all. But I got a sense of what my Black friends had experienced and were still feeling in our own country. There were hugs and tears all around as we parted. But when I said goodbye to Killian, I lost it. I told him, "You meet a lot of people in your life, but I can truly say I enjoyed every minute I had with you." He was a wonderful gardener, and I learned so much from him. I hope all of them are still alive and they survived the violence and difficult economic hardships that, after we left, President Mugabe inflicted on this beautiful country and its people.

Chapter 51

Before serving in Zimbabwe, George had worked in Washington as the senior Turkey desk officer in the Bureau of Southern European Affairs. He was exposed to a broader perspective of major international issues while I had time to take care of delayed maintenance issues at our home. During this time, Iraq, under the leadership of Saddam Hussein, invaded Kuwait. Turkey played a critical role in assisting the international effort to oust the Iraqi army. George was very busy coordinating the State Department's role in policy decisions between the Pentagon, State Department, and our embassy in Ankara.

During this domestic assignment, I was very fortunate to join George in making an orientation visit to the three countries handled by his office: Turkey, Greece, and Cyprus. We paid my way so I could travel and participate in some of the diplomatic activities at each post. In Turkey, at the embassy in Ankara, we stayed with the deputy chief of mission, Marc Grossman, and his wife, Mildred Patterson. While George was in meetings, a Turkish employee took me to the market and the old city, which had existed for hundreds of years. The buildings were terraced on a hillside, and I still remember the smell of exotic spices. I had my camera and took lots of photos.

From Ankara, we traveled to our small consulate in Adana, an important trading center in Turkey's southeast in the Kurdish region. I couldn't believe how isolated it was, surrounded by desert with camels in and around the city. What a contrast from Ankara, and not a place I would like to live in or visit again, as I am not comfortable in lonely, desert environments. But the staff was warm and welcoming, and government housing was very nice.

After Adana, we went to Istanbul, one of the world's oldest cities. Our consulate general was in one of our country's oldest diplomatic buildings, dating back to the 1700s. The architecture was beautiful, but the building was expensive to maintain, and there was talk of giving it back to the Turkish government. The consulate had its own boat, and the consul general took us on a ride on the Bosporus, which was filled with ships from around the world.

Our final stop in Turkey was Izmir, the famous trading city on the west coast. While George was in meetings, the wife of the consul picked me up in the official car with a driver and took me to the biblical city of Ephesus, a two-hour drive away. The city and its Roman ruins are famous for the site of Paul's speech to the Ephesians. The stage in the amphitheater where he spoke is still there and a much-visited site for tourists. The city also contained remnants of tile floors that had been heated in Roman times. People were sometimes buried under the floors of their homes.

After visiting the city, the consul's wife took me to a picnic lunch on a hillside at the site believed to be the last home of the Virgin Mary. This was where biblical historians believe Jesus had asked his mother to be taken to after the crucifixion. Looking out the window on the way back to the city, I was transported back in time when I saw a man in what I thought to be traditional dress riding a donkey with his feet almost touching the ground. At the time, I didn't fully appreciate my visit to Ephesus, but later when I learned more about the region and its history, this memory is one I'll always treasure.

Chapter 52

For our next stop, we flew from Turkey to Athens, the capital of Greece. George had meetings, and then we went to the world-famous Acropolis and visited the Parthenon. I love all periods of architecture, except modern buildings. It was a very dry season. As we came into the city, I saw a different type of home-building. As I remember, every house had a water storage tank built on it. A garbage strike was going on, and the hotel manager apologized for the trash that had not been taken away.

Greece had a famous history and is considered to be the birthplace of democracy. Many consider the world's greatest philosophers to be Aristotle, Socrates, and Plato, all Greeks. Homer wrote about the Trojan War, and we have his *Iliad* and *Odyssey* on the bookshelf in Kentucky. I know a little about Greek history. My husband isn't writing this book, but George is the historian of the family. He would have a lot to say about modern Greece and Greek history.

Close to Athens near the port area is the famous Marathon battlefield. In 490 BC, the Persians attacked Athens and landed their army there. The Greeks defeated the Persians and won a surprising triumph against overwhelming odds. After the battle, the Greek army commander sent word of the battle to Athens by a runner who ran nonstop twenty-six miles to deliver the news. When the runner arrived, he shouted to the crowd, "Victory!" and collapsed and died. To this day, marathons are run all over the world, and the distance is twenty-six miles.

Last stop on our trip was Cyprus, which had been divided into a Greek and a Turkish side since Turkey invaded in 1974. We flew to the island and landed in Nicosia, the capital city. We were taken to our hotel, and later, the ambassador hosted a reception for us. We talked about our trip and political events. I knew the island had been divided by UN peacekeepers into a Greek Cypriot side and a Turkish Cypriot side. I felt this was wrong, and the people in Cyprus should learn how to live together again.

During the conversation, I noticed the lady next to me had a beautiful brooch on the lapel of her jacket. I'm a serious collector of beautiful brooches. I interrupted the conversation and said, "Where did you get the brooch you are wearing?" She told me it had been made by a local artist, there were three more left, and there would be no more. Instantly I was on a mission to have one. The next day, I got a car to take me to the artist's address. I bought one just in time, as the artist was leaving for Europe to help with his grandchildren because his son had died.

We had been given permission to visit the Turkish side of the island. When I mentioned that we planned to travel the next day to the Turkish controlled side, a hotel worker, with a crestfallen look, explained that he could go to the highest hillside near Nicosia, look over to the Turkish side, and see the roof of his house that he had not been able to visit for sixteen years.

Chapter 53

After Cyprus, we returned to Washington, and after a day or so, I drove to Pineville. I had to see Catherine and Ana Maria, who had been taking care of her. Ana Maria was the wonderful woman who had come to work for us during our time in Nassau. She was now a part of my Kentucky family. We took care of each other, and she was a hard worker like me. We went up the hill to cut locus posts to use in different projects. We made a skid down the hill to slide the trees to an old log road. Of course, brother Jim and Uncle AY helped cut down the trees. It really wasn't too hard. I like to make work fun whenever possible.

After three great years in Zimbabwe, George was doing one year as a National Security Affairs Fellow at Stanford University, his senior training assignment. I went out once to see him. I got to see my dear friends Craig and Doris Leverault. We have remained friends throughout the years. Doris has done some beautiful sculptures. Craig had a very successful career in engineering. But their most important achievement was a beautiful baby girl. Tanya is a beautiful and successful young woman now. She works in the film industry

I was glad not to have diplomatic responsibilities. I gave birthday parties for my family. Uncle Joe was still my hero even after meeting so many famous people. I love all my family, all of them, but being part of a mountain clan has its downside. Mammie and Aunt Della always defended the family no matter what the circumstances. It's called unconditional love. My mother told me once, "Ann, I think you might have been wrong." But she never said it in front of other people. I was hers, and I could do no wrong.

My mother has been gone from me for so many years now, but I still talk to her, and when I have been in great pain, I have wanted my mother. So many things have been missed, all because of a damn drunken fool. Because of her lack of education, I couldn't get her away from him. I made sure my Catherine would be an educated woman and never take abuse, either verbal or physical, from any man. I was blessed with a good son-in-law and a beautiful, very spoiled granddaughter. I love spoiling her at age five. It's so sad that some of my family never saw Catherine. Lots of family left me never having seen Grace Ann.

My Kentucky home is beautiful. Nothing the State Department could ever give us for a residence could ever be as lovely as my mountain home. But it was time once again to go overseas, this time to a new part of the world: Bahrain in the Middle East!

Uncle Robert and Aunt Dorothy visiting the U.S. Embassy in Harare, Zimbabwe

Uncle Robert and Aunt Dorothy departing with George to inaugurate a U.S. funded assistance project.

Uncle Robert, Aunt Dorothy, and Catherine having a champagne brunch on the Zambezi River.

Robert and Dorothy overlooking Harare, Zimbabwe.
They said their trip to Zimbabwe was the highlight of their lives.

Participating in Zimbabwe's elephant relocation project. I'm holding the dart gun.

A sedated elephant ready to be loaded aboard a truck for transport to a less populated part of the country.

Standing with my visitors from Germany, the two Claudias, by a caution sign found only in southern Africa.

The Claudias at Victoria Falls, Zimbabwe. At certain times of the year raincoats are issued to tourists because of the amount of spray.

Catherine in her school's athletic attire standing in front of an enormous plant in our yard.

On safari in Zimbabwe.

Lorin and Diana Rambo at the embassy Marine Corps Ball in Harare, Zimbabwe.

Sitting with my close friend Dr. Terry Robinson during his family's visit to Zimbabwe. Sadly, my soulmate passed away before my book could be published.

George and Jill Robinson enjoying a boat ride on the Zambezi River.

With Jill, her son Ryan and daughter Krista, and Catherine at Victoria Falls.

The Robinsons and Catherine taking a swim while boating on the Zambezi. They're in the "cage" which protected against crocodiles.

John and Philicia Collins, with their friends from Colombia, ready to depart for a trip to Jeffrey's village.

John and Philicia, friends starting from our first
diplomatic assignment in El Salvador.

Chapter 54

In the summer of 1996, our family went overseas once again, this time to the country of Bahrain, a small island nation located in the Arabian Gulf, next to Saudi Arabia. Here, George served his second assignment as a deputy chief of mission in support of Ambassador David Ransom, for whom he had worked in Washington while serving as senior Turkish desk officer. David had been appointed as our ambassador to Bahrain the previous year when George, after leaving Zimbabwe, was doing his senior training at Stanford University's Hoover Institute. As his Hoover assignment was nearing its end, George noticed that the DCM job in Bahrain was coming open, which offered the chance to serve in a different part of the world and allow Catherine to attend the Bahrain School, a US-equivalent high school operated and funded by the US Navy.

George and Catherine arrived in Bahrain's capital, Manama, ahead of me and were settled in what was at the time the DCM residence. They immediately observed that the house was unsatisfactory, having a small living space, but more importantly from a security standpoint, it was located next to a Shia Mosque off a causeway that offered just one way in and out from the main highway. Having goats and other animals roaming next to the house along with unscreened young men herding them, not to mention the potential for antigovernment demonstrations centered around the mosque, required urgent State Department action to find us a new residence. This was done without delay, and my family moved into a guarded compound, which offered safer, larger, newly built homes suitable for hosting representational events.

The day after George and Catherine arrived in Bahrain, David Ransom invited them to his residence for lunch. This provided an opportunity for David to welcome them before the workweek began and to introduce them to George's new office management specialist (OMS), Betty Thrasher. Betty had joined the Foreign Service later in life after her children were grown and, after her husband had, unfortunately, passed. She wanted to travel and have some adventure, so she went to her first post in Rio de Janeiro, Brazil, and then came to Manama. George and Betty hit it off right away, and she really liked Catherine after overcoming her initial surprise at having our daughter as part of the lunch group. Betty would prove to be a key front-office figure who provided outstanding administrative support to David and to George throughout his assignment in Bahrain. Iris Mayo, David's OMS, who had worked for David and George in Washington, also attended the lunch.

George told me later that Catherine stole the show. She proved to be witty and fun and asked good questions about Bahrain and her new school. The highlight, however, was when she told David that she really liked his house in Washington. David and his wife, Marjorie, owned a home off Connecticut Avenue that was right next to the National Zoo. They had had us over for dinner when George worked on the Turkish desk, and Catherine loved hearing the sounds of the animals, especially the lions roaring at night. She told David that he and Marjorie had the "coolest" house in all of Washington. Everyone enjoyed that description from someone whom Betty later described as a very special, mature young lady!

Chapter 55

I arrived in Bahrain about two weeks after George and Catherine, bringing with me our dog, Simba, and two cats, Don Quixote and Baby. Before leaving Kentucky, I had to get the required travel documents for our pets and health certificates, and I had to plan for help to take care of our home in Pineville. I was glad George and Catherine had told the General Services and security officers that the first house wasn't going to please Mom. They found another house, and I was very pleased. This was the first time in years I could walk in with our pets, get a tour of the residence, and crawl into a clean bed. The residence was beautiful for entertaining and had the biggest crystal chandelier in the foyer I had ever seen in a private residence. The floors were all marble with high ceilings, with a wrought-iron balcony overlooking the large entryway. And we had a pool!

Before arriving, I knew little about Bahrain or the Arab world. There was no Foreign Service Institute seminar available to me, so I just learned what I could to prepare as best as possible. I knew, for example, that Bahrain was close to Iraq and that years before, Saddam had invaded neighboring Kuwait. There was still tension in the region and concern about terrorist activity. We were also close to Iran, which threatened US commercial interests. On top of that, we arrived just a few days after the Khobar Towers bombing next door in Saudi Arabia. Our entire time in Bahrain would be affected by terrorist concerns.

Despite these worries, Bahrain was known for its gold souk (market) and other "shopping opportunities," as George would say. It was also possible to get tailor-made clothes, buy rugs, and experience desert excursions with camel riding! Bahrain was also a very relaxed Muslim country in which women could drive, choose to cover themselves like Saudi women, join gyms, shop without escorts, and hold government positions. I was told that moderate, conservative dress would be fine, meaning when out in public, I would wear long skirts and cover my arms. I chose not to wear pants.

At the new residence, I was hoping to have a great chef because this was a house made for entertaining. I was looking forward to once again seeing Ambassador David Ransom. Since I had last seen him, he had been given this well-deserved ambassadorship and had been in Bahrain a year before our arrival. George told me later that Ambassador Ransom had said to him that we would have an invitation to everything but that I wouldn't have to attend if I didn't want to. David's wife, Marjorie, was also a Foreign Service officer. She was serving in Syria, so that made me the most senior woman at the embassy. David and I had in common a love for Corvettes, and he had his shipped to Bahrain.

One of the secrets to being happy in the Foreign Service was to ensure that people had nice housing. That's one thing I can say for the US government: for most of our overseas service, we had good housing. Often our personnel were far from home, maybe for the first time, with children. A home away from home makes a soul feel safe and secure. No, we didn't get a Mercedes with drivers to attend functions. We had to drive our own cars most of the time and walk from the parking lot.

The tone at the embassy was set from the top down. If we had a great ambassador, people would be happy. It sure made a difference. We have served with ambassadors who really cared about their staff and those who didn't. The ambassador's wife was an important person at an embassy. I wanted her, as well as the ambassador, to make us proud. We stood up whenever the ambassador entered the room. I hope this protocol is still practiced and things haven't gotten too casual.

Chapter 56

Catherine went to the Bahrain School, an international school run by the US Navy. Thank God, she didn't have to wear a uniform there, which she had hated wearing at her previous schools. She was happy in Bahrain and helped me prepare place cards and seating charts for dinners, and she stood in receiving lines with us. She was a natural because she had been doing all this since age five or six, even greeting guests in French and Spanish. It was hard to drop her off at school. The navy security personnel came through with sniffer dogs before students could enter the building during daily checks for explosive devices.

My surface and air freight shipments arrived, and I could put my personal touch on our residence. I hung my paintings and displayed my sculptures. I put treasures in the curio cabinets and, most importantly, placed my photos on shelves. I didn't travel with my fine china because George was deputy chief of mission, so the silver, china, and crystal we used were representational and supplied by the State Department office that supported official housing overseas. A woman named Martha Persinger at the State Department was especially helpful in sending me the representational items I needed. I had to keep an inventory for breakage, and damaged items were sent to the State Department for replacement. I was responsible for US government property inside of the residence and had to sign a paper to this effect.

Running an official residence was lots of work for me: planning menus, shopping for food, setting tables for formal dinners, ordering flowers, and so on. Thank God, there was staff to help me, but I made the decisions. Yes, it sounds glamorous, and it could be, but my feet were very sore at 2:00 a.m., when all the guests had gone.

Chapter 57

Before long, I had the chance to meet Sheik Isa bin Salman Al-Khalifa, the Emir of Bahrain. George had accompanied Ambassador Ransom to meetings with His Highness and found him to be warm and personable. We were invited on one occasion to dinner at one of his residences. The Emir's protocol chief called to make the invitation, and I accepted. He called back later and asked if we had children. Catherine was going with us. Here come the Staples!

When we arrived at His Highness's residence, a red carpet was laid out, and to my surprise, Sheik Isa was waiting for us as we drove up. We entered the residence, and three beautiful young ladies were in attendance, dressed in Asian dress at the Emir's palace. One of the women took photos of me, George, and Catherine, then another photo of us with His Highness. I presented him with a book about the famous Tennessee Walking Horse. He was very pleased with the gift, being a man who appreciated horses and most likely bred Arabians.

It was time to be escorted into dinner. I was surprised but pleased we were the only invited guests. A long red carpet led to the large dining room. I remember gilded chairs. George was seated at the head of the table, Catherine was to the right of her dad, and I was seated to George's left. His Highness was seated two chairs from Catherine. He was a giant of a man but small in stature. My daughter is petite. Sheik Isa said his wife bought his shoes in the boys' department at department stores! He and Catherine bonded immediately, and they began telling each other jokes about short people! Catherine at one point told him that dynamite comes in small packages. We had a wonderful time. I went to the powder room, and to my surprise, there was perfume in very large bottles, maybe pint sizes. It was the most beautiful bathroom I have ever seen in my life.

Before we left, His Highness gave me a briefcase and its combination. George said we shouldn't open it as per State Department restrictions on accepting expensive gifts. He had to take it to the embassy and turn in everything for eventual shipment to Washington. When we got home, Catherine and I took the briefcase and sat in the middle of the bed. Inside were three Rolex watches with diamond bezels, a beautiful set of pearls, gold bracelets with precious stones, and beautiful canary diamond earrings. It was overwhelming for Catherine and me. George said we couldn't keep anything and turned it all in at the embassy. His Highness must have known the embassy policy. I'm sure there was no inventory, but it was left up to us to turn it in. My husband goes by the book. He is very strict and correct. I guess he would be described as an "officer and a gentleman." He had his diamond ring passed down from his grandfather, and he purchased a Rolex for himself in the 1970s, but I will never have a diamond Rolex, and I will never forgive him!

George and Ambassador Ransom later went to a large official meeting hosted by His Highness. Sheik Isa said during his speech, "Catherine Staples told me dynamite comes in small packages." Ambassador Ransom looked at George, who explained that Catherine had said it at the dinner we attended.

Two weeks later, Catherine got off the school bus screaming in pain. She had to go to the hospital with appendicitis. One day, George answered the phone, and a voice said, "George, this is Isa." George was taken aback. Sheik Isa had called to check on Catherine. All of this happened while we still faced danger from Saddam Hussein in Iraq and potential terrorists from Iran. People back home wouldn't understand that even in dangerous situations, one could have a good life.

Chapter 58

The US Navy's Fifth Fleet was and is today headquartered in Manama. The Fifth Fleet was responsible for military security throughout the region with a special emphasis on deterring Iranian threats to shipping in the Arabian Gulf and acts threatening to neighboring countries. The commander was Vice Admiral (three stars) Tom Fargo, who was well liked by George and Ambassador Ransom. I also liked Admiral Fargo and his wife, Sarah. Admiral Fargo was under the overall authority of the Central Command commander, Marine Corps four-star general Anthony Zinni. Men in uniform always make me feel safe, and I was very pleased to see the close cooperation in Bahrain between our military and diplomatic personnel.

Gurkhas provided extra security for the embassy. These were the famous fighters from Nepal contracted to provide security at many embassies in the Middle East. Once we were invited to a party at their large residence, and I was excited to accept. They were very nice men who took their responsibilities seriously. The more security, the better in that part of the world.

Halfway through our assignment, I had to return to the US to help my family with a medical issue. On my return flight to Bahrain, a special person came into my life. A lovely woman named Nora, who was going to Kuwait, sat next to me. She was a teacher at the Kuwait International School. We started talking about our lives. When a flight attendant would come by, we would ask for a couple of cordial bottles to drink. We got a little tipsy and started talking about hurts and losses in our lives. After a while, we would look for an attendant we hadn't seen before and get more Drambuie, amaretto, or Kahlua. We got crying drunk together! When George saw me and my condition, he whisked me through the airport straight to the car. He didn't want anyone to recognize me. I had a copy of the prose poem "Desiderata" by Max Ehrmann, but Nora gave me a better one, and it hangs on my bedroom wall. Nora and I formed a bond and remain in touch to this day!

Chapter 59

It was good to be back in Manama, but soon after my arrival, I had to terminate my Indian cook. I had earlier said, "I would sell my soul for an Indian cook." Wrong! He drank, and our guards talked about his behavior. I went shopping one morning with him. I said, "Ashook, you're drunk." I grew up around people who drank too much. So went my dream of an Indian cook.

I eventually interviewed Eddie, a great chef but with an ego to go with it. He was from Sri Lanka but had never worked in a private home before. Eddie had been a chef, a demi chef in hotels, a pastry chef, and so on. I said, "Eddie, are you sure you want to work for me?" I had my doubts, but I filled out a contract and put in the job description as a cook. He refused to sign it until it was changed to "chef." I told him he had an ego but that was okay with me. I like people who have confidence.

After about a year, Chef Eddie had enough of working at a residence. He said he had made a mistake and preferred working in food and beverage industry. However, he told me, "Mrs. Staples, I will not leave you, but when your time is up, I will leave also." There are times now when he calls from Sri Lanka to catch up on our lives. If I were rich, I would try to get a visa to bring Eddie to work for me in Pineville. I have to take into consideration that we both are aging! Some of the people I would have loved for him to have cooked for have left me. I can't bring myself to say they are dead. I hate that word. I just can't see them, but I can talk to my loved ones who have gone before me. Their spirits are with me and are my guiding angels.

Raj, our house manager in Bahrain, was from Mauritius, a small island nation off East Africa. She was wonderful, and I liked her so very much. The staff was starting to come together. But it was beneath my new chef to walk the dog or clean out the cat's litter box. He helped me do a lot of dinners and buffets. He carved ice sculptures for the center of the table with blue lighting for added effect. I felt I was on a Carnival Cruise Line voyage, where ice sculptures are often seen on the buffet tables. We did great presentations of food for plate serving at a formal dinner. I taught Raj and Eddie some of my recipes. I used a ruler to properly line up every piece of crystal, silver, and china on the table for a formal dinner. I was in my glory to plan and make these events happen.

George would usually come home from the embassy, rest, and get dressed for dinner. He never knew all the work involved with dinner. Now, if he reads this, he will say, "Why are you writing about these things? No one cares to read them." I think these details demystify the myth that planning cocktails and entertainment is easy. If I enjoyed a dinner invitation at someone's home, I always thank the people who pulled it off. I know what goes on behind the swinging doors!

Here's an example of a gala event in Bahrain. I was invited to a wedding party for about four hundred women. I was often put in awkward positions because I didn't have enough information. This was one of those times. I drove myself and had a difficult time finding parking. All the women were arriving in abayas, traditional black robe-like attire. I wasn't expected to wear traditional clothing, but I explained earlier about conservative dress, and I always tried to respect the culture. I had on a long black shirt and long-sleeve blouse. I collect shawls and brooches. I often wore my favorite shawls from an antique store and a very old antique brooch that was from George's grandmother. I liked my long strand of pearls with earrings to match, not the post earrings but the kind that hung down from my earlobes.

After the receiving line for this event, all the ladies changed out of their abayas. I had never seen so much jewelry before. I recognized diamonds, pearls, emeralds, rubies, and more. I saw more gold bracelets and bangles than I had seen in the downtown gold souk. They were wearing lots of ladies' suits I assumed were made in Italy or other design locations around the world. Dinner was served buffet style on very long tables, with lots of floral arrangements and the most food I had ever seen for one occasion. Approximately four hundred women ate about only one-fourth of the food. I was seated at a table for diplomats. I knew maybe five women at my table. Admiral Fargo's wife, Sarah, must have been present. There were just a few non-Arab women at the event.

I could hear music but didn't know where it was coming from. Persian carpets had been placed end to end to make a runway about seventy feet long for dancing. The music continued, and we did a version of the Stroll from the sixties. We danced to the end and returned to pass the ladies just starting at the beginning. At some point, I realized the band was behind drawn draperies. There were men in the band, and they weren't allowed to see the women without their abayas. So, we never saw the band, but the band played on.

At about midnight, the bride and groom arrived. It created a huge scuffle since the women had to get back into their abayas because of the presence of one man. As I left through the exit line, the bride thanked me for my gift, but I had learned no one else had given a gift because it wasn't expected. Outside, everyone's driver was waiting except for one lonely and embarrassed American woman. I was upset when I got home, and George and the embassy protocol officer heard directly from me how upset I was not to have had a driver, and not enough information about what was specifically expected at the reception.

Chapter 60

I was loving my new residence in Bahrain. Thanks to George and Catherine, I met Matham Al-Ali, who was a very interesting young man. His family owned the residence the embassy had leased for us before I arrived. We became friends and worked out at the same gym. I had learned about Islam from reading *The Complete Idiot's Guide to Islam*. I'm not joking because I learned a lot from the book. King Isa was a Sunni Muslim, and the Al-Ali family were Shias. In Bahrain, the Shia were the majority of the population, but the Sunnis were in power. I was told by a friend that Matham's family was the third richest in Bahrain.

The Shia split with the Sunnis dated back to the time after the death of Muhammad the prophet, whose revelations from God formed the basis of the religion of Islam. After his death, his nephew Ali was expected by some to succeed as leader, but others believed that ability, not family ties, should have been the deciding factor. Feuding developed followed by violence between factions, culminating in the death of Hussein, Muhammad's grandson. The split between Sunnis and Shias continues to this day.

It was exciting to be immersed in a new culture. I was seeing and being exposed to wealth that I didn't know existed. I now know that the first oil in the Middle East was discovered in Bahrain. We visited the museum on the site of the discovery. At times, I felt it was obscene to have such wealth. Sheik Isa's country was wealthy but nothing like Saudi Arabia, which was completely different from anything I had ever experienced.

I loved meeting people and learning from the people I would meet. I met a very interesting man from Pakistan who worked at the embassy. When workers came to our residence, he was their supervisor. We had time to talk and drink tea.

I had some previous knowledge of how Pakistan became a country. In 1947, India was divided, and the northern part of India became Pakistan. Use your imagination and try to think what it must have been like to leave your ancestral home and march north to make a country because Muslims and Hindus couldn't live together. The relationship between India and Pakistan remains too complicated for me to understand and explain. Historically, in my opinion, it has never been a good thing to divide countries. Time has proven that to be true. For example, the dispute over Kashmir has never been settled.

Many Pakistanis in Bahrain worked for the government and other businesses. Lots of doctors and nurses were from the Philippines. The doctor who did my knee laparoscopy was from Manila. But many of the nonprofessional laborers in Bahrain and other Middle Eastern countries, and there are thousands of them, are not treated well and are sometimes abused. But they come to work and then send money home to their families, who might otherwise be completely destitute.

Chapter 61

A number of senior US four-star generals came through the country while we were in Bahrain. I had to host them once at my residence, and security was a big deal. I counted twelve-armed military security people in the back of the residence, the side yard, the front of my residence, and on the roof and at the front gate. They were doing a security check before the generals arrived. A man ran up to our private living area who wanted to know where the security phone was located. I had to get George. I knew the location of the secure phone but not where he kept the key. The generals were great. Eddie and Raj had made and served the food beautifully.

Once George became deputy ambassador and later an ambassador, residence support from Washington was a very different experience for me. In Bahrain, I was getting help with senior decorators in charge of the furniture, and there was a decorating budget. Later in Cameroon, a senior decorator visited, and I asked her to stay at the residence instead of going to a hotel. I wanted her to teach me more about decorating. But the greatest thing was getting to visit a warehouse in DC and select art for the residence.

The art program that supports our residences overseas is called the Art in Embassies program. Paintings by American artists are on loan to the program by for the term of our assignments. When selected for an ambassadorship, you get to select what you'd like to have shipped to your new post to be displayed in the residence. Soon, it would be our turn to have this experience. We were on a fast track. What a great time I was having!

Chapter 62

Don Quixote, our black cat from Kentucky; Simba, George's black Labrador; and Baby, our little white cat, lounged around the pool and back porch at our home in Manama. They could come inside the house anytime, but we locked all three away at night in a fourth unused bathroom to protect the furniture. George always let them out in the morning and gave them food and water. George loves animals, and I tell him he loves animals more than people.

Don was mine. My brother Alvie found him beside the road in Kentucky. He was about five days old. Some people are superstitious about black cats. I fed him on a bottle, and he slept close to my back to stay warm. When I left for El Salvador, he went with me. He became a world traveler.

In Bahrain, the veterinarian said, "Mrs. Staples, Don Quixote might not make it back home." Don was getting old and forgetful. He would mistake another very similar house for his. Once I went looking for him and found him locked in another house, crying. I said, "Don't cry; I'll get you out." I got a key from someone and got him out of the house. I told the vet my old man would make it home. He did in fact come home to Kentucky.

My friend Nora visited me in Bahrain, and we had a great experience. We had our photos taken on a camel. I think we went to see a camel race. I know for sure camels are nasty and spit horrible juice. I might describe it as being like chewing tobacco that people chew and spit in Kentucky. We tried smoking flavored tobacco in a bong-type system. This was in a special park environment with carved, traditional benches that we sat on. We could try different flavors of tobacco. We shared a Kodak moment. I have beautiful photos to commemorate our smoking experience.

A very special event during this assignment was when George and I were invited to go on board the USS *Enterprise*, which was paying a port visit to Bahrain. My baby brother, Bill, who was retired from the navy, had served on the *Enterprise*. He would be happy for me to be on board an aircraft carrier. There was no ambassador in the country yet, so we had to do this hardship duty! I wish I could remember every detail of the tour. I think we were invited on board because Admiral Fargo was in charge of the Fifth Fleet. I got to go on the bridge and see the air-to-air missiles down below. It drives me crazy when politicians talk about rebuilding our military. We already have the best and most well-trained men and women in the world. Some people explained their jobs to us, and they were obviously well educated, as they could explain their jobs in detail I could understand. We had a formal luncheon in the admiral's private dining room. I will never forget this experience. It was a long way from Pineville, Kentucky!

Ambassador Ransom had a traditional Christmas event at the residence. His wife, Marjorie, and their three beautiful daughters were in Manama. It was a family tradition to read from Charles Dickens's *A Christmas Carol*. During events like this at the residence, I commented on the beautiful rugs and framed, ornate jewelry used as wall hangings. David told me that he and Marjorie had collected great jewelry through the years, especially during their tour in Yemen early in their careers. This wasn't just gold or silver but more traditional beads and crafts from local artists. David and Marjorie planned to publish a book after photographing their collection.

Chapter 63

All too quickly, Ambassador Ransom's time was up. I was very sad to see him go back to Washington. Unfortunately, ambassadors usually can serve only a three-year assignment, and then they are replaced. As they say, "To everything there is a season." David was missed by many. I was anxious about what the new ambassador and his wife would be like. There was work to be done following a regional security evaluation, and we needed to find a new ambassador's residence. This would take some time and work, but there was time before the arrival of the new ambassador.

George was appointed acting ambassador, and during that time, we had a very important visitor coming to Bahrain, former Secretary of State James Baker. We were invited to a state dinner hosted by the Bahrain government. I was very excited and looked forward to meeting Secretary Baker. I instantly liked him. I was seated to his side, as was protocol. The dinner was opulent, with many different courses of food displayed down the center of the table. Maybe thirty people were invited. Servers took our plates, and we told them what food we would like to try. As usually, there was more than enough food, enough to feed sixty people. Early on in Bahrain, I was told it was the traditional Arab way to show hospitality from back in history. I was hoping Secretary Baker wasn't too disappointed that there wasn't an ambassador in the country to greet him, but he knew George from when my husband worked with him in Washington as a senior watch officer. George and I were diplomatic veterans by now. I think Secretary Baker was sincere in being glad to meet. If I had ever had the chance to vote for him, I would have done it.

It was time to find a new residence for the new ambassador. I attended a meeting to begin the process of looking for a new house. I found a perfect house that was under construction, and I met with the owner to explain that we needed a new ambassador's residence. He had built the house for himself and was reluctant to let the embassy have it for a long-term lease. After I put some "southern charm" on him, he agreed.

In my mind, I was back in Zimbabwe moving furniture and finding new properties. I got warehouse employees to move everything from the old residence. I relocated everything I could to the new house. American taxpayers would be pleased. I had the library drapes remade. The furniture was beautiful with wonderful fabric and wooden tables. Most everything fit beautifully. I called this place my finest hour with arranging and decorating. There was a spiral staircase to the second floor. Ambassador Ransom's staff came to organize the new kitchen. Tomas, his chef, was very good.

In setting up the house, I pretended this residence was ours. I made an office for the ambassador and arranged the desk, chairs, and flags where I would have placed them for George. George would say I was going into too much detail, but this was my way. I made an en suite for the master bedroom with a white sofa and put everything in place the ambassador and spouse would need on arrival. The foyer was grand, and I put a big round table in the middle. I took a very large art deco vase from my residence to make a very large floral piece for the center. Eddie, my chef, and Tomas, Ambassador Ransom's cook, made beautiful finger food to be passed to guests.

And then entered Ambassador Johnny Young and his beautiful wife, Angie. I had feared some woman with no taste and no class would arrive. Wrong! Angie started where I had left off. There was more to do. The ambassador had already been in charge of embassies four times before in other countries. Angie started putting her own touches on her new home. She started accessorizing with beautiful fabric and pillows. Ambassador Young and Angie were very special human beings. We were very lucky to serve in Bahrain with Ambassador Ransom and Ambassador Young.

One day, Angie and I went to a Majlis, a huge reception to which citizens of the country and diplomats were invited. This was an event for senior government, business, and diplomatic women hosted by Sheik Isa's wife. She was dressed beautifully with jewelry befitting her position. I always give my clothing and my accessories a lot of thought. This was one of those times when I said, "Where is the jewelry I inherited?"

Angie and I arrived at a large palace with the ambassador's driver, Jasim. We were taken to be introduced to Her Highness. She greeted Angie; this was the first time they met. We were escorted to a French provincial love seat that was gilded with a bright finish. Women were swinging incense from brass lanterns. This was definitely a high tea experience. Pastries were set out on our table. Before meeting Her Highness, we mingled with the other women. There were several round, three-tiered stands with large bottles of every perfume one could imagine. We could try anything we wanted to spray and smell. Before we left, we were given large +++++++++++++++++++++++++++++++++shopping bags of nice boxes, candy, and perfume. I'm sure there were other things, but I can't remember all the gifts.

Angie was a great help with looking after Catherine when it was prom time at the high school, and I was not in Manama. The Youngs were a good team, and I was very proud we were together in Bahrain.

Now it was time for us to leave. President Clinton nominated George to become the next US Ambassador to the Republic of Rwanda.

Ambassador Johnny Young

Angie Young, the wife of our Ambassador to Bahrain, and I getting ready for a special event at the ambassador's residence.

Preparing to deliver cakes on behalf of our embassy for sale at a charity event.

A close up of our cakes highlighting the friendship between the United States and Bahrain. The bake sell was a great success.

An unforgettable waterpipe moment with my friend Nora.

Chapter 64

Upon leaving Bahrain in the summer of 1998, George was appointed ambassador to the Republic of Rwanda, in Central Africa. I had said in El Salvador that one day I would be married to an ambassador and live in an official residence. Little did I know how much work it would take to get there.

We were going back to Washington for the official swearing-in ceremony in the Treaty Room on the seventh floor at the State Department. As my old California buddy Jerry Faulkerson would have said, "Hip-hip hooray, here comes the Staples family, clear the way."

This was a big event for us. Hosting a swearing-in ceremony would be expensive, but who cared at this point? I was thrilled because members of my family from Pineville would be there, as well as Marian Bichelmeir and Terry Gilliam from Cincinnati, and George's uncle Bill Staples and aunt YGean Staples Chambers from Gary, Indiana. George's sister Milly Staples was also coming from Sacramento, California. My aunt Della was with me. There was also our daughter, Catherine; cousin Jackeline Jordan; and my Uncle Robert Knoppe and Aunt Dorothy from Shelbyville, Kentucky. You will remember them from their visit to Zimbabwe. My running buddy Lucille Palmer was in attendance. Her husband, Larry, couldn't join us. They have been our close friends since our days together in Uruguay. State Department friends from El Salvador days John and Philicia Collins came to the ceremony as well as Admiral Fargo and his wife, Sarah. I was especially pleased that Ambassador David Ransom came since George's work with him in Bahrain helped make this day possible.

After the swearing-in, Catherine and I returned to Kentucky. She finished her senior year at Pineville High School. I was excited for her. I wanted that graduation experience for her, connection to a senior class, and making friends for life. However, it never really happened for my daughter with her return to Pineville. I thought Catherine, who played tennis, and her cousin, who was a cheerleader, might be friends and double date as I had done with my cousins. But Catherine was the outsider, and Mom couldn't fix that for her.

Catherine graduated with honors from Pineville High School and won a small scholarship from our Rotary Club. Now we had to start looking for a university for her to attend. After visiting several, we thought James Madison would be a good fit. It had a nice, beautiful campus, and for the first two years, she would be living in a dorm. However, this proved to be a difficult time for Catherine. I took her to Harrisonburg, Virginia, and helped her get settled into her new life. I cried for the next six hours as I drove home without any food or bathroom break. This proved to be very difficult for Mama Jo Ann. After some life-learning exposure, I diagnosed myself with "empty nest syndrome."

Before going to Rwanda, I had to attend a two-week ambassador seminar at the State Department. When I left home to drive to Washington, Don Quixote was lying on the back rock porch. I told him to be there when I came home. I can't remember too much about the seminar, except when I heard about Osama bin Laden for the first time. When I returned to Pineville, I carried my luggage in, hugged and kissed my daughter, and asked, "Where's my old man?"

Catherine said, "Mom, he died."

I told Catherine, "You don't joke about something like that," but she said it was true. We held each other and cried.

Don was buried in front of my lilac bush. Brothers Jim and Alvie, Catherine, and Tina were at his funeral. You heard me right. They had a real funeral with eulogies and singing. I couldn't attend, but my family made me very proud. Brother Jim preached at the funeral!

Eva and I enrolled at our community college to improve our computer skills. We had only rudimentary knowledge. We had fun and laughed a lot. We didn't leave that computer class with advanced skills, but we did get a 4.0 grade for the course. I was also taking a creative writing class with a great teacher. I wrote three papers that I remember. One was about the fear of public speaking, one was about an unfulfilled life, and another was about the life of artist Vincent Van Gogh. I wished many times in my life that I'd had time to go back to school for more education. However, I never could break away from my duties at the State Department. As dear friend Marian would tell me, "Such is life."

Chapter 65

After settling Catherine in at college, George and I arrived in Kigali, Rwanda's capital city, in September 1998, four years after the 1994 genocide in which more than seven hundred thousand people had been massacred. This would prove one of our most difficult assignments, as we had to deal with a nation of traumatized survivors. Rwanda had a long history of communal violence and numerous refugee crises, but nothing like what happened in 1994. Survivors often had to combine families and to care for and educate many orphans. Businesses were destroyed, and the country was dependent on large amounts of international aid for survival. Helping this country to recover and heal would be the most difficult challenge we faced in our time in the Foreign Service.

The Belgian colonization of Rwanda began in 1919, after WWI, and continued until Rwanda became an independent country in 1962. The Belgians did not help the ethnic problems; in fact, they caused many of them. Feelings of resentment multiplied because the Tutsi were given authority and power throughout the country. In 1933–1934, the Belgians conducted a census in order to issue ethnic identity cards, which labeled every Rwandan as either Hutu or Tutsi. This decision created an apartheid-like system rooted in myth.

Three ethnic groups lived in Rwanda. The Twa were Pygmy-like people who were probably the first inhabitants of Rwanda. They were living as hunters and gatherers and still lived in small groups. I met Pygmies in Zimbabwe and Cameroon, and I have some of their pottery. The Twa number about number percent of the Rwandan population and had no part in the genocide.

The Hutus were the majority ethnic group and worked mainly as farmers. They had been in Rwanda and the African Great Lakes region for centuries. The Belgians, however, favored the Tutsis, who had migrated to the area from the Ethiopian region. They were taller and had what the Belgians considered to be more European features. Even though the Tutsis were a minority, the Belgians gave them key government positions and greater educational opportunities. This created jealousy and resentment among the Hutus that festered, eventually resulting in numerous ethnic conflicts and eventually mass murder in the 1994 genocide.

The Rwandan genocide was a human tragedy of enormous scale that was prepared well in advance by the Hutu government through years of government-sponsored politics that promoted ethnic hatred. We can all learn from this tragic episode in human history that dehumanization and hatred of our fellow man can lead to horrific events that destroy not only societies but also our humanity.

Upon arriving in Rwanda, we were met by George's DCM and taken to the residence. We met the staff, who had food prepared for us. I liked the residence. We were up on a ridge, with a view of homes down in the valley. Two huge gardenia bushes sat on each side of the patio entry steps. The fragrance was heavenly. I went to work to make the residence as nice as possible because I would be in the country for only about a month on this first visit.

I spent a lot of time in Rwanda but never full time. I did my duty for God and country in helping us have a nice home for entertaining. Before going to Kigali, I had a meeting in Washington, and a woman in the relocation and housing office brought me up to date on the condition of the ambassador's residence in Kigali. The structure had been looted in 1994. Everything had been stolen. She gave me a door handle to make her point because that was all that was left. Toilets, tubs, and fixtures were nonexistent after the genocide. Some work had been done with basic furniture and repairs. There was so much left to do to turn the home once again into a functioning official residence based on "Jo Ann's way"!

A normal event after arriving in a new country was the famous windshield tour. It was eye-opening to see buildings riddled with bullet holes. Government offices had almost no files on procedures or how offices should operate. We were told they had to ask another country for correct protocol procedures for receiving a new ambassador. There was no American business community. Lots of places were burned out. A few hotels and a couple of restaurants were open. George would be busy, but that's the way he liked it!

I had a project, and I was ready. First was counting the residential inventory. That would include silver, crystal, china, and the condition of every piece of furniture. I had a General Services officer contact Martha Persinger in Washington to update my inventory because I would need some replacement items and new pieces added.

I asked the General Services officer to get a truck and some helpers, and I wanted my new gardeners to go with me. We were on a mission to find rich dirt, plants, flowers, and a couple of nonproducing small trees. I thought Rwanda must be Eden. I recognized lots of things, but they were twenty times larger than what I had ever seen. Salvia was as high as eight feet tall. Groves of bamboo and banana trees were everywhere. Now we had to buy pots for planting inside and outside the residence. I met a woman who had a nursery and raised beautiful long-stem red roses. I placed an order for forty about every two weeks. I was told by someone that this nursery was located at the source of the Nile River, which began in Rwanda and ended in Egypt. Other countries dispute this claim, but I think they are wrong.

The next thing to do was help plan a reception for us as the newly arrived ambassador and wife. We also hosted a reception for the embassy staff so they could begin to get to know us. George was busy with nation-building. The country was going to need a lot of support from the entire international community. Though not because l was married to him, I was certain he was a good choice as ambassador to this war-ravaged country.

George had a good working relationship with President Paul Kagame. The First Lady, Janet Kagame, belonged to the Rotary Club. We danced together at a Rotary Club event. I usually know instantly if I like someone, and I thought she would be a good First Lady of Rwanda. Her life must have been very hard during her husband's secret trips from Uganda back into Rwanda prior to the genocide. He was the leader of the Rwandan Patriotic Front, which eventually came into Kigali, stopped the massacres, and liberated the country. He eventually became president.

I spent a year and half of the three-year tour in Rwanda. I found an old schedule of events I had planned and events to attend. It would be impossible to write about many of them, but I will share the very special ones. For example, I was going out of town, and my driver said, "Mrs. Staples, would you like to see Paul Kagame's house where he lived before he became president?" I said I would very much like to see it. The driver took me to an average-looking home in the north of Rwanda, near the border with Uganda. I walked up to the front of the house, but the group I was traveling with took me around to the back. I saw a very basic underground bunker. When I went down the steps, I saw just a hole with sheets of tin and poles to support a roof. President Kagame was tall and slender, and I wondered how he could stretch out and sleep there. He used this place to hide out when he was leading his soldiers back and forth from Uganda during the fight against the previous government that carried out the genocide.

The next time I saw President Kagame was just prior to our permanent departure from Rwanda when he and his wife invited us to tea. Their home in Kigali was not luxurious or ostentatious, but rather just a simple, clean, ordinary home. George and I liked Paul Kagame, and he was working hard to rebuild Rwanda. Now with the passage of time, he has remained president but has been attacked by some for authoritarian practices. I still believe he had good intentions and was the right man for this time and place in Rwanda's history.

Chapter 66

During my first visit to Rwanda, I met the most famous American woman living in the country, Rosamond Carr. I developed so much love and respect for her over the next three years. In 1998, I was fifty and Roz was about eighty-six years old. To me she was elegant, sophisticated, and charming. Roz was friends with Dian Fossey, who was famous because of her study of the silverback gorillas. A movie was made about her life. Roz and I had private, intimate talks in her bedroom in Gisenyi. There was no age barrier; we were just two women sharing life stories. Roz told me about her husband, Kenneth, the famous African game hunter and filmmaker, and their difficult life together. Kenneth left her basically alone and with no money when he went on long hunting trips. He was much older, and they didn't have children.

I met Roz about four years after the genocide. Roz had started taking in Hutu and Tutsi children as they came back to Rwanda from the refugee camp on the border with Congo. She told me someone brought a five-month-old baby to her. Roz initially said, "No babies." She had no way of nursing them. A woman working with her said she would nurse the baby. It soon became apparent Roz would need a building for the orphanage. I don't know the exact time frame, but when we met, there were about 120 children. The woman who thought she would never be a mother was now a very proud mother. I saw Roz but not often enough. I loved every minute we spent together. When I had visitors, a trip to see Mrs. Carr was always on the schedule. I often helped if she asked for it. She wrote a book called *Land of a Thousand Hills*, published in 1999. It is a wonderful story about her many years in Rwanda.

On one of these occasions, maybe after the first year of knowing her, Roz gave me a list of medicines she wanted me to acquire. She said, "I don't expect all the things on the list."

When I returned to Pineville, I had an appointment with Dr. Glover, my gynecologist. I gave him the list and asked if he could help. About a month later, he called me and said, "Mrs. Staples, everything is ready." I brought the items back with me on my next trip to Kigali, and soon everything was ready to be put on the shelves in the orphanage dispensary.

Roz's right-hand man was a Rwandan named Simbagari. I would be remiss if I left him out of my book. I have a photo with Simbagari and me putting medicine on the shelves. I think he and Roz were platonic friends. He was a key figure in Roz's life, and she was able to do more because of him. I know he was great with the children. He helped Roz run the orphanage and had worked for her before Roz began caring for the children.

There were two little boys named Desire and Director that Roz was especially attached to at the orphanage. One was Hutu and the other Tutsi. My cook was Hutu, and my housekeeper was Tutsi. Our driver, John Charles, was Tutsi. My gardeners were Hutu. How did they live together? I have no answers except they needed to work, so they had to try to get along. That's all I can come up with to answer my own question.

In addition to having the pleasure of meeting and getting to know Roz Carr, George and I were invited to attend a wonderful Easter lunch at the US-owned Sorwathe Tea Plantation. We had a nice visit with Cally Alles, the manager, and his wife, Ameithe. This was my first time to see and be told about the processing of tea. The view was wonderful from the Alleses' home. I could see fields of green tea growing down in the valley. Cally would become a good friend to George during our time in Rwanda.

Chapter 67

After almost a year in Rwanda, we had a special visitor heading a delegation from Washington. Ambassador Richard Holbrooke, famous for his success in brokering the Dayton Peace Agreement that ended the conflict in the former Yugoslavia, accompanied by his wife and famous author, Kati, and Wisconsin Senator Russ Feingold, came to see what was happening in post-genocide Rwanda. I had heard about Holbrooke, but this was my first time meeting him and his wife. As our UN ambassador at that time, he had come to learn more about Rwanda's recovery and to lay a wreath at one of the genocide memorials. Because my husband was the ambassador to Rwanda, I had the pleasure of hosting a breakfast for the delegation. Holbrooke was a charmer and complimented me on the art in the residence. He loved art and focused in on the one he liked best, which unfortunately wasn't mine. It was part of the Art in Embassies program's selection that I could choose from now that George was ambassador.

Years later, Richard Holbrooke died from the wear and tear on his heart from overworking as our special representative for Afghanistan. He had helped end the wars in the Balkans, but Afghanistan was a bridge too far for him. The White House and many others expected he could perform miracles in resolving conflict in Afghanistan and pressuring Pakistan, but a peace agreement could not be reached. I never trusted Pakistan. Afghanistan was a landlocked country that needed trade routes to the sea, and those led through Pakistan. Farmers in Afghanistan had been growing poppies for many years. Opium is made from poppies. What kind of crop could we teach the Afghanis to grow that would make more money than poppies? Nothing!

At another point in our assignment, I had to host two special dinners for delegations of congressional staff members: one from the House International

Relations Committee and the other from the Senate Foreign Relations Committee monitoring our policies on Rwanda. I liked meeting the young staff members, and I think they liked being invited to the ambassador's residence.

Chapter 68

Bill Mellott was the embassy's regional security officer (RSO) responsible for keeping us safe in Rwanda. The former government's soldiers who had carried out the genocide and were hiding in Congo had placed a bounty on the US ambassador. Four years after the genocide, Rwanda was still a dangerous place.

For our entire three-year assignment, we had a security detail following us wherever we traveled. We also had soldiers guarding our residence around the clock. They were part of the Presidential Guard force. The country received heavy rains, and the guards had no shelter at our residence. I asked the embassy to build a shelter for them, and it was done and much appreciated! Mother Teresa said, "There are no great things, only small things done with great love." I have been in positions where I have done small things that changed many lives.

I can remember George speaking at the National University of Rwanda's first graduation ceremony after the genocide. I was a little anxious that some deranged person might try to shoot us. I saw Bill in the audience, and he was watching the crowd. I felt a little better because I knew he was armed. Concern about safety was one reason I didn't stay in Rwanda full time. The other reason was that I had a daughter back home in the US at university. Catherine had never been away from us. There was an ocean between us, so I couldn't get in the car and visit her. However, she would be spending school breaks in Kigali, and that made me feel better.

I was so busy during my time in Rwanda that once I had seventeen events on my calendar in one month. I was ready to go home to check on my daughter, our home, and my friends and family. Before leaving, I took Pascasie, our cook, and Isabelle, our housekeeper, to see Roz and the children in the orphanage. I liked to do special things for our staff because they took care of us.

During one of my visits to Rwanda, I met the Al-Noor family. I was invited to a luncheon by Shenaz Al-Noor, who managed the Umubano Hotel, one of only two hotels then operating in Kigali. When she introduced me to others, she said, "I want you to know Mrs. Staples isn't like any other ambassador's wife you have met before." I was taken aback by that statement. What was an ambassador's wife supposed to be like? I was accessible, accepted invitations from some of my staff to visit their homes, liked wine, and loved to dance. I've thought about that question through the years.

The Umubano Hotel had a club, and when I went there, Shenaz would send her driver in the Mercedes for me. There was a special section with security. George would never go dancing with me at the club. He felt he had to set a more official example as an ambassador, so it wouldn't be appropriate. I did all the official duties with him, attending hundreds of events, but I needed to dance and do things outside of the embassy.

Chapter 69

On April 6, 2000, the sixth anniversary of the 1994 genocide, we attended a National Day of Celebration in Kibungo Prefecture, where President Kagame was going to speak. Every year a different location was chosen for officials and the public to gather to commemorate the start of the 1994 genocide and its victims.

The drive was long, with no places to stop for bathroom breaks. When we arrived, an usher recognized our car flying the American flag. I said, "I need a bathroom." There were no porta potties. This called for drastic measures. The usher found a hut. A woman took two yards of material from around her waist, which was common in making a skirt or protective clothing such as an apron. Two women held up about a yard of material to cover me. I thanked them and said, "I can pee in the bush or at the White House. I'm a flexible woman." Disaster avoided!

Another time I went to Kibuye with George and Catherine. Kibuye is a lovely city on the shores of Lake Kivu. On Saturday morning, I awoke to the sights and sounds of Africa. I heard the mourning dove for the first time since Zimbabwe. I felt like a child on Christmas morning. Our rooms faced the lake. I enjoyed my coffee and being in Rwanda.

George and I had come to Kibuye to read and rest because our assignment in Rwanda was very stressful and demanding. This was my first time visiting the lake. As we entered the patio area for breakfast, we met some people from Kigali. Mr. Gasana, the head of Rwanda's National Human Rights Commission, was also there with his nephew, Mr. Nyombayire. They asked if I would like to join them for a visit to Bisesero, where a lot of people died during the genocide.

I joined Mr. Gasana and his nephew and a woman who had survived Bisesero. I saw and felt Africa as someone who had learned to love her. I saw what had become Africa to me. For example, I saw a woman with great posture carrying very heavy loads on her back and head on her way to market. As we drove up a winding road and gained some altitude, I saw a beautiful lake to my right. I love the vegetation and banana trees of Rwanda. I looked out the window and noticed a rainbowlike pattern on the water with brilliant colors of pink, turquoise, and lavender. Mr. Gasana and my other companions couldn't explain why this was happening, but it had a calming effect. Then listening to the conversation in the car, I began to realize what I would soon be seeing. Once more in my life, I had gotten in over my head—I volunteered for something without enough information. I was feeling a little queasy in my stomach and wondered how I would handle seeing the remains of hundreds of human beings.

I was told with the help of translators that approximately fifty thousand Tutsis and moderate Hutus came to Bisesero in April of 1994. Only about one thousand survived. I had read about Bisesero in a study published by Human Rights Watch entitled "Leave None to Tell the Story." Before we left Washington to go to Rwanda, we visited the United States Holocaust Memorial Museum and attended a reading and book signing by Philip Gourevitch for his book *We Wish to Inform You That Tomorrow We Will Be Killed with Our Families: Stories from Rwanda*. I read every page and personally felt it explained very well the truth about Rwanda's tragedy.

Bisesero is in a mountainous region, and people came there thinking they could survive. I recalled reading about Pickett's Charge during the Civil War and some battles my uncle Joe told me about in the Pacific during WWII. It wasn't always true that if you held the high ground you would win. The poor people of Bisesero were backed up the mountain with no weapons to fight back except rocks and sticks.

When we arrived, we left our two cars and approached the area. There were ten people in our group, and I was introduced to the architect in charge of the genocide memorial and twelve of the survivors. I was the only one in the group who couldn't speak French or Kinyarwanda. Three Rwandans spoke English, and they were very kind to help with translations. I gained a very clear idea of the architect's hopes and dreams for a memorial project.

The first stop was to see the remains of hundreds of people who had died in the fighting. We got to the entrance of a very large, framed structure made with poles and blue tarpaulins. I hesitated before entering, took a deep breath, and found some courage. I knew Rwandans were very stoic people who didn't show their emotions outside of their homes. Inside were stacks of bones on raised platforms about waist high. All were separated into different body parts. Everything hurt me, but the small skulls of children were most difficult to see.

After viewing the remains, we started our climb to the top of the hill. Everyone was concerned about my knee from an old surgery. My husband made a point to let them know I might need some assistance. I used the walking stick of one of the survivors who had taken charge after their leader had been killed. I thought, I am from Pineville, Kentucky, and a descendant of Wilderness Trail pioneers and rough mountain people. I am a daughter of the American Revolution. Being tough is in my genes, but I had never witnessed anything like Bisesero.

The architect explained his plan for a memorial as we made our climb. I wanted to help him with his project. He wanted to bury most of the remains, which were stored with tarps over them. He believed that people needed closure, a word I do not like. There will never be closure for the deaths and deep hurt some events have caused in people's lives.

At the top of the hill, the architect hoped to create a guest house for visitors with two mirrors for the survivors and the killers to look at themselves. Those brave survivors fought for three months with sticks, stones, and machetes. They held the high ground but had to fight well-trained, armed men. Such bravery should be remembered. As we prepared to leave, I returned the walking stick and asked Mr. Gasana to help translate my thoughts. I said, "I am proud to have used the walking stick of such a brave man."

What a mess the colonists had made, too often in the name of God. Where would Africa be today without interference from outside forces? We will never know because history cannot be changed. How could the international community and the United Nations have let this happen in Rwanda? What happened to the promise of "never again"?

As we descended, each person was left with his or her own thoughts. Mr. Gasana had been very helpful the whole morning. As we drove, I saw a very intimidating and very overcrowded bus approaching us on a one-way road. We managed to pass without touching sides, but there were a few tense moments. I said to Mr. Gasana, "That was a Kodak moment." He did not understand, so

I explained that it meant a special moment that should be captured on film. A few miles later, I saw a woman, alone on a distant hillside, walking on a narrow footpath, and Mr. Gasana said, "Is that a Kodak moment?" He translated to our other companions, and as we laughed, the tension of a stressful experience was left behind.

Paths have taken me on many journeys. The hillside paths of my childhood were the first lasting ones in my mind. We walked the hillside paths or the creek beds. My father could drive us part of the way by dirt road, then have to return to the creek bed. When I was about six, we had better roads and electricity. It would take a long time before we had gravel. Eventually, we got a paved road. In Africa, there were footpaths and dirt roads.

After Bisesero, I needed a break. I wanted to go home to check on my tribe in Kentucky!

Chapter 70

During our time in Kigali, my sweet baby girl, now attending university in Virginia, got together with her friends in the dorm and made Christmas gifts for every child in Roz's orphanage. Catherine came to Rwanda for Christmas and was there to pass out the gifts. It was quite a party. Roz was so pleased with what Catherine had done for her kids. As a family, we have worked hard together in this Foreign Service life.

One long weekend, we took our house guest Krista to Lake Kivu. Krista was Terry and Jill Robinson's daughter, who had visited us when we were serving in Zimbabwe. Now she was all grown up, and what a lovely pair she and Catherine proved to be. We went in the evening, which was the perfect time to visit Lake Kivu for a boat ride because that was an idyllic time to be on the lake and see its islands, which vary in size. We went with Mr. Nyombayire, our captain and owner of the boat; George's driver, Jean Charles; and our Rwandan bodyguard Bosco.

Our trusted captain took us to one of the islands where mining had been done in the past. We went ashore to search for treasures. He told me, "This island was known for its beautiful white and black marble." Of course, I could not leave without a sample. It was great fun to be out on the water, checking out the shoreline and enjoying the great calm that came with the end of another "day to remember in Kibuye." During the ride, I was a little concerned because water kept coming in by my feet. Our captain, however, kept assuring me all was well as he kept bailing with a plastic cup. I asked him if he knew the story of Robinson Crusoe. He said there are many Robinson Crusoe stories and told me, "Do not be concerned because in the worst-case scenario, if we were stranded, I have the skills to help us survive the night."

We returned from the ride at "dusty dark," as we say in Kentucky. I had five rocks to add to my collection. We had beautiful photos to remember our day, and they are among my favorites. Catherine and Krista were beautiful, and I loved the photos of us together.

Before we left Rwanda, Giora, Denise, Sharon, and Michelle Israel came to visit us. We had all first met in the Bahamas when Sharon and Catherine were in first grade, and we've remained friends through the years. Denise later brought the girls to Kentucky. I was so pleased to have them visit us then, and we had snow. Now the family was with us in Rwanda. We were on the tarmac to meet them with our driver, Jean Charles. I admit I cried with joy. They came to see us after having visited Tanzania and hiking Mount Kilimanjaro.

Catherine, who was a theater arts major in college while I was in Rwanda, was working, when she visited us on her summer break, on a very important project that involved Rwanda's street children. Lots of children lived on the street having been orphaned by war. Catherine and the children were, with the help of USAID funding, creating a play to draw attention to the suffering so many children were experiencing following the genocide. Catherine was involved in every aspect of the play, from producing to casting, directing, staging, props, and clothes. It was necessary to have translators. Krista worked with Catherine to help in any way she could. Sharon and Michelle visited them on location. I went a couple of times, but George wasn't invited until opening night because Catherine didn't want anyone to know she was the US ambassador's daughter.

Catherine asked our staff to help her. We washed, ironed, and selected used clothes, walking sticks, and hats for her stage props. She put together a small reception before the play started. A deputy minister of health attended, and the play had television and radio coverage all over Southern Africa. We were very proud of what Catherine had accomplished.

While the Israels were visiting us, George hosted a business luncheon for Rwandan business leaders to meet Giora. We also visited Roz at her home in Gisenyi. The Israel family really enjoyed her; the young American women were meeting a legend. We visited two of the genocide sites, which was very emotional for everyone. Denise's mother was a survivor of Auschwitz, the World War II Nazi death camp in Poland. My good friend had remained very active with the Jewish community in Miami and spoke to groups about the Holocaust.

Now here comes my big disappointment. Remember my architect friend in Bisesero whom I wanted to help? I was hoping Denise and Giora would help with raising some funds in the Jewish community in Miami. Wrong! I learned that Jewish people don't believe in preserving remains. I was crestfallen.

Chapter 71

Once I had the pleasure of spending a couple of days in Roz's home. It was not her home of choice, but because of the guerillas roaming back and forth on the Rwanda and Congo border, it was too dangerous to live in Buniole, Congo, her home where she lived before the genocide and raised flowers. I never got to go there with Roz, but I vividly imagine her picking her pyrethrum. It was a time when a woman could carve out her own place in history. I had my time in Africa. I got to see and feel some of Roz's experiences in very remote and untouched places.

To visit Roz, I hitched a ride with Major Richard Skow, our defense attaché, and spent time with Roz. He dropped me off at Roz's house. He had a motherly crush on Roz! He wasn't the only one. She was charming! We had a great photo opportunity at her house.

On our return trip to Kigali, Major Skow and I got our cameras out. We pulled over to take in the view and a photo of his favorite volcano. We were up on an escarpment, looking down in a valley. On our next stop, I saw several people coming up a very steep, narrow path from a village. Then something magical happened. I saw an old woman holding a large golfing-type umbrella. In Rwanda, they are used often to protect against sun and rain. I was so struck by the character of the woman's elderly, wrinkled face that I wanted to take her photo. There was no way to determine her age. I was pointing to my camera and to her, and she let me take her picture. I turned around to go back to the SUV, but something made me stop and turn around. She was right behind me. I took another photo, a full body shot. I couldn't express my feelings with words. I assumed she spoke Kinyarwanda. I reached out and ever so gently touched her face. There was such an overwhelming desire to hug her. Why do moments like this happen on rare occasions? They have touched my heart for all the days to come in my life. Who would have thought on that morning, I would have met such a special human being?

Soon, I was back at my desk, writing and thinking about another special day in Rwanda. I had an overwhelming urge to find the old woman with the golfing umbrella. Then my rational mind told me to keep moving forward. We were always working, as Ambassador Staples liked to tell me and his staff.

I can remember one occasion at a cocktail evening at the residence. I stayed too long talking with a group. George would get close to me and say, "Jodi, move around and talk with our other guests." He insisted we not linger too long with Americans; we were there to meet diplomats and government officials. He would also start to get anxious if I had a couple or three flutes of champagne. I married a born military man and a perfect man for the State Department.

Another example of actions an ambassador must make sometimes involves close personal staff. George's driver, Jean Charles, was a Tutsi and had lost all his family except one son. He had lost more than a hundred members of his extended family. He would drive me for my official duties when George didn't need him. Jean Charles was a very quiet man, who had his Bible with him all the time and read it while he waited for me and George. One day, as we were driving to an event, we passed a bridge. He said, "Mrs. Staples, in 1994, there were bodies stacked up behind the bridge that eventually flowed into Lake Victoria in Uganda."

Poor Jean Charles had PTSD and no help for it. One day, George got a call that he had attacked his wife. We couldn't believe it! I went to see her, and it was very serious. George terminated him immediately. Jean Charles is an example of everyone we met and worked with in Rwanda. In the end, everyone to one degree or another was traumatized and could sometimes act in an unexpected, even violent way. Just the week before, George had spoken about domestic abuse at the embassy. I wanted George to let Jean Charles have another chance, but he would not make an exception.

Chapter 72

Iwant but don't want to write about a visit we made in Rwanda with Giora, Denise, and their daughters, Sharon and Michelle. We went to a genocide memorial at a very large church on a hillside. When we walked in, I was shocked to see people left in the spots where they had been killed. They still had their clothes on over their bones. One woman was draped over the back of a church pew. She has never left my mind. I can still see her dress. I think it was a floral pattern. I was very concerned and wanted to know why the remains hadn't been buried. As a designated genocide site, it had been left for people to come and see what was done. I'm sure things have changed after all these years.

Later after retirement, I was diagnosed with PTSD by Dr. Vivian Fliman, a PhD clinical physiologist I was seeing in Cincinnati, Ohio. I said it was bullshit, as it seemed everyone was getting a PTSD diagnosis. She said, "It's true for you." We spent many hours together. She had me do a "tree of life." I drew a tree with branches. At the top was my birth date. All the branches listing the good things in my life were on the right tree limbs. On the left side were all the traumas and bad things. After looking at the tree, I believed PTSD was true. I understand PTSD can result from one experience or more, with a cumulative effect.

The State Department, unlike the military, provided no place to go for group counseling. I accompanied George when he went to Congress with the head of the State Department's Medical Division to testify about how the State Department had limited assistance programs. He informed a congressional committee about the steps the State Department was taking to help those suffering from PTSD. Beth Payne, a Foreign Service officer who worked with us in Rwanda and was later injured in Iraq, suffered greatly from her experiences.

She gave me a coloring book of mandalas to color figures and designs that calm and help heal.

Before leaving Rwanda, I had a last wish. I wanted to hike into the forest and see the famous silverback gorillas and maybe into the area where Diane Fossey had lived. There would be an armed military escort for protection, and that was fine with me. I was used to security. I wanted to see the gorillas but was told not to look them in the eyes.

Denise, who is a serious, almost professional photographer, and family were also ready for an adventure. George, however, would not let Americans visit Rwanda's Volcanoes National Park, due to intelligence that the guerrillas were on the move—not the kind on four legs but the two-legged kind. I lost my opportunity to see the silverbacks forever, not to mention my disappointed houseguests, especially Denise, with her thousands of dollars in camera equipment.

My knees have kept me from hiking since 2008. If I return one day to Rwanda, I will have to go on a zip line over the canopy. That's not the kind of experience I was looking forward to with the silverback gorillas. With age, I am forced to compromise.

Chapter 73

Four classes of killers committed the genocide. The scale ranged from one to four, with one being the most serious. My cook Pascasie's husband was a class one, as he had been an organizer for the militias that killed people at roadblocks. There were clergy from the Catholic Church charged with genocide. It was said that some gave their church records to the killers and opened the doors so people taking refuge could be killed. They knew who the Tutsis and Hutus were. That made it convenient for the killers. People who lived side by side, went to church together, intermarried, and had children turned people over to be killed if they were Tutsi. Sons turned in their mothers because they were Tutsi. This was a complicated situation that defies understanding.

I was told the best thing to do in the absence of a court system that had been destroyed was to return to a village-type justice system. The village headmen would hear the less serious cases, and villagers would decide their fate. These were called the Gacaca courts. Of course, killers who were responsible for hundreds of deaths, categorized as class ones, remained in prison, as were others responsible for hate radio broadcasting messages such as "Hutus, do your duty."

I told George I wanted to visit a prison. I would often see prisoners on the road in work details, dressed in their pink uniforms. These were men convicted of crimes of genocide, but when I saw them on the road, they seemed so docile. I visited a prison with the deputy USAID director and a Justice Department official providing technical assistance to the Rwandan justice ministry. The prison held 7,125 inmates. Everything was clean and orderly, and the climate was nonthreatening. The prisoners slept in hammocks with canvas tops. The prison was about two acres. There were no brick walls, but there must have been some kind of barrier. I didn't think I was nervous. I felt no fear and couldn't understand how docile the prisoners were. I guess they had no place to run and no place to hide.

Remembering the prisoners and the violence they had caused reminds me of a very significant event that happened during my time in Rwanda. I was proud to be a part of a program called Women as Partners for Peace. This was a weeklong conference put together by George's public affairs officer, Ergibe Boyd. Women were invited from around the world. I think there were about a hundred women attending. I hosted a cocktail get-together at my residence. I was surprised to meet so many women from different countries. There was even a woman from Ireland.

I got to meet Ambassador Swanee Hunt, a former US ambassador to Austria and later head of a women's program at Harvard. She was the main speaker at the peace program. I couldn't attend every day, but I stood up on one of the days and asked a question: "How many of you have lived in a refugee camp?" I was shocked that more than half of the women had lived in refugee camps, and more shocking, some of them still lived in camps. The conference was a great success.

Ergibe instituted a program to send judges back to the US for training. She was a born mover and shaker. When she set her mind to it, she could find a way to make things happen. I was amazed at how she could find resources. We still talk after all these years, and she thinks George was the best ambassador she ever worked for at an embassy or in Washington.

On the last night of the conference, after dinner, I suggested we go for a eucalyptus steam and body massage, African-style. The conference was at the Umubano Hotel, so I asked the manager for champagne, glasses, and an ice bucket. Ambassador Hunt was ready for a good time. Ergibe was with us and also eager for a good time. They were my kind of women. We all enjoyed this unexpected experience at the end of a very successful conference in Rwanda.

Chapter 74

I would like someday to return to Rwanda and visit Roz's home and her grave.
I'd like to see Rwanda's development and renewal after one of history's most
tragic events. Just before leaving Rwanda, we met an attorney from Cameroon
named Bernard Muna. We belonged to the Rotary Club together, and he was
an attorney employed by the International Criminal Tribunal for Rwanda based
in Arusha, Tanzania, which was charged with bringing to justice the ringleaders
of the genocide. We were on the same flight out of Kigali, and our paths would
cross again. His family in Cameroon would become my family, especially his
sister Ama Muna. But when we left Rwanda, we could not at that time tell
Bernard that George had been selected to be the next American ambassador to
both the Republics of Cameroon and Equatorial Guinea.

Before going to Cameroon, we flew home to Kentucky. We had a month to
enjoy my ol' Kentucky home. George was starting to like Kentucky. Remember,
he grew up in Los Angeles. The remoteness and having no neighbors were
enjoyable to him, and he liked the privacy of being in the woods. I wanted a
home back with the family. George didn't care, and as long as he had his books,
computer, music, and me, he was a happy man.

It was soon time to go to Washington for George's swearing-in ceremony.
I have used "we" or "our" often because that's the way it was. People will say
Ambassador Young and Angie, Ambassador Palmer and Lucille, or Ambassador
Jim McGee and his wife, Shirley. The State Department got two for one. Some
spouses resented giving up their careers. I didn't have a big career to leave, but
I will never know what I could have accomplished on my own, and it's too
late now. However, I did get an education I could have never gotten in the
classroom. Maybe that was the trade-off.

Unlike the previous swearing-in for Rwanda, there was no time to organize a big event with family members coming from Kentucky. It was very special, nevertheless. This time, the ceremony was done in Secretary of State Colin Powell's office. We had invited friends who were in Washington at the time and people from the Cameroon embassy in Washington, whom we would see and invite to our residence in Cameroon after we arrived. I liked Secretary Powell, and he was so warm and receptive to our family and guests. Of course, everyone wanted a photo opportunity with him, and I have some beautiful photos from the ceremony. I have a photo of me with him proudly displayed in my home. I mentioned earlier what he did for Foreign Service families. He was very popular worldwide, but not everyone got to visit his office on the seventh floor in the State Department's executive wing.

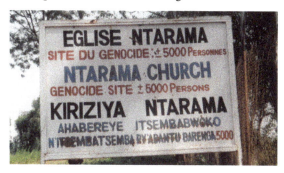

In Rwanda in 1994, approximately one million people were murdered in just 100 days. This church and scores of other sites are memorialized to honor the victims.

Remains consisting of skulls, bones, and sometimes victim's clothing are usually displayed at every genocide site. Most disturbing are the separate sections displaying the remains of children.

George's sister, Milly, with me and my sister Pauline at George's swearing-in-ceremony to become ambassador to Rwanda.

237

Walking up to the Bisesero genocide site with Mr. Gasana.

Being briefed by the architect about the hopes and dreams to establish a genocide memorial site.

I was proud to have walked with one of the genocide survivors who let me use his walking stick.

The woman that Lt. Skow and I encountered during our return to Kigali.

Catherine after distributing Christmas gifts to the children at Roz Carr's orphanage.

Roz and two of her children.

Look closely, and you will see that the child's hands were cut off.

Our family with Roz and her
assistant Simbagari.

Enjoying a special day with Catherine while
boating on Rwanda's Lake Kivu.

Secretary of State Colin Powell swearing in George to be the ambassador to the
Republic of Cameroon and to the Republic of Equatorial Guinea.

Chapter 75

When we were in Equatorial Guinea in 1985, I flew with Catherine to Cameroon's capital, Yaoundé, to see a Seventh-day Adventist American dentist. There were also lots of trips to Douala, Cameroon, during our time in Equatorial Guinea, so I knew both countries from the past. I had gone to the Art in Embassies' warehouse to select paintings for our new residence. George was ambassador to both countries now.

We arrived this time in 2001 and were met at the airport in Yaoundé by some of George's embassy staff. I would meet my household staff at the residence. George always told me that managing the residence and staff was my responsibility. They worked for me. He had an embassy to manage, and he didn't want to be involved in issues with the people working in the residence. There was always some kind of issue involving family problems, conflict between staff, or lack of money. In some ways, it was like being home in Kentucky.

When we arrived from the airport, Lawrence, George's driver, opened the door, and the staff were standing by the entry. First was Martin the maître d', French chef Mattias, Augustine the assistant chef, and Euphrasia the housekeeper. The residence was big and needed some tender, loving care. I was the woman for the job. When we entered the foyer and the downstairs official living room, George said, "A basketball team could scrimmage in here." We went upstairs to the family area, and our luggage was brought to the master bedroom, where we freshened up and then went down for food. Later, we went for a walking tour of the inside and outside of our new home. I'm not conceited, but we had worked hard for this day, and it was well deserved.

One thing really upset me when I was shown a small office that had been used by an American spouse at the embassy. The previous ambassador had given her the job of supervising the residence and staff, and she was paid by the embassy twenty-two thousand dollars a year. The ambassador we were replacing didn't have a wife at post. There was no salary if an ambassador had a spouse. That's me! I was upset as I learned later those other countries paid salaries to their ambassador's spouses, along with a clothing allowance.

I had to go to the embassy every morning to meet the guys who worked for me. Then we got on a van to the warehouse where I had an office. Once, someone in the administrative office decided that if I was going to ride to the embassy in George's official car, I would have to pay $2.75 going and coming. I wasn't paying $5.50 every day. I thought, "Screw you, people. I'll drive my car." And I did just that.

The residence needed repainting, the driveway needed to be paved, and new chair covers for the patio and upstairs porch were needed. Wow! I sent in a lot of work requests to General Services. They made the final decision depending on the money they had in the budget. If necessary, they would get approval from Washington.

When I had entered the residence, I saw the drapes and was shocked because there were four or five sliding patio doors covered by old English country-cottage fabric in red, white, and green. Who had approved that? My first goal was to try to replace the draperies. Fortunately for me, it was time to change them based on the State Department's replacement schedule. The decorators at the State Department in charge of the deputy chief of mission's and ambassador's residences almost always had their replacement requests approved. In other countries where we served, I had to live with bright red and shiny blue drapes in the guest bedrooms because there was no budget, and it was not replacement time. I lived with those damn drapes for three years. Now I put in a request, and the next day, someone was there before I got out of bed. The times were changing for Mrs. Staples.

The local staff from the warehouse didn't know what to make of the new woman in the residence. The Americans in the General Services office were very helpful. The residence had three stoves, three refrigerators, two freezers, and a locked pantry as big as a room. There we stored extra supplies, and all the liquor and wine for receptions was put away there for safekeeping. Martin had keys to everything. I didn't always trust him, but he had been at the residence for many years and had eight children, so I decided not to replace him as I had been advised.

At one point, I learned that a security team from Washington would need to take over the den on the main floor. I couldn't enter when they were working. I had the staff knock on the door to ask if they needed anything. I believed a plan was in the making for evacuation in case of a coup attempt. I had a metal door to the master bedroom. In the bathroom was a breakaway half-size door to the upstairs balcony. The family living area was off a long hallway with two metal-grill doors at each end that were locked every night. I had a radio to be in touch with the marine guard on duty at the embassy. My call sign was "Gallery." There were two local guards at our front and back gates. Security planning remains a big part of living overseas on a diplomatic assignment.

Chapter 76

My surface shipment finally arrived in Yaoundé, and our air freight was already on hand. When I finished with the residence in Cameroon, it was like an art gallery. I selected nineteen oversized paintings from the Art in Embassies program. My personal collection complemented what I had chosen. Of course, I had all my framed photos of friends and family around me. We always traveled with lots of books and music. I love all kinds of music, especially blues. I discovered Keb' Mo' and have been a longtime fan of B. B. King. Carole King is my musical favorite. I also enjoy instrumental music, especially piano and violin. I particularly like Russian composers. George introduced me to Rachmaninoff and Rimsky-Korsakov. And yes, I like country music, but the older music of Waylon Jennings, Willie Nelson, Merle Haggard, and Kris Kristofferson. My other favorites are too numerous to mention. Of course, I like some good old rock 'n' roll. I was introduced in the 1970s to Bob Seger's music by my cousin Freddy.

Would I be able to drive in Cameroon? The roads were very dangerous, and there was often news of horrific accidents. There were no rules of the road. I came to think it was the bumper on the front of the car that had the right of way. Drivers would pass on the right side of a two-lane highway, go off the pavement, and pass in the dirt. I came to believe it was a Russian roulette-type of mentality. The drivers would gamble there wasn't an oncoming car when they passed. It was very dangerous, especially on the road to the coastal business city of Douala. I decided not to drive in Cameroon.

George had presented his formal credentials to President Paul Biya, which meant he was President George Bush's personal representative in Cameroon. After a brief ceremony, he could officially get to work. There were official calls to be made on government officials, meetings with the press to explain US

244

interests, and introductory sessions with embassy personnel and their families. I was anxious to be part again of an embassy community.

One of the major issues, and one there was much to learn about, was the Chad–Cameroon pipeline project that was being built from the country of Chad to the Cameroonian port city of Douala. American companies had part of the contract to build it, and a lot of American businesses were waiting on its completion. Maybe some reading this will ask, why does the United States want to even be represented in other countries? Besides the first responsibility to look after the welfare and safety of American citizens, mostly it is about supporting the business interests of American companies. The embassy's Economic and Commercial Section was the focal point in the pipeline effort. The Consular Section looked after American citizen issues and had responsibility for issuing immigrant and nonimmigrant visas, while the Political Section followed local political issues and relationships with other countries. We had lots of responsibilities that not many people back home knew much about.

Chapter 77

Since 1989, the US hadn't had an embassy in Malabo, Equatorial Guinea. But in 2001, when George returned as ambassador, the country had changed rapidly due to offshore oil discoveries and the enormous wealth they brought. When we traveled to Malabo for George to present credentials to President Obiang, who was still in charge since our first assignment there ended in 1987, I wanted to meet the American citizens. We stayed with Exxon's senior company representative, Ben Haynes, and his wife at their residence. I was so surprised to see their home. It had been built and assembled in Texas, then dismantled to ship to Malabo. It was beautiful and generously supplied, with freezers full of food and a well-stocked bar.

In Malabo, I found our friends Tomas and Trudy Dickens. Tomas had worked with me at the embassy during our first assignment in Malabo. I was so surprised when I visited their home. For our meal, Trudy took the Corel dishes out of her china cabinet, the very set I had given them when I had left Malabo in 1987. I was touched to tears! I also found Ramona Edjan, my friend from out of the past. In 1987, she had walked down a dust road from my house with her girls after I had given her pasta, peanut butter, and other items from my pantry. What a success story she had now become. I had to laugh when I asked about the beauty shop. She had kept it, maybe for old memories. Ramona was still with her husband and was happy.

There was much work to be done for me in both Cameroon and Equatorial Guinea: find a house for us and other visitors to use in Malabo, send furniture over from Yaoundé. Was history repeating itself? In Malabo, there was no need to find another Hotel Impala, as there were new houses and a modern, new airport. This time around in Malabo, it was going to be a different adventure for me.

The reason that conditions in Equatorial Guinea had improved so dramatically since our first assignment in 1987 was that oil had been discovered. The Russians tried to find oil offshore but had discovered nothing and said there was no oil. The French didn't succeed. The Spanish had no luck. Guess what? An American ambassador wanted to encourage American companies to give it a try. They discovered oil ten miles from shore, with reserves to last an estimated fifty years.

For a special event, we traveled from Cameroon on a charter flight with Catherine, who was visiting Malabo for the launching of the Marathon Oil Corporation's methanol plant. I got to meet the former US ambassador who had persuaded American companies to search for oil and his wife. The two of them had been invited back to Malabo for the special event. I was so pleased for the people of Equatorial Guinea, whose lives had improved so dramatically since oil was discovered.

On one of my other visits to Malabo, I took Catherine back to the island and to Moka, the paradise in the sky. She had been in a Spanish preschool when she was about five. Now she was in university in Virginia. We had a great reunion with people from the past. Her playmate and friend came to visit her. He was working for an oil company. Time changes everything!

The diplomatic life had a downside. It wasn't a bed of roses. The stress and security issues were starting to take a toll on me. We had been living behind walls for security against crime and terrorist concerns for more than twenty years. Had I enjoyed living on the edge, worrying about security all these years? As my psychologist told me, "Jodi, you lived a high-risk, high-reward life." I wondered what the next three years would bring.

I remembered when Malabo in 1985 had no proper food market, just an open African-style market. Cups of beans, sugar, and flour for sale were put out on paper on the ground. Dead monkeys were hanging by their tails in the fresh meat section. A small store was run by a man from Beirut. Now there were shops, markets, and cars everywhere. A new airport had been built, and there were lots of places to eat.

The African countries I have lived in always have tribes. The president of Equatorial Guinea was a member of the Fang ethnic group, which dominated this part of West Africa, while the chief tribe on the island part of Equatorial Guinea, where the capital Malabo was located, were the Bubis. Of course, presidents are partial to their tribes. Now with the oil, I hoped more wealth would be distributed to all the people. I saw the infrastructure had changed, and there were good jobs with the American oil companies. I was so pleased because the people of Equatorial Guinea deserved a better life.

Chapter 78

George, Catherine, and I celebrated the 2001 New Year in Yaoundé, Cameroon, at the Hilton Hotel. The buffet dinner was very good. I usually ate hot food but no salads away from the residence to guard against parasite infections. Great African traditional dancers provided entertainment. The stage for the band had been erected in the middle of the swimming pool. There was a bridge-type walkway to the dance floor. What a great idea!

When we left the hotel, I was shocked to see thousands of people in the streets. Our driver, Lawrence, had a difficult time maneuvering our sedan through the masses of people. I was glad we weren't in the armored car because the windows did not roll down. I rolled down the car window to shake hands and wish the people a Happy New Year. George was concerned for my safety, but I was caught up in the moment. It made my and Catherine's New Year's very special. Making contact with the local, grassroots people makes me feel connected to them. Remember, diplomacy is all about the people!

Because of George being the American ambassador, I was a member of the First Lady of Cameroon's organization for the fight against AIDS. It was called CERAC. We all had dresses made in the same material, but I could make my own design. I was especially pleased to wear my dress to the National Women's Day parade in which thousands of women marched. My dress and headdress were a hit with the other ladies. When the driver was taking me to a special event, the people would wave to me with a thumbs-up because I was dressed in traditional African clothing. Some knew who I was because of the car and diplomatic license plates. I was so proud. If they could only have seen me back home!

I feel I can never do justice writing about Cameroon. I could write a book about my life there, as well as the people I met and some I loved. I know some loved me in return, and some have died since I left the country. I would hear about unrest from people, but there was no hunger. Cameroon was one of the few African countries self-sufficient in food, and it had the best mangos, papayas, and bananas. I can't forget the pineapple that was so good that the juice ran down my chin. Cameroon even exported food to neighboring countries and to Europe.

I asked the embassy protocol office to request on my behalf an audience with the First Lady, Mrs. Biya. This office ensures that correct formalities are followed. For example, for dinner invitations, the office will advise on correct seating of officials who will attend. I was told the First Lady didn't usually meet the ladies of the diplomatic community. I had seen her but never had had an opportunity to talk with her. I was given a date and time.

I would need what I had learned in my public affairs seminar to handle what I was about to experience. Lawrence drove me to the presidential residence and opened the car door for me. The press was outside. I was escorted by protocol to be introduced to the First Lady. There would be three people in the room, one man being the interpreter. The meeting was great, including a nice glass of champagne. We were both relaxed and talked about our families. I think Mrs. Biya's mother was still living. We had fun and laughed often. There was a photographer at some point. I didn't pay much attention to him. What was going to be a twenty-minute interview turned into about seventy minutes. The second glass of champagne was even better. I really liked the First Lady, and we talked about each other's lives. We held hands, and we made eye-to-eye contact with my hands on her shoulders. I don't remember any part of our time together when we talked about politics.

When I made my exit, about a dozen microphones were put near my face. I was confident I could handle the situation. The reporters had lots of questions. I said, "We were just two women who talked about our families, our work, and our interests, and we laughed often." They wouldn't accept my answer because they wanted to believe there was more to our time together. I learned in a media seminar at the State Department that just because you're asked a question, you don't have to answer it.

The next day, Mrs. Biya and I were on the front page of the *Cameroon Tribune*. Three photos of the First Lady and me took up the whole of page fifteen. We laughed, had a great meeting, and formed a bond. I have no more to say. There are copies of the newspaper here in Kentucky in my file.

Chapter 79

George had a good working relationship with President Paul Biya during our three years in Cameroon. Mr. Biya gave George a large presidential medal of recognition before we departed the country. During our time there, President Biya was invited to the White House for a meeting with President Bush, and George also participated. The discussions included Cameroon's support for the US invasion of Iraq. Looking back, I wish we had never invaded.

Because we had met Bernard Muna from Cameroon in Rwanda, we were eventually going to meet all the Munas. They were a very famous family. Their father went to school with no shoes. He became a teacher, then headmaster, and eventually prime minister. Ama was the last of seven children and the only girl. But when we left Rwanda, we couldn't at that time tell Bernard that George was selected to be the next Ambassador to the Republic of Cameroon and also to the Republic of Equatorial Guinea.

George and I received an invitation for dinner at Akere Muna's residence. He was a well-known attorney in Cameroon. The staff served appetizers and champagne. Normally, I like to make eye contact with people, but I guess I didn't on this occasion. A very interesting woman entered, and I shook hands with her. She said, "We've already met." I was so taken aback because she was Ama Muna, the only female in the Muna family with six brothers. She had been helping in the kitchen, then had left and changed clothes.

That night, Ama and I formed a friendship that would last a lifetime. So many good things happened to me because of this friendship. I saw places in the country that I would not have if it were not for that friendship. Ama took me to her home in Bingue, about two hours from Yaoundé. The home of her mother and father where Ama was raised was there. Ama had a home in Yaoundé as well as a place in her village. The village home was her second home, and her father lived there for several years before his death. The home was a walled compound with two houses. One belonged to her brother Dr. Wali Muna. Ama was with her father when he died. I had not met her at the time of her father's death. He was a former prime minister and leader in Cameroon's independence movement. According to African custom, people would come during the week to pay respect. Ama had to feed them and give them something to drink. She told me about a thousand visitors came each day. That would be about five thousand from Monday to Friday. On Saturday and Sunday, thousands more visited. My dear friend was so exhausted she went into seclusion. She told me something her father said that helped her in difficult times: "The music is always playing; you just have to listen."

Dr. Wali Muna, Ama's brother, was a cardiologist who got his medical degree from the University of Washington and later studied internal medicine at Johns Hopkins and cardiology at Yale. He returned to Cameroon and built a hospital. He shared some of his adventures with George. He told him that when he was a student in the States, he drove an eighteen-wheeler to help with college expenses." He was a huge man in stature but so kind and gentle.

A few years later, on a return visit to Cameroon to see Ama, I got sick. Wali took me to his hospital to see an endocrinologist. My thyroid had stopped working, and he helped me get treatment. He was also our local medical advisor at the American embassy for twenty years. Dr. Muna said he was sleeping on the same mattress he had shipped from the US when he returned home after attending Yale University. I made a request to the Administrative Office to give him a mattress when we had an embassy sale. I don't know if my request was approved.

Dr. Muna's wife, Teresa, had a wonderful gift shop with lots of African "stuff." I liked so many things, but some were very heavy, and I had a US government shipping allowance. A metal lion sat on the floor of the shop. I wanted him! He wasn't for sale. He had been in the shop for twenty years. I sent in reinforcements to help with my negotiations with Teresa: Ama, George, and Dr. Muna. Long story short, George bought the lion for my birthday. The price came down from twenty thousand to seven hundred dollars. She had priced the lion so high that no one could buy him. He is now keeping guard in our condo in Cincinnati.

Daniel Muna was a medical doctor in Douala, Cameroon. He had a clinic and helped a lot of people. I came to know and care about the whole Muna family. Brother George was an aeronautical engineer. John had gotten a degree in agriculture from the University of Tennessee. I miss Ama every day, and she is always in my thoughts. We keep in touch with WhatsApp.

Chapter 80

Ama received the title of Mafor, a designation held by a distinguished woman who coordinates with local rulers called Fons about how to improve the lives of their people. Ama's responsibilities covered about thirty-two areas of the country. She received the title at a huge African ceremony with more than five hundred people attending. There were dancers wearing beautiful headdresses and costumes, spears, drum music, and more.

There is a very elaborate induction ceremony when becoming a Mafor. Ama ordered a whole chicken and bottle of champagne to eat and drink before the ceremony started, as it would probably last all day. The event started out by getting Ama dressed inside our room. Several ladies attended Ama; I was an observer. Ama was dressed in special clothing for the occasion, part traditional fabric on the bottom with a royal purple/red material from knees to shoulders and lots and lots of shells stitched into the fabric. She wore a hat and a four-inch leopard belt to match. The finishing touch was a garland made of branches. A horse's mane was tossed over her shoulder. She was taken into a dome structure about ten feet tall covered in leaves. The head Fon gave her instructions about her responsibilities. Afterwards, all the women began walking in a line. I was third, another woman was first, and Ama was in between us. I had my own horse tail, which is used when dancing to drum music by throwing it over each shoulder.

When the ceremony was over, everyone went to a very large courtyard. Try to imagine a very large haystack structure but made out of leaves and branches. Three Fons were up on a platform. Daniel was there because he was head of the Muna family. He was the oldest, and in Africa, that carries a lot of responsibility. I was seated next to him, and we watched the African dance company. Daniel made a speech because his sister was being honored. Some weeks before,

I was given the title of Mafor by the Fon of the province of Bamenda when I visited Ama in her village. I was one little Mafor compared to the honor Ama had just received, but I was so pleased to have the title.

For some reason, I was always approached to dance when I visited African villages. The custom at this event was that everyone got into a circle. Someone passed a walking stick to me, and I was to take it to the middle of the circle and dance. Then I would take the walking stick to someone else, who would come into the circle. I came from a dancing family. I can't remember not dancing. I was having a great time, drinking champagne and the local brew as well as eating traditional food. I was dressed in beautiful African fabric from the village of Kumba for Ama's big event. Different fabrics are used for ceremonial occasions for different provinces.

There was another secret ceremony that few non-African women ever got to see. Ama asked the Fon if I could be part of the ceremony. Ama told me later, he had asked her, "Why this woman?" She said it was just about love. He gave me permission to attend the secret ceremony. I don't think Steven Spielberg could duplicate what I saw and experienced. The props and setting would be difficult for me to explain. The women were old. I couldn't tell if they were age sixty or a hundred. Their feet were so mangled, some couldn't wear shoes. Later, I would send shoes back to them. Remember, this was part of a secret ceremony. I could never explain or recreate the room and the ceremony.

The next morning was crazy. The Fon wanted to know, "Who was this woman [me!] eating our food and drinking our beer?" No men were allowed in the secret ceremony. I'm sure he knew what had happened. He just wanted to meet me. We had to find something to cover my head. I used one of Ama's dresses. I was told I had to keep my head lowered, and Wali Muna, who was there to support his sister Ama, told me that the Fon had mystical powers. The Fon from Kumbo also came to the ceremony and told me, "You have a temper. You have to learn to swallow your words." He gave me the title "Keeper of the Land." He said, "Wherever you are in the world, you have to take care of the land." I asked him to say a prayer for me and touch my head. He asked me to bring my husband to visit. I promised him I would bring George, and later, I kept my promise.

Afterwards, Ama whisked me to the car and said, "No one touches the Fon, and he touches no one." Without knowing, I had committed a faux pas. Then we started laughing. She should have told me. Some of the best times in my life have been unexpected. Lots of things have been planned, but it's not the same as when something spontaneous happens. The older women from the night before took me to see their garden in the village. They gave me two types of garden tools. I have them here in Kentucky, and I use one of the homemade hoes. It has a short handle, and one must bend over to dig with it. I heard it said in Africa that as long as a woman can bend from her waist, she isn't old. A man must have made that lie up.

After the event was over, we went to Ama's home in the village. The side of a steep hill to the left had been terraced. There was seating to enjoy a huge waterfall. I could hear it from my bedroom. The next morning, we walked out the security gate and took a walk through the village. A man was sweeping his dirt yard with an African broom. He was playing his radio and said good morning. I felt as if he radiated happiness. Sister Ama and I walked to a bakery and got two beers and a loaf of fresh, crusted, baked bread. We drank our beer and picked the crust off the bread. Ama told me she owned the bakery. She was a woman of many surprises. On occasions like this, I wondered, *Who has the best in life?* Maybe those villagers sweeping their yards with an African broom made of straw, listening to their radios, and greeting us were much happier than lots of Americans. You can't miss something you never had. I saw happy people in simple surroundings.

Chapter 81

Before leaving to return to Yaoundé, I wasn't looking forward to the bad drivers, bad roads, and congestion. Ama's driver drove too fast, but I had ridden with him before. When I arrived back in Yaoundé, everyone had missed me, and I had missed my surroundings.

It was time to go to work at the residence on what would be my biggest gardening project. I had lots of ideas, but I needed good workers who could visualize my plan. The warehouse staff and other workers at the embassy were ready to help me. Of course, I had to run everything by the embassy's General Services Section.

I requested two hundred stakes to be cut and sharpened on the ends. I needed lots of heavy string. I wanted a couple loads of rich dirt. The workers who would be helping me couldn't see my vision yet! My gardeners helped me stake out my walkway and flower beds. Now they understood my request for the stakes. I mapped it all out, and the guys started digging in the flower beds and using the rich dirt I had requested. Someone thought up the idea of knocking out a five-foot section of wall in the upper garden to make steps down to a landing and continuing to another level. It was a huge project to make steps of rock and cement.

The lower level by the tennis court had standing water that ran down a steep slope from the upper garden. A rock mason made a half gazebo up against a wall with room for two chairs and a half table fixed to the wall. I divided the garden into two sections with a wall made from wire and a rock path to meander through the garden. The garden had lots of flowers, plants, and small trees and a couple of fruit trees. The embassy electricians put in beautiful lighting.

The local workers had gone home and told their wives about the garden project, and the wives asked permission to see it. I was thrilled they came to see my dream come true. When we entertained, our guests liked to take their drinks and walk through the garden. The project wasn't very expensive. I had permission to use people on embassy payroll and tools, and vehicles from the warehouse to improve the residence. The US dollar was strong, and the exchange rate was great, and I had the backing of the ambassador!

During this time, I was still traveling to villages. George said he wanted Americans to get out of the embassy to get to know a village and meet the people. He felt very strongly that his staff shouldn't come to work, go home, and not get to know the people. It was good for morale, and it was also important for Cameroonians to get to know Americans.

Chapter 82

O n one special occasion, I planned a day for all Americans to visit the residence in Yaoundé. This included our Peace Corps volunteers, missionaries, and other Americans working in the country. The main reason for the gathering was that they needed a briefing from George about our security programs. If they needed to be evacuated because of a coup, national disaster, and so forth, there were designated American homes where they could seek help and protection. The embassy needed to know how to find Americans in an emergency. This wasn't a new policy. The Foreign Service has always had the responsibility to protect American citizens.

An ambassador and his wife had a lot of responsibilities, running the gamut from monitoring the treatment of Americans arrested for fighting in a bar to addressing displeasure from the host country and domestic violence. We knew right away if something happened involving Americans, such as when one of our Peace Corps personnel was in an accident. Sometimes, the Regional Security Office could handle a problem, but George was always notified by the marine on duty at the embassy. If we were at a restaurant, Lawrence, the driver, would be called and he would notify George. If we were at a reception and someone needed George, he would break away and check in immediately. That was our life.

We have always tried to make Sunday a quiet day. I would read the embassy unclassified newsletter and write cards to friends and family to be put in the diplomatic pouch, which were then sent to the mailroom at the State Department in Washington and then into the US mail service.

On one Sunday, at about 4:00 p.m., the marine guard called us and said there had been an accident on the road to Douala, Cameroon's second largest city. American schoolchildren and teachers were on a bus returning to Yaoundé from a school outing to climb Mount Cameroon. The school bus driver had pulled out on a blind hill and hit a car, and there were many injuries and even deaths. Lawrence picked us up, and we raced to the hospital. There was no proper ambulance service. George and I were in a waiting room. People were bringing children in by car and in the back of trucks. George went to the back of the hospital where the kids were being treated to try to get information for anxious parents.

Identifying the children was a problem because they had been separated from their backpacks. George knew some of the children by sight. He learned that an American student and the Moroccan ambassador's son had died. They were friends and had been seated together on the bus. Colonel Scott Rutherford, our military attaché, was pacing and in a panic. He truly was as white as a sheet. George went back two times to the treatment area, but he couldn't tell Scott his son was dead. I told George to tell him, but he couldn't say the words. Finally, he told Scott he would check one more time. He told Scott that his son was one of the two boys who had died. The Moroccan ambassador was also waiting. Maybe the doctor gave him the news.

In the next day or two, I went to see the Moroccan mother who had lost her son. She lived down the street from me. My guard watched me as I walked to her house. Her guard was watching for me. I wanted her to know I was close by if she needed help in any way. The king of Morocco sent a plane to bring the family home for the son's burial. I saw her once after the accident, but soon afterwards, she returned to Morocco permanently.

About twelve children were injured, and unfortunately, an American teacher had a severed arm and bled to death before she could get to the hospital. It was a horrible experience, but I wanted to be there. I have never written this down or talked to my psychologist about it until now. I will discuss this with her. I have been in therapy since we retired. This tragedy is something I will never forget.

Chapter 83

I had a really good Cameroonian friend named Maureen. Her father would bring me vegetables from the countryside. All I had to do was call and she would be there for me. Mostly I needed an interpreter and a friend; Maureen was both. I have beautiful photos of her.

One time, we went to the African market to shop for bargains, and I visited a tailor to pick out material to design my own clothes. It was a luxury for me to have tailor-made clothes. One day, I arrived at noon, not knowing about the Muslim prayer time. The streets were filled with people praying. It wasn't like Mecca in Saudi Arabia, but I had never seen so many people dressed in white clothes.

Maureen came to visit a friend in the US and came to DC to visit me. We drove home to Kentucky. Maureen met a lot of my family and dear friend Eva. I'm sure none of them had ever met an African woman. We had a wonderful drive back to DC. I took her back to her friend, and I bought her a teal jacket.

Maureen sang in a trio of young women. The embassy called on them when we needed singers. I guess that's the way I met her. During her visit to Kentucky, I wanted her to sing for my family members. Uncle Joe had tears in his eyes. Brother Jim was filled with emotion. My sister, Pauline, would later come to Africa, and Maureen was a great friend to her.

Maureen didn't tell me before she traveled that she had gotten sick. Why not? I could have helped her. I am friends with a Black family in Pineville, and introduced Etta, one of the family members, to Maureen. We went to Etta's church, where she sang for them. For some reason, I could not understand why Maureen didn't want me to know she was not well. She died later in Cameroon. I had not known how much this would hurt me to write about her until I started writing. She was a true friend. The next time, I return to see

Ama, I will ask to be taken to Maureen's grave "if the good Lord is willing and the creek don't rise." You must say this the country way; forget grammar. I will visit and hope Maureen's other family members are well, especially her father. God bless her soul.

Gladys Viban was another special woman I liked and respected very much. She worked at the embassy as the public affairs assistant. She was with me on many occasions with and without George. When I was invited to the official opening of a computer school, Gladys went with me. We arrived with the US flag flying on the vehicle. I had a traditional meeting with the director, was given a walk-through, and met the students. We had samosas (bite-size food) and champagne for the toast. I was given a certificate making me godmother to the computer school. Gladys was with me to help, but most importantly, I needed her support and for French translation. Cameroon is part Anglophone and part Francophone. The visit went well, and I was very proud to represent my country. Gladys was a valued member of the embassy staff for years and was part of the advance help for events at the ambassador's residence. With her help, we accomplished a lot together.

After a visit to the cities of Garoa and Marowa in the predominantly Muslim northern part of Cameroon, Gladys presented me with photo album I cherish. Her words written in it are as follows: "*Dear Ambassador Staples and Mrs. Jo Ann Staples, You have touched thousands of people in Cameroon through your thoughtfulness and understanding. As for me and my family, you have both been a real source of strength and encouragement. I shall always draw fortitude and inspiration for the wonderful memories you have indelibly printed in my life. May love, joy and peace always attend you.*"

Chapter 84

Gladys was appointed elder in her church, and I was invited to attend the ceremony. Maureen was waiting for me when Lawrence pulled up. She took me around the side of the church and to the front seats. I had been to some happy church services, but this was special. The singing was too good! When the induction part was over, the good times had begun. I saw Dr. Indube, the dean of the medical school, dancing down the center of the church. People were up and dancing in place or up front and in the isles. If you were in your seat, you were dead! A good time was had by one and all, especially Mrs. Staples. I was so glad to have been a part of Gladys's special day. I was the only one invited from our embassy to attend.

Among one of the special happenings in this assignment was when Pauline, my one and only sister, came to Cameroon. George asked me what I wanted for my anniversary gift. I said, "None of my immediate family has ever visited us since we have been in the Foreign Service, so I'd like to have my sister visit." I was so pleased when she arrived safely. She had never traveled outside of the US. This was my best present ever. During her time in Cameroon, we went to the marine house for a party.

The US was building a new embassy. I was talking to Richard, the project manager, and he said, "I have to fly back to the US to find an office manager. It has to be an American citizen who can pass a background check."

I said, "Richard, wait a minute. I want you to meet my sister." He met her, and right away, based on her qualifications from previous work with construction companies, he offered her the job.

Pauline went back to Knoxville, put her furniture into storage, and came to Africa. I was elated. During our adult life, we'd had very little time together. We were working briefly at the same time in Cincinnati, but she got transferred to

Louisville. She then met her husband, Jim, and moved to Shreveport, Louisiana, where she lived for the next eighteen years. She didn't have any children from this marriage. The marriage ended in divorce, but something good came from this union. Sis got attached to her mother-in-law, and they have a love for each other that has lasted many years. Pauline moved back to Knoxville with Bill, her new husband, though they eventually got a divorce too. Sis was always head of the household. Her husband, Bill, just had a chip on his shoulder. I will say no more. Bill died, and as I said before, my grandmother told me, "If you can't say something good about the dead, don't say anything at all." My sister was free to travel.

After Pauline arrived in Cameroon and started her new job, I helped her put together a pretty apartment. My sister lived for the next year and a half just a block from me. We had to find furniture from the local economy, but there were no furniture stores. Instead, you had to find a vendor on the street and request a sofa made to order. Pauline's apartment came together nicely. We had such great adventures and made lasting memories. My friends became her friends, especially Maureen.

Pauline found a church and got involved in an orphanage after meeting a couple of nuns. She helped by providing shoes sent from her church in Knoxville. She was always helping women with cottage industry projects and trying to empower women. My sister is a giver and helper. That's what makes her happy. The men on the embassy building site loved her and her office staff. One of her projects was buying a small stove like a hibachi, which she gave to a poor woman she met who would roast and sell peanuts. Sis asked the men on the job site to save their whiskey bottles to put the peanuts in. A small business was started.

The men on the site were complaining about no good laundry service. Pauline bought a washer and dryer for Maureen to do their laundry. Pauline had many more accomplishments, but I love this one! She taught the owner of a restaurant she frequented to make her meat loaf. He put it on his menu, and it was a big hit. She attended many embassy events, and we could be together. My sister is a good woman and, to this day, still speaks emotionally about out time together in Africa.

Chapter 85

Before leaving the story of my time in Cameroon, I must mention one other sad thing, though it is difficult to write about.

I returned to Yaoundé about seven years after our assignment ended and stayed with Ama. She had one son, Fami, whom I liked very much. I called him "my banker" because he would exchange US dollars for francs when I needed more money. He always wanted to know if I needed anything because I was alone when Ama had to be at her office.

After George and I retired, we were in a restaurant in Lexington, Kentucky. George had done a search on Ama Muna to see what was happening with her in Cameroon. George said, "Jodi, Ama's son has died in an automobile accident." I was sick to my stomach. He was only twenty-six.

I called Ama and got more details. She said, "I didn't know how to tell you." It happened late at night, and a friend was driving Fami's Mercedes on the Douala Road to Yaoundé. I wrote earlier about my fear of that road, which was the reason I decided not to drive in Cameroon. The news was terrible. I couldn't be with my dear friend because my health wouldn't permit me to return to Cameroon. I've always felt guilty that I didn't receive the tragic news in time and hadn't tried to make the trip to help Ama.

Chapter 86

George needed another job. He liked being ambassador to both Cameroon and Equatorial Guinea, but our three-year assignment had ended. I loved what I was able to accomplish with the people and my own personal growth. George and I were very different people. When he felt he had done his best to promote US interests, he was ready to bid on another position. We returned home, went to the State Department, and made some connections. Normally, the procedure is to bid on positions that are available because people are in rotation cycle, and some are retiring.

George had heard of a new position available at NATO Headquarters in Belgium. The interested individuals would have to have an ambassadorial rank. I think in the State Department that would be about the equivalent of a three-star general. We were in Washington when George got an interview with General Jim Jones, the Supreme Allied Commander Europe stationed in Mons, Belgium, who was back at the Pentagon for consultations.

I asked George if I could go with him. He called, and General Jones said it would be fine. Not too many things get me excited but having the opportunity to meet a four-star general and visit the Pentagon was a special opportunity. I wanted to look my best. I wore a beautiful dress, my pearl necklace, and my mink coat. Because most of our assignments were in sub-Saharan Africa and Central America, my coat spent most of the time in a fur storage facility in Knoxville.

It was great being met by military officers and taken to meet General Jones. We went into his office, and after he spoke with George about NATO issues, a more relaxed conversation began. I mentioned that I was a Jones from Kentucky. We talked about his family background. He asked George a very direct question as to why he wanted to work for him. George told him that he had worked years ago in NATO and wanted to be involved once again in helping the alliance meet today's challenges. I said, "General Jones, come and visit us sometime in Cameroon." That was the end of the interview.

We drove later that same day back to our home in Kentucky. Catherine was home, waiting for us. She said, "A General Jones called for you." When George returned the call, General Jones told him, "The job is yours." It happened so quickly, and we were very pleased.

My baby girl went back to university, and we went back to Cameroon to finish our final months before permanent departure. It was difficult to not tell Ama that we were going to NATO, but she was a government minister in the Cameroonian government, and they didn't need to know just yet that we were leaving. I liked being a part of the First Ladies CERAC organization. I never wanted to be an ambassador, but I liked being the ambassador's wife. I would have liked to be one of the senior decorators at the State Department. I even wanted to own a bar in a tropical location, but I didn't get the opportunity in this diplomatic life.

Chapter 87

One final note I want to share about being in Cameroon is what we did for our national day celebrations. I helped pull off three big Fourth of July events in Cameroon. I got so tired of the standard Fourth of July receptions. They are boring except for the fireworks. We had to attend other countries' Independence Day celebrations. They seem to be held most times in gardens with long speeches. I hate it when my high-heeled shoes sink in the ground as I try to stand on my toes. Well, that's part of the job, but I wanted to make our celebration special. I thought there should be a theme that celebrated an everyday American, grassroots-type experience.

I knew we needed a committee to brainstorm ideas. We decided that one reception would be like a state fair. We used a very large rectangular room at the Hilton. We had tons of Fourth of July decorations at the warehouse. We received a message from the president that George would read. We got a big tub for bobbing for apples, a cotton-candy machine, homemade ice-cream cones, and so on. Someone found a wagon with a fold-down back gate. We had bales of hay delivered and made a corral, and someone found two horses we could use to set the scene. The end of the room had a back entrance, and we used that to bring in the horses, hay, and wood into the Hilton. Yes, I'm telling the truth! I think George must have asked for permission from his tennis partner, who was the manager of the Hilton. To cap it off, we had cooks making hamburgers and hot dogs with all the condiments. I'm sure there were kegs of beer. The reception was a great success and set the tone for the next two Fourth of July national day receptions.

I had promised Catherine we would go to Hawaii for her twenty-first birthday. We were late, but I did keep my promise. I took a break from Cameroon, and we traveled to Honolulu. We had a wonderful vacation. I love history, and it was great to see the Pearl Harbor National Memorial. The USS Arizona's visit there was very emotional. I am sure there would not be a Pearl Harbor memorial without Elvis Presley, who did the first benefit. I thought about the young man from Kentucky who helped take bodies out of the ruins of the Arizona, my beloved uncle Joe North.

That might have been the reason for the next Fourth of July receptions. Part of the money for these events came from the American companies operating in Cameroon. Once again, we had a committee to plan the event and they decided on a Hawaiian theme. George approved an order of about five hundred Hawaiian leis to put around the necks when greeting our invited guests. The guest list grew to about eight hundred. I had bought Hawaiian dresses for me and my sister, Pauline. She's a great seamstress. We had videos to show the dancers we selected to learn how to do Hawaiian dancing. Pauline made the tops and bottoms from material with Hawaii patterns. The practice sessions paid off, and they danced beautifully to the music.

We made big platters of tropical fruit for the buffet. That was easy to do in Cameroon. Island-type drinks were served in pineapples. I didn't try the roasted pig! Small sandwiches and other food were available, and the usual bars were open. I know it was a big event and different. A photographer took pictures when people entered. It was great being and working with my sister. Of course, in all these events, the embassy General Services staff, carpenters, and electricians helped. I always want to acknowledge the Americans at the embassy and the local staff. Really, I don't know how you could make an embassy function without these people. As I mentioned, we come and go, but they stay for years.

For the third and final Fourth of July event, I wanted a "Down the Mississippi" theme. I had always wanted a Scarlett O'Hara dress like in *Gone with the Wind*. I couldn't jerk down the drapes as she did in the movie, so I had a local seamstress create southern belle-type dresses for me and Pauline. Materials were readily available but no green velvet! I had to settle for black. Pauline made me a fan to complement my dress. I put a brooch on a black velvet ribbon to wear around my throat. My sister likes to tease me that she is like a peacock and loves a lot of color while I'm like a penguin because I prefer black and white. Pauline wore a light blue satin dress with accessories to match. We had to dance with very large hoops.

I'm still amazed at the effort that went into making the reception come together. I always know members of the local art community. We had a mural of a paddleboat going down the Mississippi painted. The ceilings were high at the Hilton. We had the carpenters prefabricate the balconies. They were hung as high as possible on the wall and painted black. We even found Spanish moss to hang from the balconies. I think this was my favorite of the three receptions we hosted during our assignment in Cameroon.

George had the duty of closing the bar and saving beer and beverages so we could move them to the residence for another reception for the American community the next day. I was told it wasn't necessary to invite our residence staff to the reception at the Hilton, but I insisted. They were all dressed beautifully. I wanted them to be included to show appreciation for all their help and the late nights cleaning up after big events, which could take hours. It could be 2:00 a.m. It was too dark and dangerous to find their own transportation, so I had Lawrence see them safely home.

We invited Tomas and Trudy, who were still living in Malabo and doing very well financially, to stay with us and go to the reception. They loved it. When leaving the hotel, I asked one of our embassy's local employees what he thought of the event. He said, "Mrs. Staples, I have nothing to compare it with."

The French ambassador was behind me. He said, "How do we follow this?" Bastille Day on July 14 is their national day. He had ten days! This was my biggest event ever in my memory. George thought we hosted about 1,100 people. It was truly a team event. Kudos to everyone.

Keep in mind, I had to make some of the same events happen in Equatorial Guinea. We had two countries to take care of because we were accredited to both countries at the same time. We had closed the old embassy in Equatorial Guinea and then reopened another a couple of years later. Lots of things had to be shipped or flown to Malabo, and we had to find a residence for us and visitors. Security concerns, of course, also had to be resolved with anything we bought or rented. It makes me tired just writing and thinking about it all. How about happy thoughts? Let's go to the beach, my happy place.

Chapter 88

Cameroon had two beaches: one, Limbe, with black sand; and the other, Karibi, with white sand. I enjoyed getting away to them every chance I got. They reminded me of El Salvador, which also had black and white sand beaches. I assume any country with white and black sand beaches has volcanoes.

I really liked the Russian ambassador's wife. I am sure we could have been friends, but we couldn't talk to each other without an interpreter. I just couldn't see us on the sand at Karibi with a male translator between us. She sent me her specialty food at Christmas, and sometimes, she would arrive at our residence with a special treat for me.

Women have been more or less the same when I've met them. The country doesn't matter. They are homesick, miss their families, and want a better education for their children. I'm part feminist and like being a woman. We should receive the same pay for the job as male counterparts. I've worked too hard, worked like a man when I couldn't get help, and lifted more weight than I should. I wonder if that's the reason for my many health problems, especially since I have aged. I believe in many instances a woman is the right person for the job, the simple reasoning being that women give birth and do the majority of the work raising children. Mothers will think hard and long about going to war. Of course, there have been exceptions down through history.

I celebrated my fifty-seventh birthday in Cameroon. I think this was the best birthday of my life. I invited my favorite people to the residence for a late supper. Some had never been to a late supper. It started about 9:00 p.m. We had a birthday cake (chocolate, of course), small kebabs, and snacks to get everyone ready for my favorite club. I picked all of the guests. They were my favorites, and most were Cameroonian.

I invited about fifty people to a late supper and birthday cake. About 11:30 p.m., we left to go dancing. I had been to the nightclub Caesar's three times before. The name, famous in Roman history, will be remembered forever. Inside, there were security guards dressed like Roman soldiers. The music was loud, prerecorded, and nonstop. My sister, Pauline, was present, as were Ama, Dr. Muna, Jadine (a Foreign Service officer), Gladys, Bernice (a great friend who worked for the National Oil Company), Akere Muna, Ellen (George's secretary), and Dr. Ndube (from Gladys's church). Gary from Geovic, an American mining company, also came. I will tell you about him later. Others who came were two of my friends from CERAC, the members of the First Ladies organization, George Muna and his wife, and the minister of defense. Kina, the embassy nurse, was one of my favorite people and also joined us.

At Caesar's, you didn't have to have a partner. People just got up and danced until they needed some refreshment and to rest, then hit the floor again. I danced until my hair and clothes were soaked. The champagne was always flowing at our table. Everyone just danced the night away, and no one cared about official titles or positions. Lawrence picked me up about 4:00 a.m. I went home and pulled my shoes off in the foyer. I couldn't walk upstairs, not another step, in my shoes. You can understand why this was my favorite birthday celebration. There was a time in Camelot when everything was perfect.

Chapter 89

One evening there was a cookout at the marine house, where the members of the embassy's marine detachment live and a place where Americans can go for different events hosted by the marines. Typical events include pool parties, movie nights, volleyball, and so on. Ambassadors and spouses like to attend these events to show support for our marines.

That night, as I was having a drink at the bar, I started talking to a man who seemed like Atlas. The weight of the world was on his shoulders. His name was Gary Morris. His company, Geovic, had invested nine million dollars trying to get approval for a cobalt mining project. He was hitting nothing but road-blocks, and the proposed project was not being approved. I said, "Don't leave tomorrow. Have you been to the embassy? My husband is the US ambassador. He can get you a meeting with President Biya. I bet the president doesn't know about Geovic." George went with him to meet President Biya, and soon thereafter, the contract was signed to start mining cobalt.

It was time for some work and fun. Ama and I decided to have an art exhibit together. One of the major artists displaying his work was from Senegal. Ama knew him and arranged for him to come to Cameroon. He came with twenty-five paintings. Three were very large. In order to ship them to Cameroon, the paintings were taken out of their frames. The carpenter from the embassy made new frames for their display. My dining room was reserved for Cameroonian artists who displayed their art. We used the living room and foyer for the Senegal artist's paintings.

We invited lots of diplomats as well as government officials. Ama knew who to invite from Cameroon. My private collection and the pieces from the Art in Embassies program stayed in place. I asked the carpenters to make frames for wall hangings and about twelve easels to display paintings on the floor. The house and patio were a perfect place for the exhibit. I had large white pedestals made when I first arrived and selected clay pots to hold tropical flowers. These were put on top of the pedestals. I used birds of paradise, elephant ear leaves, and huge ferns.

I selected fabric and table linen for the patio tables and chairs. I asked the decorators in Washington to have new table linen made for me. For formal events, special linen was sent from Washington. Early on in Cameroon, I asked for the upstairs balcony to be screened. The balcony was above the patio. We put lots of plants up on the balcony, which I used for small groups. We used the dining room and patio often. People loved to walk in my garden.

The music addition to the residence was wonderful. I asked the electrician if there was a way to have music in the whole house or just the dining room, a switch to take the music to the patio and the den with the library. I had control of where I wanted the music to be heard. He did it for me. I've never had that arrangement again.

Chapter 90

One morning, I got a note from my housekeeper, Euphrasia, that said, "*Mrs. Staples, my husband died last night. I have no mother or father to help me, just you.*" Lawrence took me to her house located behind some other houses along a dirt road. She had three children, and the place was very small for five people. When I entered, my eyes had to adjust because there wasn't a window. I found Euphrasia on the floor. I didn't recognize her because someone had shaved her head. She told me it was a custom to shave a woman's head when her husband died. Her husband's brothers came and took her little television, radio, and so on. It was also a custom to give food and drinks to visitors. She had no money.

I had Lawrence take me home. I got the kitchen staff to start making small sandwiches, plantain chips, small, sliced wieners with toothpicks, some potato samosas, and so forth. I gave Lawrence money to buy soft drinks and two cases of beer. I asked him not to tell the ambassador, who had said not to have Lawrence buy beer because he didn't believe it would be appropriate.

The funeral home would not come to get the body until it was paid. I think I paid to pick up her husband's body. In my mind, it was the equivalent of about thirty-five US dollars. An obstacle was that she needed transport to get her husband's body back to their village. I had done all I could to help her, but I couldn't use a US government vehicle. I didn't ask because I knew what George would tell me.

Later, I went to check on Euphrasia. She wasn't eating, and her little son wanted her to eat before he did. I saw such love for his mother on his face. I wanted her to save face in the community. She had some status because she worked for the American ambassador at his residence. She didn't have to worry about her job. She was a great housekeeper. When I returned to Cameroon a few years later, she was a grandmother and still working at the residence.

Chapter 91

I loved being in Bingue, Ama's village, where such interesting things happened. One morning, at about 6:00 a.m., I heard people outside. They were lined up to talk with Mafor Ama. In that position, she was a key advisor to the Fon king and was a powerful decision maker in her village. She was sitting on a special chair and was dressed to receive people. There were so many requests for many different reasons. Ama talked to me later and told me they wanted a goat, money, wedding help with renting tents, chairs, political favors, and so on. I asked, Ama, "How can you do this for so many?"

She said, "They expect me to continue what my father started." I wondered how financially she could continue her father's traditions.

On another occasion, Ama had eight people for dinner. I had asked my staff to make a carrot cake for me to take. Ama's brother Daniel was at the table. I remember a priest being one of the guests. He told jokes about the Nigerians, whom he described as being very smart talkers and con artists. They had conned the priest with a deal for seeds that would cure AIDS. Everyone had a story about their own experiences with Nigerians.

During dinner, one of the guests asked me how many times I had been to Kumbo. I said, "Maybe three."

He said, "You have been there two times," and gave me the details. I realized he was from the government. I was very disappointed because I thought when I was at Ama's, I was free from all the security. I couldn't be mad at her for informing officials because I loved her too much. I had forgotten I was the American ambassador's wife. The government felt I needed protection.

The dessert was served, and I was very proud of my contribution of a carrot cake. I was seated next to Daniel, who took a very small piece as did everyone else. My cake idea was a mistake! When big platters of fruit were served, everyone took large portions. They preferred fruit.

I remembered a conversation with Dr. Wali Muna, Ama's brother, the cardiologist. He had told me before that when the Western diet was introduced into the country, there were no European diseases. High blood pressure, heart disease, diabetes, and weight problems all came with prosperity. I loved Dr. Muna and his wife, Teresa. He died after I left Cameroon.

Chapter 92

In Cameroon, as in other countries, women's issues are very important, and I was taught an important lesson about giving interviews to the press. A young woman wanted to interview me. I wanted to help her with her career. I asked our public affairs officer to be with me for the interview. The questions were good, and I was pleased with my answers. There were more than thirty questions. One question was "In your life, have you ever encountered a situation of sexual harassment and/or male chauvinism?"

I said, "Sexual harassment, sure. I think in most places of work, women always experience harassment. Women should know how to deal with it and overcome it."

We talked about many important topics, my feelings and concerns, and my life and responsibilities as the wife of the US ambassador to Cameroon.

The interview lasted for more than an hour. I was very confident in my answers. The public affairs officer said it was a good interview. We were promised to see a draft before it went to press. When I saw the headline in the paper, it read as follows: "Women Should Know How to Overcome Sexual Harassment in the Workplace, Says Jo Ann Fuson Staples, Wife of the US Ambassador." The sexual harassment question and answer lasted about a minute, but there was so much more to the interview. Why did she focus on a small part of the conversation? Lesson learned to be careful with the news media.

I will never forget participating in Cameroon's annual Women's Day celebration. I didn't know what to expect when I got up that morning and got dressed. We were all to wear the same material, and I designed a copy of a very nice dress I had bought in Bahrain. It was long and straight with sleeves.

Lawrence was trying to get me close to the viewing stand. At one point, it became necessary to walk. My friends were keeping a place for me in the stands. I could see Maureen, my faithful friend, always there for me. I recognized some of the CERAC ladies. I had a good seat for viewing the parade, and I was quite surprised with the number of women in the march and in the stands. The media estimated there were thirty-six thousand women. I had never experienced being in this kind of an event before. I was very touched by the handicapped people who paraded in their wheelchairs and on crutches, making an effort though it was very difficult. A reporter asked me if I really thought this day had brought any change in the lives of Cameroonian women. I really couldn't answer that question, but if women are able to come together and celebrate, then that is a positive thing.

Chapter 93

Let me tell you about two more very special visitors. I have always liked our programs developed by the State Department's cultural affairs office in Washington. Depending on the country and what kind of event the department would like to promote, they sponsor photo exhibits, art exhibits, jazz groups, gospel singers, and so on. They travel to give public performances in other countries. It can be lots of work for my staff with the food, embassy and warehouse staff helping with invitations, podiums, chairs, microphones, sound systems, and very tired feet. The cultural affairs office also works closely with embassies to coordinate student exchanges and the International Visitor Leadership Program.

For example, one of my favorite experiences was being involved with the visit of a jazz trio featuring an outstanding vocalist by the name of Cynthia Scott. The group gave a wonderful performance at the residence with close to a hundred people in attendance. It was an event by invitation only, as attendance at these types of events were highly sought after. The embassy maintenance personnel, electricians, and warehouse personnel were responsible for the setup of chairs, the stage, and lighting, and I had refreshment areas in two locations. The performance was a huge hit, and everyone enjoyed the evening.

I really enjoyed meeting Cynthia. After the show, I asked her if she would like to come upstairs and watch a short DVD of Johnny Cash reflecting on his life. She especially liked his words about death and how in the end, it was just final and that was that! It gives one a lot of food for thought.

I was also told that General Jones was going to visit Cameroon on his way to South Africa. George has a way of bursting my bubble sometimes, but he didn't this time. Some of the diplomatic community wanted to know why the general was coming to Yaoundé, especially the Russians and French. He was coming because I invited him. Oh, I was sure there would be people wanting meetings with him. I was given time for his visit. I asked the gunnery sergeant if the marines off duty could be invited to the residence. I wanted to make this happen for them. It could be a time they would never forget. My sister, Pauline, was also invited. We have always loved a man in military uniform! General Jones was a career marine. He was commandant of the Marine Corps before becoming NATO's supreme allied commander. It was a great small gathering, and General Jones's photographer captured and shared special photos.

Chapter 94

Some final thoughts as we depart Cameroon and Equatorial Guinea. Our family loves animals and we were traveling with three. Don Quixote, my black cat who had died, was not on this assignment. Simba was getting a gray beard. Baby, our white cat, did not come home; he got sick. The doctor couldn't tell why, and he died in four days. Poor Baby was very sick. I think he had eaten a gecko, a lizard-type animal, in the garden. George was very sad. I hated to tell Catherine back in school in Virginia. Baby is buried down in the second level garden by the gazebo under a bronze plate with his name. I hope his marker is being taken care of by the gardeners.

We didn't have a residence or embassy in Malabo. We did have a nice house I found to stay in when we went to Equatorial Guinea. The changes in this once-poor but now oil-rich country were a big surprise. There was a new airport, and flights were coming in daily. In the old days, the big event was going out to the airport on Saturday to see the Iberia Airlines plane come in from Spain. The roads were great, especially to Moka. There was even a pull-off viewing area from the main road. There were good restaurants. I didn't get to use it, but today, there's a flight to Annobón with a hotel for business or holidays. A new embassy has finally been built in Malabo, and the US ambassador in Cameroon no longer has to cover two countries.

Our next assignment was to Belgium. George traveled from NATO's military headquarters in Mons, Belgium, with General Jones about twenty days a month. I spent time at home in Kentucky, taking care of what I considered family responsibilities. George had a difficult time leaving our dog, Simba. A very nice family with a young son took him. It was the right decision. The family sent photos to George and corresponded with him until Simba died a few years later.

Chapter 95

I would like to write a bit about Anthony Bourdain. My heart hurts because of his death. He was a famous chef and world traveler who for many years had an award-winning show on CNN. He was on my bucket list of people I wanted to meet. I wanted to believe l could have approached him about taking a trip to Africa. We could have traveled to Cameroon and Equatorial Guinea. I feel there was such a connection because we shared a love of travel, meeting people, food, and trying to understand the world we live in as best one can.

Bourdain was a teacher because of who he was, and by watching his show, people got to travel, understand political issues, see faraway places, and more. I loved all his shows because he had the ability to get right into the present moments people were experiencing—taking us on a trip by train to Myanmar, hiking in Peru with his friend, four-wheeling in Nicaragua, recovering from a party in a hammock, or taking his famous boat trip down the Congo and making *coq au vin* with chickens that had to be cleaned under very trying conditions. He was a long way from New York with no demi chefs. He made me feel l was there in Basque Country and wanting to be with him, sharing food with his friends, using my Spanish, and having a history lesson about this unique part of Spain on the border with France. I felt like I was on the mountain with him in Armenia, overlooking the vastness and having a picnic with friends.

Bourdain wanted to go to Azerbaijan but didn't get permission. I once met a very nice Russian ambassador and his wife when George was ambassador to Cameroon. The Russian said, "You look like you could be from Azerbaijan." I feel that I am like Tony Bourdain because we learned so much about the world and the people who live on planet Earth. The Foreign Service and being part of the State Department family gave me a deep love for travel and an invaluable education. As with so many things, there is a downside to knowing and experiencing too much. I believe Tony and I became very lonesome. I sit here on a hillside in Kentucky and feel isolated both geographically and physically. There aren't many people I can talk to about my experiences, feelings, and thoughts. I don't fit in, but maybe, I never did from an early age. My world was small but very big in my imagination.

Chapter 96

Well, I thought I was leaving Cameroon, but I can't do so without mentioning Cathie Bennett. My friend Cathie came to Africa to spend some time with me. The staff at the residence did everything for her. I wanted to take care of her; she had been generous, kind, and loving to me. Now it was my turn. It feels as if we did a thousand things together.

Cathie Bennett is from Harlan, Kentucky. We met because of her electrician, John Caroll, who felt that we were two women who would enjoy meeting each other. He was right! We went for walks in the woods together. After some time, we felt we were soulmates. I don't use that term lightly. We were mountain women and shared a love of nature, art, plants, and pottery. Cathie had a beautiful art studio in the woods on the grounds of her home. We also spent some time at her family's home in Destin, Florida. They also had a home in Hilton Head, South Carolina. I liked all the Bennetts, especially her mother. Mrs. Bennett was involved in the coal business. She had three sons and two daughters. She was a powerful woman and a worker. Mr. Bennett died before I met Cathie.

We were invited to a party at the residence of John Kelly, a Foreign Service officer who worked for George at the embassy. I can see Cathie now and how she danced until sweat was dripping from her hair. George and I took her on official visits. She was at dinners, special events, and cocktail parties. I was so proud to show her off to my friends and embassy family.

There was just one problem: Cathie's family had grown wealthy in the coal business. That meant maybe we couldn't travel in the same circles. Remember my uncle AY saying, "If you can't pay your way, you stay at home." I could split restaurant checks, taxis, and a room charge, and go food store shopping, but I couldn't refuel the company plane! When I went shopping with Cathie, I got one outfit; she bought ten.

Cathie took me with her to a famous art exhibit in Chicago. We took her family's plane. I loved everything about being in Chicago. Cathie packed a bag for me from her closet, things that might complement my clothes. I wasn't insulted because I like feeling pretty. My designers are at Macy's. I love clothes by INC and Jones New York, Chico's, and Soft Surroundings. I also have clothes I designed for myself made by Indian and Muslim tailors in Cameroon and Bahrain.

We left Chicago after dinner. I will never forget the takeoff; before we gained too much altitude, it was amazing to view the city. I have had time in small aircraft, but I don't remember anything so spectacular. I can't describe it and do it justice. Cathie had given me a special memory. I have nice memories of George and me having dinner at her home in Harlan. She has three beautiful daughters. Those were fun times and good memories.

I remember meeting Sherrie and Marco, friends of Cathie, at her home. We got to be friends, and George met them later. Through Sherrie, George, after retirement, got to be involved with ProLiteracy, a nonprofit organization focused on improving adult literacy in the US and worldwide. I went to its headquarters in Syracuse, New York, but it was George they were interested in for his international experience. That was okay with me. I retired to my home in Kentucky.

Marco was in the coal business, and Sherrie was a retired educator. Once, we flew to New York for a long weekend. It was such a fun time. What I remember most was that we had fantastic seating to see the musical *The Color Purple*. At the end of the musical, there was the longest standing ovation I had ever experienced. No one wanted to leave. Everyone stood and applauded, and it continued for ten minutes. My thanks to Oprah Winfrey, whose financial support made this event possible. What a great gift she gave us to bring this play to Broadway. There is a disadvantage to living outside the US and in developing countries. I've missed a lot culturally. You can't have it all in life. We make choices.

Chapter 97

A ma gave a going-away party for me in Bingue. It was so much fun with lots of food, drummers, and dancers in costumes. Some of my same friends from my birthday party attended. Pauline was there, and we danced with Ama. The party lasted until about 4:00 a.m. Some people got drunk, but a soup was made to break a hangover. I don't get drunk, but there have been times, I could have used the recipe for some friends and family.

I liked taking my guests down the river in a dugout canoe. Catherine and I were the first to make the trip. We were up front, and a man from a small nearby restaurant was paddling the canoe. He stopped and pointed out a huge tree close to the river. He pulled the canoe onto the ban; we got out and went close to see and touch this giant. It reminded us that trees are living things.

Laurie, my dear friend from Kentucky, came with her daughter Brandy to visit us. Brandy had been living with her aunt Julie in Paris. Laurie had stopped over to see her sister and pick up Brandy for a mother-and-daughter vacation with us in Cameroon. We went on the river trip, and Laurie recorded their experience with her camera.

My sister, Pauline, went down the river for the ride and to see the huge tree. I said a prayer because it was necessary when one is confronted by something so spectacular. I got to enjoy the experience of having been there. The river is a great way to end this part of my story. There's a short tale I like to share as I have always liked rivers:

"... So–this–is–a–River."

"*The* River," corrected the Rat.

"And you really live by the river? What a jolly life."

"By it and with it and in it," said the Rat. "It is brother and sister to me, and company, and food and drink, and (naturally) washing. It's my world, and I don't want any other. What it hasn't got is not worth having, and what it doesn't know is not worth knowing. Lord! The times we've had together. . . ."

I read these words, taken from a 1913 story, *The Wind in The Willows*, in a brochure for my trip to Alaska.

Wearing my traditional dress and participating with my friends in celebrating International Women's Day.

With Gladys Viban, a special friend, at her church where she was made an elder.

George and I wearing gifts of traditional dress during a visit to the Cameroonian village of Kumbo.

Standing with a Cameroonian elder.

Enjoying the art show at our residence with Ama Muna, my African "sister."

George having fun celebrating at my birthday party.

Special Cameroonian friends at my "one year old" birthday party.

Leaving a nightclub after my birthday party. Kicking up my heels
with Bernice, Ama, Pauline, and Maureen.

Speaking, with household staff standing behind me, at the farewell
gathering of embassy personnel before departing Cameroon.

Chapter 98

In 2004, we went to Belgium when George was assigned to NATO as the State Department's diplomatic advisor to General Jones, the former commandant of the US Marine Corps, who was then serving as the Supreme Allied Commander Europe (SACEUR). The first American general to hold that title was Dwight Eisenhower at the end of WWII. He had to oversee the rebuilding of Europe and the challenge from Russia at the start of the Cold War. General Jones's job was much different from the work required of his predecessors.

NATO today has expanded to include former Soviet Bloc countries, and General Jones had the responsibility to ensure cooperation and close coordination between their militaries. Besides worrying about the continuing pressure from Russia, he had responsibility for developing the NATO training mission in Iraq that built a new army as that country began recovering following the fall of Saddam. In addition, General Jones oversaw NATO's military assistance programs in Afghanistan. These jobs required a full-time travel schedule to Iraq, Afghanistan, and NATO member countries to meet with heads of government and defense chiefs. George was his advisor on the best way to work with these leaders while also looking out for US interests. His work with General Jones required him to travel on average twenty days a month.

In moving to Belgium, I didn't know what to expect, but I was not happy. In Mons, there was a beautiful residence that, for years, had been provided to senior State Department officers holding George's position. I never got to see it! It was too much upkeep for the embassy, located thirty miles away in Brussels, Belgium's capital, so it was sold to the Dutch government. General Services didn't want to send people to Mons from Brussels to maintain the residence.

While still in Cameroon, we were invited to visit Mons, had dinner with General Jones, and met the secretary of the navy, Gordon England, and his wife. Secretary England gave me one of his official navy coins (now proudly displayed in my display case with other treasures). That was when I learned there would be no official residence, no staff, and only a small amount from NATO for hosting official events. I went back to Cameroon and asked for separate maintenance allowance, which would allow me to live in the US in an official capacity while not requiring that I live in Belgium full time.

That didn't mean I was without responsibilities. I returned often to my home on the mountain in Kentucky. When I returned to Belgium, it was difficult to find housing in Mons. Everything I found was rejected because of security regulations. There was an apartment I liked very much, but it was just off the street with not enough setback, a security violation.

George found a nice house, but it was too far out of town. He made the decision when I wasn't there. Now I had to request furniture from the military. I had to beg, borrow, and steal. "Steal" is an exaggeration, but it was difficult. The house was beautiful, and I loved the floor plan, with a beautiful atrium and skylights. George had a small air freight shipment of limited household items and a small surface shipment. I put in enough decorative accessories in the shipment to make the house look very pleasant. George's shipment of books was the added touch. I made it into a comfortable home for George. Now I would have time to work on our home Kentucky. Things had a way of working out, which I didn't understand at the time. A lot of military officers' wives chose not to stay in Mons because of their husbands' travel schedules. I had other things I needed to do at home. It would have been a challenge to live in Aulnois, a French-speaking village close to Mons, and to be alone a lot due to George's travel schedule. My French was *un peu* (a little).

The Belgian government owns a château in Mons that has been the home of the Supreme Allied Commander Europe since 1969. This was now the residence of General and Mrs. Jones. I loved going to the château, called Grendelbien. This helped fulfill my need to be around beautiful architecture, furniture, and paintings. The Joneses were a beautiful couple. I remember asking about a painting in the den from their private collection.

I was invited to a ladies' luncheon hosted by Mrs. Jones at the château. Most of the ladies were military wives. One was the wife of General Stein, a three-star American air force general. I was enjoying the conversations, especially the
" 'ish general's wife. Most talked about life after retirement, the jobs that their

husbands would have, and how they would spend the money. They assumed a high position in private industry would make up for the years getting by on military salaries and the time spent working to support their husbands. I never had enough money and learned that some ambassadors' wives from other countries were paid a salary, plus a clothing allowance.

Chapter 99

George gave me a bit of a history lesson about Belgium not being in a good location strategically. Flat and sandwiched between France and Germany, Belgium historically had been fought over by numerous armies for centuries.

I would get my art fix in Belgium. I took visits to Bruges, Ghent, and Antwerp. I have very vivid memories of the church in Antwerp where Rubens is buried, Saint James, which was opened in 1658. There were instructions on behavior and silence as we entered. I never feel so close to or believe in God more than when I'm in a church or cathedral, or immersed in a natural setting, especially a prehistoric forest. I asked a woman for paper so I could copy the words written outside the church, which are as follows:

"We give you a cordial welcome. Your interest in this church and its art treasures gives you credit. By special request of many visitors, we dare to ask you as well as your guides to speak in a subdued voice. Silence is a token of respect. Silence communicates its message. Silence is the music of the heart that admires."

I have too many art books. George tells me I don't have to buy a coffee-table-size art book for every art gallery or exhibit, but I do because they give me pleasure. How did these artists come to be in their lifetime? I will never understand. How are cathedrals constructed? I've read many of Ken Follett's books and still can't understand. His book *Pillars of the Earth* explains the construction process and is a favorite, as I can escape to another time. I like journeying back through time.

We went to the painter Rubens's home where he had his studio. In his bedroom, we asked why his bed was so small. The guide said, "People believed at that time that sleeping in a sitting position is better for health."

There was an opening to look down into the gallery from the second floor. I bought a print of his studio, and everything in it was a painted in miniature. I wondered how this was possible two hundred years before photography would begin until years later, when I found my answer on the internet: he painted them himself. I have the print on my wall in the condo in Cincinnati.

Ghent is a medieval city. I loved the canals and architecture. I like reading medieval history and am fascinated by all types of structures. The twilights and sunsets must be spectacular with the reflection in the canals. The city was spectacular. We had only a day, which was a mistake. I'm truly sorry I didn't have more time to explore this fascinating city. We also ran short of time in Bruges, where I had hoped to buy a piece of famous Belgian lace to take home to my friends. Unfortunately, I couldn't decide because there were just too many choices.

Chapter 100

While in Mons, we took some leave and went to Munich, Germany, to see "little sister" Claudia; her partner, Claus; daughter Lara; and beautiful Marie, Claudia's mother, who lived in Augsburg, Germany, which is also where Claudia is from. I met Claudia when she was about eighteen. Her family loved my brother Alvie, who was in the army and stationed in Germany. Oma, Claudia's grandmother, really loved Alvie. Al and Claudia went their separate ways, but we have remained friends for years. She visited me in Zimbabwe, and we climbed the Dolomites in Italy with my daughter, Catherine. Marian, Claudia, and I had an adventure in California seeing the coast highway by van. We three took a sponge bath out of melted ice in my cooler. So many good memories.

While in Munich, I once again got to see Claudia's daughter Lara. She was a baby the first time I had seen her, and now she was a young girl about eight years of age. We took the train from Munich to Augsburg to visit Claudia's mom, Marie, whom I loved. During the visit, Claudia translated. Marie was now a grandmother. The day passed too quickly. In the past when Maria and I were without Claudia, she would say, "Now the great silence begins." I could say, "*Wie viel Geld?*," "*das ist schon,*" and "*du musst essen.*" That means, "how much money?" "that is beautiful," and "you must eat." Somehow, we managed to communicate and laugh a lot.

While I was in Augsburg with Claudia and Lara visiting Marie, Claus and George went to Dachau, the famous WWII concentration camp. I had no interest in going there. We three ladies had a wonderful day. We had wine, fruit, champagne, and good freshly baked bread. I know I was a Roman in a past life. The next day, Claus, Claudia, Lara, George, and I took the train out of the city and had lunch at a beautiful lake.

After visiting friends in Munich, George had to go to London for meetings with the British Foreign Office. He and I went by high-speed train to London, passing under the English Channel through the "Chunnel." I was a bit apprehensive going under the water but very excited to see London again. During a previous trip with Catherine, we got to see hedgerows in the countryside, ancient stone walls, livestock, and other pastoral sites. During another stopover while George was in meetings, we visited Windsor Castle before we traveled on to Africa.

In London, we stayed at a lovely hotel right on the Thames. I could look out and see the Parliament building and Big Ben, and I was within walking distance of the British Museum. I went to the museum, hoping to see paintings by Gainsborough, and I was not disappointed. Sometimes, I felt that Catherine and I had better experiences than George because we got to tour historical sites, shop, and meet different people while he was usually in meetings.

Chapter 101

After visiting Claudia, we flew from Munich to Moscow. The time had come to see Russia for myself. George has an incredible knowledge of history and knew lots about the country. Because of the assignment to NATO, George knew our deputy chief of mission in Moscow, and he helped with our itinerary. I must admit to having been very excited.

After clearing immigration control, we took a taxi to our hotel, the famous Hotel Metropol, right off Red Square, where Lenin and other historical figures stayed at the start of the Russian Revolution. We were on a private trip, not official government travel. I liked it that way. We were, however, still traveling on diplomatic passports, so I'm sure when we arrived, the KGB knew we were in Moscow. I didn't care if they followed us. I was here to learn all I could. I wanted to see museums, get a feel for the architecture, and eat great food that I hoped would be different. I also wanted to travel by train to see the countryside and meet some people.

The wide roads going into the city were just as I'd seen in images from the past. Moscow had all the upscale stores I recognized from Paris, New York, and Buenos Aires. I think the drive into town was about an hour, just normal freeway driving, but let's not forget rush-hour traffic. There was all the good and bad that comes with development.

I was anxious to get to the Pushkin and the Hermitage Museums. I had heard about those two art museums for a long time. Pinch me because I must be dreaming. The Pushkin held especially beautiful paintings. I remember some very large ones, but I didn't know who the artists were. I kept looking for a name on the paintings, but there wasn't one I recognized. We learned that most of these artists had never been allowed to exhibit outside of Russia.

Our guide was wonderful. I told her about my childhood and the fear the Russians were coming to take my country. I told her about the fear of radiation and how we were told to get under our desks in case of nuclear attack. I didn't know much about Russia, but I knew about people putting shelters in their backyard. I must have seen this on TV because I was in grade school, about seven or eight years old. We got our first TV about the same time. This information must have been for people living in large cities.

The tour guide said something I have never forgotten: "When was young, I never knew you Americans existed." I've thought about this many, many times. Was her world that closed in? Mine was very limited in some ways. I started learning about geography in the fourth grade, and we were about the same age.

We went to another museum in Moscow, and to my surprise, I saw displays of the Seven Wonders of the World in miniature. Maybe the average Russian didn't get to travel, but they knew about some things outside of Russia.

We went to St. Basil's, the Russian Orthodox cathedral. I bought beautiful incense holders on chains with brass hangers for beautiful red globes. I have them proudly hanging in my formal living room in Kentucky. They weren't expensive but are priceless to me. We did normal tourist things. We also went to the Sunday art market in Moscow, and George came away with a beautiful etching of what we thought a rural country home in Russia might look like. I had my photo taken with a Russian artist. I love going to open air markets when I travel. I would also recommend, for example, the Sunday market in Miami. One of my favorite artist proofs came from Miami.

In Moscow's Sunday market, George bought a beautiful lacquer box with battle scenes of St. George slaying the dragon. Mine were boxes for special jewelry with artistic scenes painted on them. I bought two beautiful Russian reproductions of Mary and Child icons. They are in my bedroom at home.

During our time in Moscow, I asked to visit a cemetery. I like them because they are sculpture parks to me. On this special occasion, I got to see the standing monument to Yuri Gagarin, the first man in space, with his image carved in stone. I stood by the right side for a photo opportunity. I have it framed on my buffet in a wide, gilded frame. Famous Russian poets, political leaders, and even Khrushchev's wife are buried in that cemetery.

In Red Square, we visited the State Russian Museum and the Kremlin Armoury, with its spectacular displays of incredible royal carriages, historical military weapons, and costumes. Crowns, scepters, chalices, and, my favorite, the biblical bindings, including one from 1499, were on display. I saw the military weapons of the fifteenth to the seventeenth centuries. The display case linings were of red and green embroidery fabric. Almost five centuries have passed since the armory was first mentioned in the old documents that have survived to our day. I wish I could return to Russia, but at this time in my life, because of medical issues, it would have to be on a flight with first-class accommodations.

After a wonderful stay in Moscow, we prepared to leave for Saint Petersburg. All our arrangements were made in advance. I was very happy and grateful to everyone who made our trip to Russia so life changing. I left thinking about the history of religion after all I had seen and felt. I had been inside a Russian Orthodox church. There were many throughout the country. I think religion never left the people, and despite the years of Communist rule, the people never lost their belief.

To travel to Saint Petersburg, I requested that we travel by train. Our driver took us to the train station and checked our baggage while we waited in the car until it was our time to board. I don't like to be separated from my luggage; I'm always anxious when I feel out of control. As bundles of bags were being loaded, I reflected on how similar it was to travel in Africa. I told myself to be calm. The driver had our tickets to Saint Petersburg and our passports. I also don't like to be separated from my passport.

For a while, it seemed as if everyone was boarding except us. The driver returned, and we were taken to the first up-front compartment with a sleeping area above our seats. We were on the overnight train to Saint Petersburg, which departed at about 4:00 p.m. Our personal attendant brought us coffee in a pewter holder with a glass insert. I put my nose to the window because I wanted to see the countryside, which never happened because it was getting dark.

Military personnel were outside in the corridor. It was very crowded, and they were laughing, drinking, and having a good time. Shouldn't they have been in another part of the train? I went to the bathroom and asked to pass. They must have known we were Americans. My mind started to work, and I thought, *Are they there because of us? Is it my imagination?* I didn't see other people in their compartments. I don't remember talking to anyone else. This didn't feel right, but our attendant gave us food and made our beds.

I felt like Laura in the film *Doctor Zhivago* when we arrived at the station and saw the mass of people, push carts, and belongings carried in assorted bundles. I bought a mink hat in Moscow. My friend Cathie from Kentucky had loaned me a mink oversize collar to complement my wardrobe. In America, train travel was popular in the past. With the development of cars at an affordable price, people didn't travel by passenger trains as before. Trains became mostly for cargo. Maybe my fascination with trains came from watching coal trains as they passed where we lived when my father was alive. During the night, I looked out into total darkness. Where were the Russian night lights? I was confused. I didn't realize at the time that outside of major cities, Russia was underdeveloped.

I remember our morning arrival in Saint Petersburg as being very early. It wasn't daylight yet. We paid a porter to handle our luggage. We were staying with our American consul general, Karen Malzahn, who had worked with George years earlier in the Operations Center at the State Department and, later, in Bahrain, where she had replaced the Economic Section chief before we left. Her apartment was tastefully decorated. I was surprised how spacious and open the floor plan was, with beautiful large windows.

We were near the curb, waiting for Karen because she was caught in traffic. I was having some pain issues and took a rest. I must have overtaxed my body in Moscow. We had a prearranged schedule by the same tourist company as in Moscow. I am sure we had some surveillance, but it didn't bother me. I think soon after our arrival, the authorities knew we were truly just grateful visitors. Being in Russia made me feel safe. I didn't have to worry about a purse snatcher or about getting lost and looking for directions. I was just enjoying the ride.

Chapter 102

In Saint Petersburg, our tour guide took us to visit Catherine the Great's country house and other historical sites. Two things are permanently etched in my memory. One is our visit to the WWII memorial. In 1941, three huge German armies attacked the north, center, and south of the Soviet Union. The northern force was stopped on the outskirts of Saint Petersburg, then known as Leningrad, and German forces surrounded the city, which was cut off from the outside for nine hundred days. During these terrible days, over a million soldiers and civilians died. People survived by eating their horses and even tree bark.

George and I went to the site where thousands of the people were buried. The Russian people suffered unimaginable hardships. My heart hurts for the people, especially the mothers who gave birth to these sons and daughters. I think that some of these people who are now grandmothers and grandfathers are still living to tell the stories. In human history, from my understanding, I don't blame "the people." I blame the leaders and politicians. A poster I have seen of an old Native American comes to my mind. He had one tear running down the side of his face. He was maybe sad and angry for the loss of his sons, native land, and traditions. That one tear is very significant in my life.

Now I was ready for my art appreciation event. We entered the Hermitage Museum. Our tour guide was very knowledgeable. My husband and daughter now have a better appreciation of art museums and exhibits because of Mama Jo. I think I brought the love of paintings and sculpture to my family. It would be pleasing to me to think I might live long enough to take my granddaughter, Grace Ann, to the Hermitage.

I was not disappointed with our visit to this famous museum. We were awestruck and overwhelmed, and immediately realized there was too much on the schedule. We had planned five other stops but asked for them to be canceled. I would think it would be possible to find an example of the most famous paintings in the world on display in the Hermitage. I am an admirer of Corot. I can recognize his paintings by the white flecks of paint on the canvas. We entered a room, and I said, "George, I think there is a Corot on the right." Then I looked down the wall, and there were more and more. The whole room was just paintings by Corot. There were other rooms like that, with the works of many, many famous artists.

I also saw a painting I never expected to see except in a book. They had on display Rubens's *Return of the Prodigal Son*. It was part of the Hermitage's private collection. As my friend Tomas would say, "Mrs. Staples, it's too good." It takes a lot to excite me. I do not scream and shout like some women. I get very quiet and reflective. That doesn't mean I don't feel it inside.

We went to the gift shop—as George likes to say to Catherine and me, "another shopping opportunity." I bought a sixteen-by-twenty copy of *Return of the Prodigal Son* on canvas, a print of a convent where Czar Peter the Great sent his sister to live out her life, and a print of St. Basil's Cathedral in Moscow with the famous onion domes. I think this architecture must be unique to Russia. Oh, I cannot forget my three purchases of reproductions of Fabergé eggs for my daughter, son-in-law, and myself. I also have a reproduction of an egg with Catherine the Great's carriage inside it in miniature.

That evening, I wasn't feeling so well. I stayed in Karen's apartment while she and George went to the ballet. I'm sure any ballet in Russia is great. The famous Bolshoi is in Moscow. There, I was in Russia, and I had to pass on seeing the ballet! Maybe I needed some quiet to mentally prepare for my return first to Mons and then to my home. Our daughter, Catherine, took tap and ballet lessons. Our five-year-old granddaughter, Grace Ann, is also showing some interest in ballet.

Our trip to Russia was a great experience for George and me. It will always be one of the highlights of my life. Far too soon, we had to leave and with regrets because we didn't have enough time to see everything.

Chapter 103

George's work with General Jones took him to Afghanistan, Iraq, and other hot spots of the world. I needed to be at home in Kentucky, and I didn't like being away from Catherine. My friends complained about being separated by states. I was an ocean away from my baby girl. I also had a very sick aunt Evelyn at home. She has been battling groin cancer. She loved art and painted beautifully, so once I arrived home, she was expecting a full report.

Evelyn was my aunt, but we were about the same age. My uncle Clyde was my grandmother's son by her second marriage. I loved both my aunt and uncle. They were married when she was sixteen, and by age twenty, she had four sons and was an outstanding mother. She went back to school, got her GED, and worked in social services and the school system. Uncle Clyde was a coal miner and liked to make a few jars of good moonshine. I have had the good fortune of having known some strong women in my life.

During a visit to Belgium for a NATO foreign ministers meeting, Secretary of State Condoleezza Rice asked George to come back to Washington to become the next director general of the Foreign Service. This was a high-level assistant secretary of state position.

Well, here we go again. I had to find an apartment and move some furniture, paintings, and decorator items from Kentucky. I found a beautiful apartment with two bedrooms, an office, two and a half bathrooms, and a dining room/ living room with a kitchen that was large enough to make space for a small table. A large balcony could be made into a greenhouse with a table and two rocking chairs. I could do some entertaining on a small level. The library was perfect for some of our book collection.

The director general of the Foreign Service was responsible for assignments, policies, retirements, and recruiting people to staff our embassies abroad and offices located around the US. It was a huge responsibility from the office that enacted policies affecting over sixty thousand people. It was particularly difficult for George, as he had to make sure our embassies in Iraq and Afghanistan were fully staffed with personnel willing to serve in war zones. George was traveling a lot, with many overseas trips. I was happy to be home and to also have a beautiful apartment in Washington without the responsibilities of managing a residence overseas. But then tragedy struck.

Soon after the assignment began in Washington, I received word that my baby brother, Bill, had been diagnosed with throat cancer. Thank God, I was back in Washington when he got sick, and I received the call. The doctor in Florida said it was very serious and told Bill to get his affairs in order. George and I said, "No way. Come to Washington for treatment." Bill and his wife, Sue, came to live with us, and George helped get him into Walter Reed hospital. Bill was retired from the navy, so he was eligible for admission to this world-famous military medical facility for treatment. One morning, Sue and I went to see Bill, and Dr. Coppit, a well-known military throat specialist, came in to see him. I was holding one of Bill's hands and Sue his other as Dr. Coppit said, "Bill, you have stage four squamous cell carcinoma throat cancer."

Bill asked, "Am I going to die?"

Dr. Coppit said, "Bill, I'm a surgeon, and we're going to have a team look at this."

I have always believed in angels and prayer. Bill was no celebrity in this world, but we had so many friends and family praying for him. My sister asked for help from her church in Knoxville and her friend in Louisiana. Bill's friends in Florida, my friends in Africa and many other countries, friends in Washington, plus friends in California were praying for Bill. There had to be hundreds of people responding. We will never know the exact number, but I believed it would help us in our hour of need.

For the next few months, I was on the DC Capital Beltway taking Bill from Falls Church, Virginia, to Walter Reed. The doctors were desperately attempting to shrink the cancer. Dr. Wilson, the chief of the radiology department, was wonderful and so kind to me. My sister, Pauline, would come to Washington as often as possible to see Bill. Other family members were devastated after learning about Bill's diagnosis. Brothers Jim and Alvie loved him so very much. Nothing pleased me more than when the three brothers got together to listen to country music and drink Budweiser, Jack Daniel's, or Jim Beam. We had only each other and no parents after I was twenty-four years old. My baby Bill was fifteen when he saw Mom shot by Bob Gambrel.

My poor baby Bill was very sick but very courageous, and he was ready to fight this cancer. I would make an egg for him, but he would throw it up most of the time. He was losing weight but still fighting. No matter how sick he was, in the morning, he would shower, put on his clothes, and shave, even in the darkest times. He had to have his hair combed before going out; that's a family thing. His clothes were kept nice. I would iron his shirts. I had been his protector all his life and wouldn't let anyone hurt him. We kept chugging along lie the train in the children's storybook *The Little Engine That Could*.

One morning Bill, Sue, and I went to Walter Reed. Bill and Sue went to another office. I decided to go by Dr. Wilson's office and see how much shrinkage of the tumor we had. He pulled up the latest scan on his computer screen. He asked me for Bill's name again. He thought he had pulled up the wrong screen. He was in disbelief because the cancer wasn't there. Later, he told me it was the biggest cancer he had seen and now it was gone. I ran down to the hall to find Bill and Sue. I gave them the news, and we got in a huddle, hugging each other and crying. My brother went on for six years before the cancer came back with a vengeance.

Catherine was a great support for her uncle Bill during his seven-year struggle with throat cancer. Matthew, her husband, was always good to Bill. She loved all three of my brothers, but Bill, who called her "Cat," was her favorite.

Chapter 104

After Bill's treatment at Walter Reed, Bill and Sue returned home to Florida, and I went home to Kentucky. Evelyn was still fighting her cancer. Maybe she didn't get dressed every day in street clothes, but she retained her elegant self. She would dress in silk pajamas and could do some amazing head wraps after she lost her hair. My uncle Clyde would say with adoration, "Mother, would you like a cup of coffee?" Her home was small, and I called it a jewel box. Evelyn's mother, brother, and sisters were helping with her care. She went to Lexington, Kentucky, where she could stay with her sister when she was having treatments.

I took a painting of mine to put in Evelyn's bedroom on an easel. On the next visit, I would change the painting for another one. I rotated art books and art magazines for her. I didn't want to clutter her bedroom. I liked the magazine *Art & Antiques*, and Evelyn liked the *American Art Review*. Evelyn was a great cook, and my uncle liked to help in the kitchen. We got to take one trip together. We went to Shelbyville, Kentucky, to visit Uncle Robert and Aunt Dorothy. Remember, Uncle Robert had met his brother by his mother's second marriage late in life. Unfortunately, Evelyn and I never got to Washington to see the National Gallery of Art. I regretted it, but she hesitated, thought about it, and said, "So what? We had the dream."

When I got home from Russia, I went to the hospital to see Evelyn. She said, "Sit down beside me. Pull up a chair and tell me everything." She was a very pretty woman, and I loved her, and she loved me. My father's ancestors had made their way into Kentucky and settled in Little Clear Creek, where Evelyn lived.

Evelyn is buried in the cemetery at Fuson Chapel. I can see why the Fusons chose Little Clear Creek, as it is a beautiful location with hills and valleys in one of the prettiest hollows in Bell County. My uncle Clyde was lost and lonely without her. Now I must write more hurtful news.

Chapter 105

In March 2008, my wonderful uncle Robert died. I wrote earlier about our good times in Kentucky and Zimbabwe. Aunt Dorothy and Uncle Robert loved Africa. After his daughter, Mary Dean, found us here in Kentucky, we had twenty-one years of enjoying life. I estimate there were fifty family members who adored them. Uncle Robert helped Aunt Dorothy with her antique business after he retired from General Electric. He was our MacGyver and could repair anything. Robert and Dorothy were like the *American Pickers* on the History Channel. They had a van and traveled for enjoyment, looking for that next treasure.

On one of Uncle Robert's visits to Pineville, we went for a drive together. Normally, we were never alone because he was so popular. He told me his heart was out of rhythm, and no doctors had been able to correct the problem. I understood that the extra burden he was carrying was quickly wearing his heart out. I didn't say anything, and he didn't elaborate. We just got quiet and rode down the mountain. We never talked about it again.

Uncle Robert's funeral service was very special. My husband, George, is a fantastic public speaker and spoke at the funeral. Catherine and I think he speaks better than President Clinton. He got so attached to Uncle Robert. Both had a love of adventure and history books; I also always have a book with me. I felt Uncle Robert and I were alike in ways that can't be explained. He was cremated.

Aunt Dorothy did well considering the loss of her husband. They were partners in everything. Aunt Dorothy by now had outlived her husband and three of her children. I cannot fathom that much hurt.

Aunt Dorothy started a five-year plan of everything she wanted to accomplish. George had found the location where all the antiques were collected and stored for decorating new Cracker Barrel restaurants around the country. He had a connection to get us a private tour by invitation only. Aunt Dorothy had enough antiques to decorate twenty restaurants, so she looked forward to that tour. She was a charmer and loved beautiful things but finding something she loved pleased her the most.

Aunt Dorothy was ready to travel with us. George watched a Ken Burns documentary on our national parks and wanted to buy a motor home to travel the country. I said, "It isn't my dream, but buy one if you want one." George did and we had some nice trips. But sadly, Aunt Dorothy did not go with us.

Chapter 106

On June 7, 2008, Catherine had a beautiful wedding in a million-dollar setting. The venue was at Pine Mountain State Resort Park, the oldest state park in Kentucky. Uncle Robert couldn't be there. He died just a few months too soon. His nickname for Catherine was Petunia. Aunt Dorothy came with her daughter Donna. My wonderful aunt Della didn't attend. Mr. Madon, the mayor of Pineville, was there, as was my friend Dr. Glover, who came from Knoxville. The Ebie family from Chicago and Kathleen and daughter Juliette from Nassau were also there. They had been to Pineville lots of times. Kathleen came early to see if I needed help. Juliette was a bridesmaid for Catherine's wedding. Matthew, my son-in-law-to-be, came with his parents, who were at our home for the first time. I can't mention everyone, but all were very important. Brother Bill didn't make the trip because he was still very ill.

I arranged a breakfast buffet at our home for everyone. Our home didn't have much parking, so we got a limousine from Knoxville for the day to shuttle people from White Church, my mother's family church and the oldest in our county. The driver had to make several trips. It turned out beautifully.

Pine Mountain State Resort Park, the wedding venue, is very special to our community. Each year, during the last week of May, we have a big event for our small town, the Mountain Laurel Festival. High Schools from throughout Kentucky send princess candidates to compete in a beauty pageant that lasts the weekend. The events include a parade, street dance, and breakfast at someone's home for the queen candidates, who represent universities. The culmination is the crowning of the queen by the governor at Laurel Cove, in the park.

In early May, workers clean the park and our city to get Pineville all decked out for this big event. Business owners do beautiful window treatments with posters of the princess and queen candidates. A huge rock in the park has steps that lead down behind the beautiful pond. Park personnel add beautiful blue coloring to the water and make the pond look gorgeous. The mountain laurels and the rhododendron bushes are in full bloom. No price could be put on a venue like this. Catherine was married in the park a few days after the festival, so everything still looked fantastic.

In the evening after the wedding, a deejay provided great music at the main lodge. I gave him a disc from my favorite club in Yaoundé, Cameroon. He wasn't thrilled, but he played it. Something magical happened, and the dance floor was crowded. Everyone loved the music. Cousin Bill and his wife, Linda, came from Irvine, California. They were doing their thing on the floor. Terry and Jill, our friends from Laguna Beach who had visited us in Zimbabwe, were having a great time. Jill made a big entrance at the wedding, especially with her red hat. Doris, my artist friend, carved a beautiful heart from a rare stone for Matthew and Catherine's wedding gift. Doris had been here before, and her husband, Craig, made his first trip to Pineville.

Denise Israel and her daughter Sharon, whom we had met back in the Bahamas, were present. Denise and I had never lost contact. Sharon was also one of Catherine's bridesmaids. Denise had always been into photography. Her wedding gift to Matthew and Catherine was a beautiful photo album of the wedding. The father of the groom, Dr. Bill Randolph, escorted Aunt Dorothy down the aisle to her seat in the amphitheater. Aunt Della and Uncle Robert should have been there. They'd had a previous journey to make, and I couldn't go with them. They had crossed over to the other side of life. Maybe they were watching from their "Room at the Top." That's a song by Tom Petty that my brother liked.

George's friend Jerry Rolwes, from his air force days at Hill Air Force Base in Utah, also took photos. Jerry had retired as a lieutenant colonel. George encouraged Jerry to take up photography after retirement because he was always taking photos. Jerry developed a professional photography business and gifted Matthew and Catherine with a wedding album like the ones he produced for his clients. Between Jerry and Denise, Catherine has great wedding memories.

I should mention that my daughter's best friend was a man. What to do when Catherine wanted her best friend to be her principal maid of honor? Well, it worked out great! Catherine and Eric had been best friends for about eleven years, ever since the Bahrain School in Manama, Bahrain. For the wedding, Catherine asked Eric to be her "man of honor."

We had a wonderful dinner before the dancing began. I worked closely with Wanda, the banquet manager, and I was very pleased. I have planned many buffets and formal dinners in my life. I had table floral arrangements made to order. I have been accused for many years of being a perfectionist. It is true, and I confess to being guilty, but when the cards start coming in with the accolades, George will say, "Mama J [or Jodi], you've done it again."

Aunt Della always said, "In this family, at a special event, there always has to be a family member who makes an ass out of himself." In keeping with family tradition, Brother Jim had too much to drink because his ex-wife, Tina, was there with her new husband, David. Jim and Tina were married for twenty years, but Tina would always be part of the family. Ninety percent of the guests didn't know there was a problem. Someone came to me and explained there was a problem with Jim. I went out on the porch, and two doctors who were guests were checking on Jim. I said, "He isn't going to mess up Catherine's wedding." Brother Alvie put him in the back of his car, took him to the hospital, and literally tossed him in the emergency room door. Alvie returned and hit the dance floor. He didn't miss much of the music and dancing.

Doctor and Mrs. Ebie were our guests, and when the music started, I asked him to dance with me. They are Cameroonian but have lived in Chicago for many years. I met their son Kenny at our residence when we were assigned to Cameroon. Kenny was studying there and was born in Chicago.

Catherine and Matthew danced the night away. They had a beautiful wedding surrounded by family and their friends from college. My daughter was beginning a new chapter of her life, but to me, she'll always be that little girl traveling with us around the world and making sure our boarding passes were safe!

Reconnecting in Munich, Germany with my "little sister" Claudia and her daughter Lara.

In our private compartment on the train from Moscow to St. Petersburg.

Visiting Moscow's open air art market. Another shopping opportunity!

My baby brother Bill.

Retirement recognition, well deserved, from Secretary of State Condoleezza Rice.

The satisfaction of completing with George a successful 26-year diplomatic career.

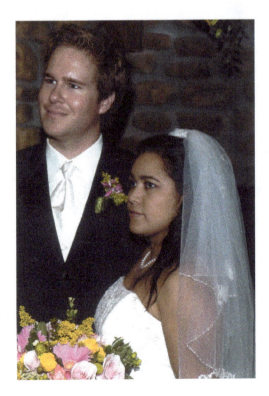

Matthew Randolph and Catherine on their wedding day.

With my friends; on my right Kathleen and daughter Juliette, and on my left Denise and daughter Sharon. The girls and Catherine met in the first grade in The Bahamas.

Catherine's bridesmaids holding her "man of honor."

Chapter 107

After Catherine's wedding, I survived a vicious grizzly bear attack in Alaska on August 28, 2008. I had traveled to Alaska for a week of trekking, sightseeing, and photography. Little did I know that my life would be changed forever.

Oh, to the poor souls who make decisions without having enough information. That was what happened to me. George and I had gone shopping at Whole Foods Market in Lexington, Kentucky. On our way out, George picked up a free magazine. That was the beginning of pleasure, pain, and trauma that would change my life forever. On Sunday morning, I was reading a good book when George came into the bedroom and said, "There's an article in the magazine for a ladies trip to Alaska with a Zen master." We had gone to a few Zen classes in Alexandria, Virginia, before we retired; I never did understand those damn koans. I always felt pressure from the Zen master to come up with a very profound explanation.

The next few weeks were a whirlwind of activity. I had to spend a lot of money and time getting ready for the trip. I started to have misgivings about the commitment I had made. George had made the call and sent the full amount in because I was told I was the last to register. That wasn't the truth because two people didn't decide until the last day. There were seven females, including me.

When I talked with Anne, the Zen master, I asked, "What are the security arrangements?"

I discovered she would be our only security. Anne said, "I am certified in Maine to use a sawed-off shotgun."

My heart sank. At some point, I realized we were going to the home of the grizzly bear in the Brooks Mountain Range in the far north of Alaska.

Anne Dellenbaugh was the owner of Her Wild Song Tour Company, a wilderness guiding business. She was a Harvard Divinity School graduate and a former Zen priest who purported to be a master of meditation and yoga practices. Her experience, however, was centered on kayak and canoe trips, mainly in Maine. I had been so enthralled with the website and brochures we were reading that I thought I would feel like Ayla in Jean Auel's book *The Clan of the Cave Bear*. On the front of Anne's brochure was a scene of two women overlooking an escarpment into a gorge. The caption said, "Touch the Wild." I was hooked as my pioneering instincts took over my logical mind. I did, however, look forward to being with Anne, as I was very interested in her possible help with my Zen meditation experience and as a way of helping with my PTSD issues from our difficult overseas assignments and my life before the Foreign Service.

For our anniversary during our assignment in Zimbabwe, I had treated George and me to a hunting safari. I was working at the embassy, and my money was burning a hole in my pocket. We had professional hunters, trackers, skinners, cooks, and even a spore man, who stuck his finger in animal poop to check the temperature and guess how long it had been since a herd of Cape buffalo, kudus, or elephants had passed through the area. But most importantly, we had security! I didn't expect a Hemingway experience with a director's chair with my name on it, but I did assume we would have an armed, hairy-chested man with a high-powered rifle. Wrong!

The check cleared the bank, and it was too late to turn back. I picked flowers from my garden—a sample of my grandmother's old tea rose, a sample of morning glories that my mother loved, and a rosebud from my new knockout red rose bush—and taped them into my journal. I was on my way to Fairbanks to meet my traveling companions. The following are notes from my travel journal as written:

> *Arrived in Fairbanks on the Eighteenth of August. It was a good trip and very uneventful, just the way I like it. Cincinnati, via Chicago, Anchorage, Fairbanks. I found the bed and breakfast, Vivian's Place, on second street. I was a little shocked by the lodgings, but everything turned out well. Anne arrived and I felt better. Slept great but very tired.*

Tuesday — 19th: Had my camera checked, went to a small museum, saw an art museum, and had a nice lunch. Two more ladies arrived (very nice) and one was a nurse. Fairbanks isn't that interesting, but I haven't seen very much, and maybe I should be more objective. So far, I like all my traveling companions. Went shopping for rubber boots (light blue) and a knife because I couldn't bring one from home. Had an hour for Jim Beam and Coke before I had dinner with the girls. The bed and breakfast is growing on me and everyone is very pleasant and excited. The B&B let me leave my extra luggage. I'm so tired of packing and unpacking.

Wednesday — 20th. Up at 6:00 a.m.—read until 12:30. Will need an afternoon nap. Have gone through my gear check for the 20th time; no joking. I'm fuckin' tired of the worry. Ain't having fun yet!!! My Last Shopping for "Things". Extra batteries, toothpaste, camp chair, etc. Soon it will be yoga time. Got to do another check of my full pack and day pack.

After we left the B&B in Fairbanks, we traveled by bus on the Dalton Highway to historical Wiseman, where we spent our first night in the old dance hall turned into a B&B. I liked the place because I had a feather bed and felt like I was in Germany with Claudia. We left early the next morning for Coldfoot. We met Dirk and his wife, Danielle, the owners of Coyote Air Service. The airport building was small and decorated to fit with the environment. It would take two flights to get seven women and all the cargo into the single-engine plane. I went on the second flight.

Dirk was our pilot for the trip to the Gates of the Arctic National Park in the central Brooks Range. On a positive note, the hour-long flight was beautiful beyond description. We had traveled a long way by bus and single-engine plane. We were so remote; I didn't think we would see anyone.

Journal entry — August 21: The first day in camp, up early for yoga and meditation, a quick breakfast, and I'm too cold and tired to write. Everything hurts!!! My whole body aches. I didn't sleep much last night. I was so cold and a bit scared. Anne wouldn't let me buy my own bear spray in Coldfoot. I had no bear spray, but in the end, she gave me one and I had to leave it outside the tent. I tied it to the tent stake and put a rock on top of it.

It felt like a wind tunnel at night. The gorge might have been cut by an iceberg. All the other women are wonderful. One young girl has been especially nice to me. She helped me with my day pack and water bag that fits in my pack with a tube running to my shoulder. I can get the tube to my mouth and drink. That gives me freedom to have my hands free. I need to use both walking poles. I was too tired to eat.

Friday — 22nd: We could hear wolves this morning. What an eerie feeling!!! Hope they stay upon the ridge. Thank God for my walking poles. Today was difficult, stress on my whole body. Anne and Sharon came by for nighttime caroling outside my tent. The wind is blowing so hard. I had frost on my tent this morning. I'm going to sleep in gloves. The hand warmers help and I'm going to put them in my sleeping bag. I will go to sleep. I am going to sleep kissing Jonathan (my good luck seagull). I had him made by a jeweler in Laguna Beach in 1975 in Laguna Beach. My daughter Catherine's bandana in my hand. Thinking of everyone in Kentucky; especially nephew Ben.

Saturday — 23rd. The women are all different. Everyone has partners with the exception of Sharon and me. I'm married and Sharon was too, but she lost her husband of many years. She's 68 and here to spread her husband's ashes. I'm 61 and everyone else is in their 30s, 40s and 50s. Lois is struggling because she had a broken foot that is still healing. Wonder what tomorrow will bring? I hope it will be hiking on flat land. Today was like climbing Pine Mountain three times, with no trees. We have lots of rocks and cliffs. There are no trees here but millions and millions of rocks, small ones!!! I feel like I'm climbing a slate bank. You have to be from a coal mining state to understand; slate comes from residue from coal; it is small and with dust. I climbed a volcano in El Salvador, hiked in a rainforest in Equatorial Guinea, walked on the Black Beach in Cameroon, but this is the granddaddy of them all.

Sunday — 24th. There is pain that medicine can't take away. I knew that before, but this place has driven it home big time. In all this vastness I have never felt so alone. I'm so lonesome I could cry. I believe there's an old country song with that title. Is it a song by Hank Williams? Bet a million I will not hear a whip-poor-will in Alaska. I miss Uncle Joe and it hurts to think of losing him. I dreamt of Aunt Addie last night. In this place of such stark beauty, so removed from life, yet there is nature of a different kind. There's so much yellow, a nice red, and the ground is gray; lots of plain old dirt, and rugged terrain. My tent has no floor padding, and the ground hurts my knees. I am always crawling on my knees for something; can't stand up in the tent. I have my body and soul pain to deal with in Gates of the Arctic National Park. Yesterday's walk was so painful coming off the mountain. Wonder what tomorrow will bring?

Monday — 25th. This not what I expected, but then on second thought I had no expectations. I wanted to go to the beach!!! A bad choice got me here. God help me finish. I have experienced such physical pain from this difficult trip. The hiking was so difficult because of the deep ruts from where the caribou had migrated, and we were late in the season so there is frost on our tents from the severe cold we experience every night and early morning.

In the morning, there's no talking. I don't know what to make of Anne. There are moments when I'm so very sorry I came on this trip. Then, I'm okay with where this trip has taken me. We ate pancakes, not the pancake house type. Sorry Sharon, our cook [this is not the other woman I befriended named Sharon], you are working under adverse conditions. Two caribou walked through the camp. They joined two more and I watched the four travel along the river together. "Where in the Hell are you, Jo Ann?" Will have to look for a weaver bird nest to determine what is east or west. Jo Ann, "you aren't going to see weaver birds here!" I saw weaver birds in my garden in Zimbabwe and out in the African bush, but not in Alaska.

Tuesday — 26th. George Brooks has been on my mind. He was my first husband and he died before I came on this trip. Ours was a pure young love. We were young but very much in love. He was in my life from 13 years of age until I was 22. Those were important years in my life. He was a very private person and a very hard-working man. His death has hurt me. I knew where he was and had his work number if I needed him. I pray for his soul. "George, if you are somewhere and know what I am think-ing let me say I'm sorry for the hurt we caused each other. There was so much I wanted to say to you when I came to see you, but your wife never left us alone. I kept one promise to you and never had my hair cut short again. You've come to me in my dreams since your death. You want me to come to you, but I can never determine upon awakening if you are alive or dead. Our good and bad times will remain unspoken. My grandmother, who I loved so very much and you loved, always said, "Speak nicely of the dead or say nothing at all."

Wednesday — 27th. Anne tells me that today we have to be silent from noon to 3 p.m. I did some housekeeping inside of the tent. I then did some work outside. From the hike the day before I got stuck in the mud. The suction pulled off my rubber boots. I washed my socks in water so swift one sock was washed out of my hand. I'm with a group of women and three of us don't belong. Anne moves around the campsite at 5:30 a.m. doing some kind of chanting. Does this purify the camp and keep the grizzly bears at bay?

I'm so cold. I can't do all the yoga movements. The Zen meditation position is difficult. I wish I could do everything but now they are too painful. I have to make it okay because I now have limitations that I have to accept. Damn!! I wish life could be like a blackboard so I could take an eraser and start all over again. Then, I'd start my life over since I can't live in the moment. I turn to nature as I always do and close my eyes and listen to the sounds.

August 27 — On our last full day in camp I asked to be on the first flight to Wiseman. I want out of here. Today will be about a seven-mile hike. My knees hurt, elbows are raw, hands hurt. The pain is beyond description in my left shoulder. I wish I could stay in camp, but I can't for obvious reasons. We have to be in groups of two to three, but that rule has been broken many times.

These are the last of the notes from my journal.

Chapter 108

On the morning of August 28, 2008, at about 6:00 a.m., I was sitting on my sleeping bag in my tent, packing everything into my main pack. I felt something rub against my back through the tent material. I knew it was a bear from the height and feeling. My thinking was to be very quiet and not to move. God, please let him keep moving away. There had been other animals moving through the campsite during the week, but this was different. If I heard something, I would turn off my headlamp, stop reading, and slide down in my sleeping bag. But this time was different.

The bear hit the canvas material hard at the bottom of my sleeping bag but didn't break through. My mind was calculating the situation rapidly. I looked around the tent for something to fight with, but there was nothing. The bear spray was outside tied to a stake, and I had two zippers to get through and not enough time. He hit the second time in the same spot. I put my back to the side where he hit the tent. The sound was loud and vicious as he came at me, his mouth open as he burst through. All I had to fight him with was my feet and my hands. He had my leg in his mouth, and I remember being lifted off my hips. I kicked him with my right leg, and he swung me from side to side. I remember thinking, "God, is this the way it is meant to be?" At some point, I started screaming for Anne.

After that, I don't remember much, and maybe that is a blessing. Was it a dream? Then the strangest thing happened. There was a man's voice behind my right shoulder. He was saying, "What are you going to do now?" That's all I remember until Jen, one of the ladies in our group, was cutting me out of the tent. She was a critical care nurse. The cooking tent was on the ground, but Sharon the cook had managed to find one knife sharp enough to cut the tent material. Jen said she could hear me moaning and saw blood. She told me later that I said, "A bear tried to eat me, but I kicked it!" Afterwards, my memory would come and go.

Jen was trying to assess my injuries and stop the blood flow. There wasn't a proper first aid kit. The other lady helping was Lois, who had a bad ankle. She had an Ace bandage. She had been to nursing school but had chosen to work in the administrative section of a medical facility. A lot of this information was told to me later. I had Ace bandages for my knees and pain pills in my backpack. I was talking but don't remember clearly what was going on in camp. It was very cold, and we were too late in the season to be doing this camping trip. Jen's plan was to keep me from going into shock. I had been mauled seriously. Two big bites on my right leg had done lots of damage, and I was badly injured on my right hand and arm. My left shoulder was slashed to the bone, and I had face, ear, and ear canal damage.

Anne said that when she heard my screaming, she thought someone was having a bad dream. Anne and Sharon made noise and distracted the bear away from me. Sharon banged two oil cans together. They ran to the cooking tent and managed to find some bear spray. They discharged it, and the loud sound and plume of orange smoke frightened the animal. He retreated. By this time, some of the other women were up and started beating on pots and pans. The bear knocked over a couple of tents, crossed over the rapid water that surrounded the camp, and looked back as if to think about returning. I would learn later that we were camped too far apart on a sandbar with rapid water running around us. An experienced Kentucky hunter said that many things were done wrong with setting up the campsite.

I learned later that after the attack, Anne was sitting on a rock as if lost in space. Anne had called Dirk, our pilot, to come quickly. His original plan was to arrive at 8:00 a.m., but he wanted to come at 10:00 a.m. because of bad weather. There was a very low ground fog and poor visibility. God bless Dirk! He had a meeting with his wife and two children, and they decided that despite the bad weather, he would try to find us. We heard him overhead, but he flew away once and came back a second time. Through a break in the clouds, he saw the sandbar and landed. I will be forever grateful to Dirk and the risk he took to help me.

I was covered in sleeping bags to keep warm, given hot tea, and talked to by my traveling partners. The back seat was taken out of Dirk's plane, and Dirk and some of the ladies used a sleeping bag as a drawsheet to lift me into the plane. During our flight, Sharon was holding my head in her lap and giving me soft kisses on my forehead. Jen was holding my legs, and the other Sharon was touching me from the copilot's seat. I asked them to sing to me. The song they sang by Libby Roderick was very helpful:

How could anyone ever tell you
you are anything less than beautiful?
How could anyone ever tell you
you were less than whole?
How could anyone fail to notice
that your loving is a miracle?
How deeply you're connected to my soul. . . .

Chapter 109

I prayed to God, my Cherokee women ancestors (I'm one-sixteenth on my grandmother's side,) my great-grandmother, Grandmother Mammie, my mother, and Aunt Della to come to me for strength to endure the pain. Dirk said it would be more painful during the descent to the oil company site. They had a medical team ready and a specially equipped helicopter to fly me to Fairbanks. The lights went out, and I don't remember the flight. The next thing I remember was the hospital with Jen and a Dr. Wennen getting me ready for surgery. Dr. Wennen had talked to George in Kentucky and told him about my injuries. I was in surgery for seven hours. The next afternoon, George and my daughter arrived at the hospital and were briefed by Dr. Wennen, and so began the long recovery that will never end.

Let me speak to you about my precious Catherine. She is a take-charge kind of young woman. She rolled up her sleeves and got busy getting Mom cleaned up; she knows her mother. Hair is very important. My hair had been left long, except for the right side of my head that had been shaved back about four inches to make room to reattach my right ear.

I was in a foggy place. I was looking out, and I was on my back. I saw a big canvas. It was from the ground to the sky. It had no margins on the right and left sides, but it was not like a piece of paper. This was very disconcerting because I didn't understand. Was it real? Was it a dream? Was I seeing the sky? At the bottom right side, near the ground, I saw the number two. Then way up high on the left, I saw the number seventeen. What did it mean? To this day, I have no understanding of this vision. What was it? If I ever get to Las Vegas again, I will bet two and seventeen.

I had another unique experience at the Fairbanks Hospital. Every hospital in the US should have a "car wash"-type facility. That's what I named it because

326

I was run through a large shower room. Someone had taken some PVC pipe and made a gurney and chairs. Ceramic chairs were built against the wall with lots of shower heads. The nurses gave my daughter a heavy-duty yellow raincoat with a hood and boots. The nurses also had raincoats and boots. I was sprayed off on the gurney. No sponge bath could clean me up.

Catherine climbed behind a ceramic chair. She was above my head and ready to wash her mother's hair. What a mess my hair was in, and she was just the person to clean it. She discovered sausage-size mud patties made from dirt, weeds, and, she assumed, bear saliva. She knew I wouldn't want my hair cut. The nurse brought scissors to cut the mud patties out. George had a motel room where he and Catherine could, if they wished, rest and shower after visiting me. A bed was brought into the room, and Catherine stayed most of the time.

Chapter 110

All my traveling companions came to see me the next day. After fourteen years, I still have difficult times because of what happened. I relive the experience often and especially late at night when I can't sleep. Anne had made so many mistakes. The first big one was at the ranger station in Coldfoot, when she wouldn't allow me to get bear spray. I had gone up to the counter to buy it, but Anne said I didn't need any. She was buying four for seven to share. That upset me because it went against everything I had read and learned about bear safety. I should have gone against her wishes, and I should have had bear spray in my tent.

I was well prepared for this trip. I came to camp on the second flight with supplies, camping equipment, and so on. Anne helped me pick a campsite. I saw bear spore by my tent. I mentioned it to her. She said it was old, but I knew better because I had seen on DVD and photos in books what bear scat looked like. This was new with bright red berries.

I assumed Anne would demonstrate the shotgun and satellite phone. Never happened. I saw a bag for carrying the shotgun, but the weapon was never taken out of the bag. It just lay there on the ground outside of the cooking tent, collecting dust. I wanted to leave, but I'm no quitter. Plus, I couldn't afford to call Dirk to come get me. What an uncomfortable situation I had gotten myself into this time. The site was wrong, and Anne's information was misleading. She might have had kayaking and canoeing experience, but I learned later that Alaska was new on her website.

Anne, Sharon, and Lois were great assistants who helped Jen. Lois gave Jen all the credit for saving me and said some of her nursing skills that she hadn't used in years kicked in. Rene, another of my traveling companions, was making hot water for tea. Her tent was the farthest from me. She didn't know what was happening in the beginning.

All the women were heroes. They were incredibly courageous. Jen stabilized me and stopped me from bleeding out. Sharon, our cook, came to Kentucky to check on me, give me emotional support, and cook for me. I love Sharon. I met her partner, Mary, in Maine. I have their photo in my kitchen in Cincinnati. Her soft kisses saved me! Our group met the following year in Booth Bay, Maine, in 2009. Jen took me sailing. It was a beautiful day to be alive.

Chapter 111

When George and I returned from Alaska, we flew to the Cincinnati/ Northern Kentucky International Airport. We went to an airport hotel for me to rest before the drive home. Marian came to view the remains. Only joking! Henry, my friend for years, came with Marian. My platonic friend Dick, whom I had known since I was nineteen, was no longer living. He would have had a difficult time with what happened to me in Alaska.

When we dove home and got near my hollow, we stopped at my brother Jim's house. He came to my side of the car. He was very emotional and said to George, "Thanks for bringing her home alive." He turned with tears in his eyes and went into his house. Before I left for Alaska, he had given me a note that said, "*Sis, thinking of you this morning. A peach for a peach of a sister. I love you, Jimmy Cecil. Have a good trip and enjoy yourself.*"

Sometime later, maybe a couple of days, I started waking up slowly. I was lost. I didn't know where I was. I saw a doorframe that made me feel a little better, then some rocks that gave me comfort. I was seeing the huge fireplace I had designed for the master bedroom because I love rocks. Then I saw my skylight in the ceiling and realized I was in my bedroom. Something had happened to me. It wasn't a dream. It wasn't a normal waking up. I don't know what to call it. I felt down the side of my leg, and the Ace bandage was there. I started to cry, then cried harder and harder. This was real and I was hurting. My bear attack had been real. George tried to calm me down, but I was lost in pain. The hurt was unbearable.

Chapter 112

I met a beautiful woman in the office of my gynecologist, Dr. Glover. Her name is Cindy McClellan. She knew a man named Bobby Drinnon, who was a visionary. People flew in from many places for consultations with him. The waiting list was years long. Cindy spoke about the hurts in her life, especially her brother's and her mother's deaths. I talked about the bear attack. She had gone to Mr. Drinnon several times and had a prearranged hour with him in Middletown, Tennessee. She was very gracious and shared a half hour of her time with me. Cindy took me to his office and introduced me to him.

I was having a very difficult time, especially regarding the man's voice I heard as I lay injured during or after the attack. I wanted to know if Bobby Drinnon could help me with the words I heard. The man had said, "What are you going to do now?" After all the things I had done in my life, I just didn't understand that question. Mr. Drinnon said maybe it was God. I said, "I talk to him often, but he has never answered me. That would be too arrogant."

He said, "What if you were so near death, you had to make a choice to give in to death or to want to live?"

That made sense to me, and I thought that answer was possible. I will always believe in angels. Cindy stayed very helpful and close to me for the first couple of years after the bear attack.

A woman at the Dallas airport approached me when Bob and I were on our way to Iran. She said, "I don't mean to bother you, but I see a woman who is very old, and her hair is parted in the middle. She is on your shoulder. She will always be with you to protect you, so you don't have to worry." She had described my great-great grandmother Goodin. I have a photo of her, and she fits the description. I prayed to the women in my family for help on the flight to Coldfoot and Fairbanks, Alaska. I will always believe they helped me survive the bear attack.

Chapter 113

After surviving the bear attack and returning home to Kentucky, I had many years of physical and occupational therapy, plus countless medical appointments with pain management and orthopedic specialists. It was many months before I could walk from one end of my house to the other, and it was a year before I could drive again. While I had no more follow-up surgeries, I still carry scars on my face, arms, hands, and legs that will always be with me. My right hand still torments me. I wear a glove most of the time. I haven't worn a short dress or stockings in years. I cannot wear high-heeled shoes ever again. I go to the beach when I have an opportunity, but I stay covered up, and I can't let the skin graft on my leg get too much sun.

Soon after I came home, Jackie, Marlene, Modean, and Cora—my aunt Della's daughters—came to see me. All four are wonderful women. They were not afraid to see me. I got news that some people were uncomfortable visiting me because they didn't want to see me after the attack. I had great care from my family doctor, Dr. Talmadge Hays. Dr. Hays told me that when he looked at my eyes, the lights were out, as I was still deeply traumatized. He followed Dr. Wennen's suggestions for follow-up care when I got home. It took eight pillows in the bed for my body to be positioned properly, two under my head, two to support my wounded left arm, two for my wounded right leg, and two for my right hand and arm. Doctors who have looked at the photos of my injuries before and after surgery said I shouldn't be alive.

As for special friends and family, it hurts that I will not see Laurie in her floral dress, bottle of wine under her arm, and a smoke to complement the wine. She died in 2009 in a terrible motorcycle accident. She had planned to teach me to ride her son Chandler's small Harley-Davidson. We were serious, and it would have happened if Laurie had lived.

Laurie wrecked her Harley late at night in Knoxville going into a steep curve. It was a battle for her trying to come off the respirator. No point in writing all the details. John, Laurie's father, came from Florida to Knoxville and made all the arrangements. He drove back home with his daughter's ashes in the passenger seat. I have tears in my eyes writing this because I can't imagine the pain. He and Laurie's sisters took their boat out and scattered her ashes in the ocean. My life would have been much richer with her in it. We would have traveled together, and I know we would have gone back to Cameroon with a stop in Paris to see her sister Julie. John and I have talked about more details for my book. For a long time, I just could never ask questions about the accident that eventually took her life. I hate this life I'm caught up in sometimes.

I liked to call Uncle Clyde and go for a visit, especially after Aunt Evelyn's death. I would request country cookin', and he was a great cook. On one occasion, he had put a wood-and-coal-burning stove in the living room. I said, "If Evelyn were alive, you wouldn't get away with the stove." Wood and coal will keep a house very hot, but it is a lot of work to keep the ash and black coal dust from settling all over everything. He laughed and said the heat pump in the house was to please her.

One fateful day, Uncle Clyde's son, my cousin Randy, said that when he went to get his son from school, Uncle Clyde was going to cut wood. He told his dad that when he got back, he would help unload and stack the wood. When Randy returned, he found my precious uncle dead on the front porch. He had a heart attack while unloading the wood. I wish Uncle Clyde had never bought the damn stove.

Hiking with the group on a hillside in Alaska

Back at the cooking tent for tea and planning for the next day's hike.

An example of the vastness of Alaska.

Thank God for Jen who save my life.

My beautiful cousins who came to cheer me up after the bear attack.

My sister whose love and support is always there when needed.

Chapter 114

Let me turn my thoughts in another direction. I have loved California since age twenty-five. I go as often as time, work, and money permit. I go to see Doris and Craig wherever they are living. I remember from when we first met and they had just a one-room place with a small kitchen to today, when they have a lovely home in Ventura, California, close to the yacht club from where they go sailing. Doris is a fantastic artist, and Craig is a well-respected engineer. They've come a long way from the old green van in which she traveled the coast, searching for driftwood to carve.

I always liked going back to Laguna Beach to see Terry and Jill. Pat and Patricia live in Northern California in Sebastopol and have a winery. Vel Miller, my artist friend from Nassau days, and her husband, Warren, live in Central California. Their home defies description. She has a studio where she still paints mostly western art. On their ranch they raise longhorn cattle. Lauren and Diana Rambo from Zimbabwe days live in Fresno, California. Robert Rackstraw, whom I loved, sadly has passed from this life. I'd sometimes meet him at Terry and Jill's whenever I returned, or we would meet at the Newport 17 restaurant. When Catherine was about three, during a visit, I wanted Robert to see my daughter. They played and he did drawings of helicopters for her, and she liked that a lot. Females of all ages loved him.

Doris and I like the Big Sur area, and we have a secret cove that's all ours. Ken and I explored the whole coast when I first got to California in 1974. I've been to Hearst Castle five or six times and have gone sailing with Doris and Craig in the Channel Islands. I've camped out in Yosemite Valley several times and have enjoyed skiing in Bear Valley.

Chapter 115

As I've said, for many years, I had been seeing a clinical psychologist in Cincinnati, Ohio, even before the bear attack. Dr. Fliman was originally from Chile, and was so kind, soft spoken, and insightful that I always and still do consider her a friend. She told me I have lived a "high-risk, high-reward life." These words are posted on my refrigerator door. I have thought about that for years.

Looking back, I think she was right. She had diagnosed me with PTSD before the Alaska trip. I told her the trip was meant to help my PTSD. God, it almost killed me both physically and mentally. After fourteen years, I am still confused and cry in the shower. Sometimes, I feel more and more alone with each passing day.

The bear attack in Alaska has changed my life forever. I am living with inoperable nerve damage, and my PTSD is very difficult to manage alone. Here in our small town, there are no support groups. I just have one little shih tzu dog. He weighs about fifteen pounds, and I was wondering when to introduce him in my book. My therapist said a little dog might help. Brother Jim said, "Sis, you need a little dog." In him, George gave me, us, the best gift ever.

George found him online. We went to Somerset, Kentucky, met the owners, and came home with Darius. Yes, that's the name I gave him. He is seven years old now. People who meet him will say, "Oh, Darius Rucker, the country music singer." I tell them he was named after a famous Persian king and descends from a very old Chinese breed. He has friends named Gator, Lobster, Lamb Chop, and Giraffe, who are his favorite squeaky toys!

I had no idea what an emotional-support dog would be like. I know he can turn into a little lion if a stranger gets too close to me. He sleeps with us, usually at my feet and near the side of my body. He knows when I cry and will come running and peek over the duvet. If there are tears, he will lick them. He has steps to get up on the bed. He's not a complete cure for my pain. I like touching him because he has hair, not fur. I know he helps, but if he has had enough rubbing, he will nip at me. Darius has taken on my personality.

George helps with Darius when I'm in too much pain. I used to walk him but not so much lately. George gets up at six to take him outside or to the pee pad. George was always an early morning person, and he loves Darius. Sometimes, Darius is overprotective. Darius takes a nap on George's shoulder. I realize now that we're just Darius's "pack," but sometimes when I can't see him, I get scared that I may trip over him. I never imagined a dog sleeping in my bed. Dogs in my family were always outside to protect your home and never allowed inside. Oh, the times are a-changin'!

Chapter 116

Friends here at home have also helped me during these difficult times. Terry Lynn Dove, who lives close by, has been a special friend, neighbor, and helpmate for years. Terry and her husband, Richard, were there after the bear attack. I knew Terry's great-grandmother and great-grandfather. She comes from a strong mountain family and calls me "lovely."

Two years after the bear attack, George took me on a trip to Memphis, Tennessee, to once again visit Graceland. I'm a huge Elvis fan, and it was a wonderful experience. I remember being in Elvis's living room with a bandage on my hand, as well as a walking cane with shoulder supports for my arms and a handle for my hand: not a typical walking stick. Inside Graceland were two beautiful stained-glass panels of peacocks. I wanted a photo of me by them, and George took what I thought would be a great one. It turned out that because of the stained glass behind me, I looked like I had a peacock on my head. Laugh or cry, that is the question! I just felt I needed to go back to Graceland. I needed to feel alive and see Elvis's home once again.

We stayed at the Little River Inn. We went to Beale Street, and I knew what I wanted to do: to dance! George said, "Are you sure?" I got up and danced, and that was the first time after the bear attack. The music made me feel alive. I had almost died from the attack and not being able to do the things I loved.

Chapter 117

How much more can this woman take? More pain on the left (bad) versus the right (beautiful) branches of my tree of life, which I drew as an exercise for my psychologist. On May 12, 2011, my wonderful brother Jim died. I remember the afternoon we found him draped over his coffee table. I could not believe he was gone. He was on the floor sitting cross-legged, his back was bent over, and his face was on the table and turned to the right. I got behind him with my back to the couch, put my stomach to his back, and slid down so I could put my arms around him. I was screaming, "Oh, Jim! Oh, Jim!"

George was trying to force a Xanax into my mouth. He said, "Jodi, you're going to have a heart attack."

I stayed in that position until the ambulance arrived. I think they must have had to pry my hands away from my brother.

I'm often angry with Jim, because every day I leave my house by the back walkway, I see the angel he gave me up on the hillside in Kentucky. When I pass the cemetery, I say, "Damn you, Jim, you shouldn't be up there in a cold, dark grave." I miss his cooking. Six years ago, his two brothers Bill and Alvie and I baked the traditional old-fashioned apple stack cake he could make so well. Mammie's grandmother must have taught her, and she must have taught Jim. There was no recipe, but Jim didn't need one. The recipe had been handed down in the family. After Jim died, Bill and I got on the internet, and there was the recipe. Ours was better because Mammie used dried apples from the old apple orchard tree. She peeled and quartered them and put them on strings to dry behind her wood-and-coal-burning stove.

I discovered a singer Jim would have liked by the name of Sissel, a soprano from Norway. She does a version of "Going Home" that would have made us cry together. I prayed he would come to me in my dreams, and he has. I'm pleased to say most have been nice dreams. They're like a visit. *Good night, brother! Where is that life force/soul that left your body? Where has it gone?* Jim would have loved an old gospel song titled "Farther Along," which was sung at Elvis's funeral. Maybe someday, I will understand why. Jim would say if he could, "Cheer up, my sister. You will understand it all by and by."

What could I do for Jim now that he was no longer present? George had gotten four tickets for us to see Jim's favorite country singer. Yes, we went to see country music legend George Jones. Jim in spirit, George, Eva, and I went for Jim's birthday in September. Years before, I had given Jim a small eagle carved by women in Uruguay. Something said to take the eagle to George Jones.

George and Eva thought I would never get near George Jones. I said, "Wait for me." I saw a bus with lots of lights. I thought that inside must be someone important. It was George Jones's manager. I told him my story, and he went and got Mrs. Nancy Jones. Nancy took us backstage to meet George Jones in person, and I presented brother Jim's eagle to him. I told him he never knew my brother existed, but that Jimmy Fuson was his greatest fan. Eva, George, and I had photos taken of the presentation of the eagle.

We talked it over and decided to fold Jim's seat over during the concert in memory of him. We had third-row center seats in front of the stage. We had waited ten months to see the show which was wonderful. Jim would have loved it.

Once, I saw Jim in a dream sitting on his front porch. We were in his swing, and I was looking to his left and he to my right. He must have been crying because the side of his face was wet. I said, "Jim, you want your house back, didn't you?" I woke up.

In another dream, I was lying in my bed facing the French doors and my back porch with a balcony on top. Jim was sitting on the porch railing with both legs balancing on the two-by-four. He got up, and I thought he was going to go by the greenhouse. I ran through the house screaming, "Jim, don't go!" I never saw him again.

I have a leprechaun in my backyard. Only three people have seen him. He is wearing a coat, hat, and pointed shoes, and he is green. He has pointed shoes. Jim has seen him. Harold Patton, a good friend and backgammon player, saw him once. Harold would get so damn mad, he could never beat Jim. I have seen the leprechaun as the little green man. No one else has ever seen him. People say we were all smoked up. I'll let the reader decide. He's real.

Jim left beautiful messages on my answering machine, and he had a great sense of humor. He left a message to say, "Sis, this is your brother Jim. I'm flying in my little Cessna today. Sorry I missed you! The mountains are beautiful. I feel like I could land on them. I would love to take you up to where God lives. My personal chef will have a nice lunch prepared for me. Oh well, we will do it another time. Just wanted you to know I love you. Your big brother, Jim." I've saved two of these messages. Jim never had a Cessna or a personal chef, but he had an incredible imagination.

Jim died from abuse of prescription drugs. He got hooked after a heart attack and other health issues. I wish he could have smoked marijuana and drunk Jack Daniel's or Jim Beam. I believe we would have had a different outcome. Jim should have had medical marijuana. I need medical marijuana, but I'm stuck with pain medication from my pain doctor and urine tests every month. I love my home state, but I detest some of the politicians. They sway with the wind and have yet to authorize medical marijuana that I desperately need.

The day before he died, I stopped by to check on Jim. He was having serious withdrawal pains and wanted some of my medicine. I said, "No, Jim, you have to manage your medicine." I got in bed and held him. When I left, I said, "Do you want anything from town?" He told me to bring him a strawberry milkshake. When I returned, he took the milkshake and went back to bed. That was the last time I saw him alive.

I'm so alone without my big brother. George Jones sings a song that says, "I will be over you when the grass grows over me." If I could speak to him, I'd say, "Don't worry, Jim; we'll keep your grave clean. Pauline and Alvie still help with decorating all the family graves on Memorial Day. The only thing missing is you. Jim, I'll never stop loving you. Please come to me in another dream."

With Alvie and Pauline decorating our
family's graves on Memorial Day.

Finishing our work on Memorial Day.

My last walk with Jim before he died.

Chapter 118

Following Jim's death, I needed to see my friends and drive the Pacific Coast Highway. I was still taking pain medication for the inoperable nerve damage from the bear attack, but the ocean air was good medicine, and all my friends are wonderful. The last stop was to spend time with Terry and Jill in Laguna Beach. I didn't see Robert on this trip. We talked by phone, but he was always paranoid that the phone was bugged. We talked about his children and grandchildren.

I was packing for my trip home when I got a call that Uncle Joe had had a heart attack. I flew there at night and got to Pineville Hospital the next day as he was about to be transferred to the Baptist Hospital in Knoxville. I went in the ambulance with him and met his surgeon and heart doctor. I think the heart surgeon didn't at first want to do the operation. The doctors just saw this skinny old man. They didn't know him and knew nothing about his life. I told them about Uncle Joe's military history, about his daily walks in the mountains, and his work in the mines and mostly sawmills before he retired. He lived with his wife, my aunt Ruby, and he was her caregiver. He did his own yard work, and he was strong mentally and physically.

I gave the best sales pitch of my life for my uncle Joe. My uncle and I talked, and he agreed he didn't have any chance without surgery. That was his best option. He came out of surgery on a ventilator. I was so scared for him and stood by his bed until my hips to the bottoms of my feet hurt. The intensive care staff put no time limit on me. Uncle Joe wasn't coming off the ventilator fast enough for the doctors. I was in tears doubting myself about advocating for the surgery. But when he came out of intensive care, I cried with tears of relief and happiness.

All the nurses adored my uncle Joe. He had rehab therapy and never missed a session. He would walk in the hallway with his therapist, and when they finished the required distance and got back to his door, she would say, "Mr. North, you want to walk some more?" He would always agree. He was a man who always went the extra mile in life. One day, the therapist said to me, "Do you know your uncle is very tormented because he thinks he killed a child during WWII?" I told her I didn't know. She might be the only person he had ever talked with about this event. We were very close, but I never mentioned it to him.

Uncle Joe and I had another six years together, filled with togetherness and fun times, especially our birthday parties.

During the sixteen days I stayed with him at Baptist Hospital, I discovered his vision was very bad. I said, "Uncle Joe, as soon as you get over this surgery, we are going to have your eyes evaluated."

We went to Corbin, Kentucky, about thirty miles from home. The doctor said Uncle Joe's eyes were very bad with large cataracts. His eye surgery was successful. George or I went down daily to his house to put in his eye drops. When the time came, we returned to the optometrist, and I was sitting in front of him when the patches were removed. He looked at his cap in his hand and said, "I can see the stitches in my cap bill." He had twenty-twenty vision again. He was eighty-six years old. He didn't need glasses, but he had some made with clear lenses because he had worn glasses for years.

On one of our visits to the eye doctor, the receptionist told us that Applebee's restaurant had free lunch for veterans. That sounded good to us, and we were hungry. Uncle Joe had worn his cap commemorating the USS *Arizona* that I'd bought him in Hawaii. People were saluting him and thanking him for his service. He had never had so much recognition. We went to the bathroom, and when I came out, Uncle Joe was waiting for me and talking to the manager. I heard him explain, "I wasn't on the *Arizona*, but I helped take some bodies out of the ship. I didn't come home for four years while I was in the Pacific."

Back at the table, Uncle Joe said, "Jo Ann, the coffee was good." I told him we were in no rush, so we could have another coffee. He got more attention, and when we started to leave, a man stood up and opened the door for us. I'm sure no one had ever given him that much thanks for his service. What a wonderful day with my Uncle Joe.

When he was ninety-two, he was taking out a small bag of garbage when he fell on a slope to the road. He broke his hip and stayed on the ground all night. He was rushed eventually to the University of Tennessee hospital in Knoxville, had surgery, and came through it. He was fragile and was put on a feeding tube. Uncle Joe's son Carson and his granddaughter Greta didn't know about the feeding tube. Why? Uncle Joe was skinny, and he used to say his grandmother said, "When you get old, you get the wasting away disease."

Uncle Joe told George he was going to die and go to hell because of what he had done in the war. George said, "No, Joe, you did what you had to do."

Uncle Joe said to me on one occasion, "Jo, why have I lived so long?" I said, "Uncle Joe, you are a good man."

He died surrounded by family at the age of ninety-two on August 27, 2012, at 8:10 a.m. Greta, his granddaughter, was in bed with him, talking and touching him in a loving way. I will repeat part of what he said to us after he came up the hollow from the cemetery after Mammie's burial: "I was good to my mother, and I never sassed or talked back to her. I feel good." And then he walked up the road to his house. That's how I feel about Uncle Joe. I can use the same words. This is very hard to write about, but I want to keep his memory alive in my book.

Chapter 119

George now has his motor home that I didn't know he wanted. I've enjoyed some of the trips. We went to see my brother Bill two or three times in Pensacola, Florida, after he returned from Washington. We had a beautiful site we liked with a beautiful view of the Gulf Coast. Bill and Sue would come and spend the night with us or drive over in the morning. George and I also had a wonderful trip to New Orleans, Louisiana.

Once we get to an RV park, it's always nice to get set up and make our site a focal point. I make it home away from home. We bring wind chimes to hang once the awning is put up, hang flower baskets, and put out a grill, a fold-up table, and fold-up director chairs. I have candles, oil lamps, and two rocking chairs. We can open a lower storage compartment door that has speakers so music can be transferred outside. George puts up with me because he knows I'm a perfectionist. I bring nice things from our kitchen to prepare and eat our meals. George knows I'm not a paper plate and cup woman!

On our trips, I find out what is in the surroundings. In New Orleans, we discovered that Tennessee Williams's *A Streetcar Named Desire* was being performed in a small theater. I love small theaters. I enjoyed being in New Orleans, but I don't always enjoy the journey in our motor home. I have too many pain issues and hitting the potholes can be very painful. We need road construction badly now! I am uncomfortable with our bridges that are in disrepair.

On one of our trips, we went to a reenactment of a WWII field hospital. Everything was vintage, including Jeeps, trucks, tents, medical equipment, food in original packaging, and authentic uniforms for soldiers, doctors, and nurses.

This reenactment was held on President Eisenhower's farm at Gettysburg, Pennsylvania. I'm always interested in decor inside and outside of buildings. Mamie Eisenhower liked pink. Touring their home, we could see that the theme was pink, pink everywhere. The living room had a round pink sofa, like those I have seen in foyers in fancy hotels. The five-star general and former president slept in a bedroom that was all pinked out, even the bathroom tub and vanities.

On another of our trips, we visited the American Civil War Museum at Appomattox, Virginia. George likes swords and bought a replica of Stonewall Jackson's cavalry sword. Jackson continued to use the same sword from his days as a West Point cadet. The museum also had Robert E. Lee's dress uniform and other interesting displays from both North and South.

We made a memorable motor home trip to the Northeast of the US, and it was very, very special because Catherine joined us. First, we went to Philadelphia to see the Liberty Bell and Constitution Hall, where the Declaration of Independence was signed. We also visited Martha's Vineyard in Massachusetts. We didn't get to do much shopping—too expensive. George inquired about a painting he saw in a gallery. The price was $262,000. We laughed afterwards. Never let anyone know you can't buy something. George got a reprieve from the gift shop! We went on to Nantucket by ferry. Catherine and I bought refrigerator art.

George knew I loved the Hudson River School of painters. He heard the largest collection was in Hartford, Connecticut, with the highlight being the Thomas Cole paintings at the Wadsworth Atheneum Museum of Art. My favorite Thomas Coles are displayed in the National Gallery of Art in Washington, DC. There are four large paintings there titled *The Voyage of Life*. I bought a coffee table art book at Wadsworth and other small items at the gift shop.

This wonderful trip up the East Coast was very special because it was our last trip together as a family now that Catherine is grown, has a husband, and is raising our granddaughter, Grace Ann.

A final note about our motor home trips. We always came home the fastest way, spending as few nights as possible in campgrounds. Once in Georgia, we checked in for the night at an RV park near Warm Springs, Georgia. The woman at check-in suggested we still had time to visit President Franklin Roosevelt's Little White House. What a surprise we found on that last part of our trip.

I think the house must have looked the same as when FDR used it in on his trips away from Washington. We saw a film describing his use of the house and how he liked to come to Warm Springs to take advantage of the spring waters to help him be more comfortable despite his polio. In the garage were three old cars that were modified so he could drive them despite his disability. I like old cars, and the convertible was my favorite. The house was small but with everything in place just as it had been when he left it. And still on display was the unfinished portrait he was sitting for when he had his fatal stroke.

Chapter 120

Soon after returning home from our motor home trip to the Northeast, George went to play golf and made his usual run to the post office and library. When he returned home, he gave me terrible news. *God! Oh God! Oh God!* It was October 12, 2017, and my brother Bill was dead! I was in the TV room, and George stood on the landing and told me that Sue called and said, "Bill has died."

I remember getting to the entry and was on the kitchen floor by the bookshelves. I had fallen down, and George was telling me if I didn't get up, he was calling an ambulance. I remember saying, "George, just give me some time."

Before he died, Bill and Sue had returned to DC to meet once again with Dr. Coppit. After his cancer had disappeared, Bill had called me after every PET scan in Pensacola. He would know I was anxiously awaiting the results. When he passed the five-year mark, we thought he had won this terrible fight with cancer. It came back during the sixth year. George retired from the Foreign Service in 2007 and we were back home on the mountain in Kentucky. We went to Washington, met with Dr. Coppit and his staff at Walter Reed, and got the horrible news about what Bill was facing. I was relieved because Dr. Coppit hadn't been deployed and would take care of Bill.

When Bill returned to Washington, I was in a treatment center in Florida to get off prescription drugs. I had checked myself in voluntarily for thirty days. I had survived the grizzly bear attack in Alaska in August 2008 but had worried that I was becoming too dependent on prescription medicines. I left the treatment center two days before completing the program and flew to DC when I was told Dr. Coppit might have to remove Bill's larynx. I might never be able to talk with him again. We were told the first time he was treated at Walter Reed that he had maxed out on chemo and radiation. His body couldn't stand anymore. At the last minute, Dr. Coppit decided not to take out Bill's voice box. We were relieved, but the bad news was he would eventually have to go on a feeding tube.

Dr. Coppit grafted a big chunk of skin from Bill's chest to the side of his neck to protect his larynx. It was just too painful to watch the decline of my dancer and super roller-skater. Bill was one of the good guys. He loved to cook, eat, and have a good time. He was the guy who would stop to help someone in need, for example, to help someone fix a flat tire or someone who had a computer problem. He was a lover of technology and new gadgets. I would say he was a genius. George would call Bill for advice on buying a new laptop and more.

On one of Bill's visits to Pineville, we passed the family cemetery, and he said," Sis, that's where I want to be buried." I arranged his funeral from start to finish. My sister, Pauline, came over from Knoxville to help with some of the arrangements. She had to leave because Bill's best friend Michael from high school and his sister Karen were coming to her house. They came from Shreveport, Louisiana, to be with us and were like family. Karen and Tony, her late husband, had come many times to Pineville. I am sure they loved Bill.

I asked our local funeral home to bring Bill home from Pensacola. I was so overwhelmed. I went to the shopping center and bought clothes for him, everything the funeral home told me to buy. His wife, Sue, and her two sons by her first marriage did not get to Pineville until two hours before the funeral. I believed Bill loved Sue. I know Bill loved her sons, Steven and James, and they truly loved him. Sue's brother Donnie and Bill were friends and loved to be together. I would say to Bill, "Don't forget Billy," Bill's only biological son.

I arranged the whole service for my baby brother. The music included Sissel singing a beautiful version of "Going Home" and the old spiritual "Farther Along" sung by Elvis. We could never have a funeral without "Amazing Grace" sung by a country music singer. Catherine said, "Mom, you have given away the funeral you planned for yourself."

When we were in Washington, Bill wanted to go to the National Cathedral. George, Bill, Sue, and I went to find a priest to talk with Bill. We left Bill alone with him. If Bill had had time, I believe he would have done what was necessary to become a Catholic. For his funeral service, I asked Father John, a priest in Pineville, to do part of the service. I asked Terrell Gibson, a Baptist minister, also to be part of the service. I think he was a cousin to my father. It was a beautiful service by both ministers of the clergy. Father John's words were comforting. My Southern Baptist family had never heard religious remarks from a Catholic priest. My dear friend Eva talked with him after the service, and my sister, Pauline, thanked him for his compassionate words. They didn't know until the funeral started that a Catholic priest would be doing part of the service. I know Bill was somewhere laughing and saying, "Way to go, Sis."

Bill's body now rests at the end of our hollow at the Tad Goodin Cemetery. That was my brother's wish, and I made it happen. It was the last thing I could do for him. He was in good company. Brother Jim was there. His mother, grandmother, grandfather, Uncle Joe, Uncle AY, and other family members are also there. Bill and Jim were veterans and have military stones on their graves.

When my grandmother died, Uncle Joe said to all of us, "I did all I could for Mom. I feel good."

Now his words come to me, and I can say, "I did all I could for Bill." To use Uncle Joe's words, "I feel good."

Chapter 121

My best friend forever (BFF), Eva Sheryl Lewis Taylor, died of the COVID-19 virus on July 23, 2020. We were best friends for fifty-seven years. I don't know where the strength or courage will come from to write about living without her. I just know I have to put her death in my book. If she could talk to me, she would say, "You'll be all right. You can do this because you were always very smart."

On July 2, 2020, Eva and her husband, Jack, came to my house to see my daughter. Catherine is Eva's godchild, as is Grace Ann, my granddaughter. We all knew about COVID and did our elbow bumps, wore masks, and used hand sanitizer. There wasn't a vaccine at that time. Eva was very tired, and her ankles were swollen. We went to the screened-in porch, sat at a big table, had the ceiling fan on, and kept some distance between us. Grace Ann was playing with all her gifts from Nana E., which is what Eva preferred to be called.

Eva was in too much pain to bend over and tie her shoes. I had/have very painful pelvic and groin pain. Jack said, "Could we have imagined forty years ago we would be talking about aches and pains?"

Eva had had health problems for a few years. The doctor had said it was COPD, but she hadn't smoked in thirty-five years! I knew that she was susceptible to pneumonia and had a terrible, undiagnosed cough. The last time she had gone to the hospital, she was adamant that I shouldn't visit her.

Jack and my dear friend got up to go home. I put out my elbow for an elbow bump, but Eva stretched out her arms and said, "Come here. Give me a big damn hug." I returned her big hug. Then she walked down my steps and out the walkway with Jack. Eva lightly touched the tops of my hydrangea and never looked back. I never got to see her again.

There were three young women from Kentucky. Judy died from lung cancer. Then there were two. With Eva's death, I am the last one left. We had planned for our deaths, and for each, there would be a big celebration of life with music and photos arranged on tables. The people who would have attended Eva's funeral could have been in the hundreds. We might have needed the funeral home for two days. Eva was bigger than life. She was a very large fish in a small pond. She was loved by many because she gave so much of her energy, time, and money. My friend Eva didn't have a lot of money, but we had enough kept back to help if we saw a need. We didn't always tell George and Jack our "business," as my grandmother would say, or what we wanted to do. Eva was there in time of sorrow to bring cooked food, homemade cakes, and her famous white chicken chili. She was a great cook. We were there for the celebrations and deaths in our families and the good and bad times all our lives. Eva is in every room of my home. There are photos, lamps, clocks, brooches, books, cards, and more. I can't forget the Elvis memorabilia. I'm so happy we made our trip to Graceland.

How do I end writing about my life and times together with Eva? There is no end because she is with me every day until I'm gone. There were times during the many years after she lost her son Jackie when she would call me. I would listen to her words, let her cry until she stopped. She would say people would ask, "How you are doing?" If you tried to tell them, they quickly changed the subject and didn't want to listen. My friend would tell me I listened as long as she wanted to talk, and we sometimes cried together. She said she knew I loved Jackie. He was everything I could have wanted in a son. She shared Jackie with me, and I vicariously got to have a son. Eva and Jack's children always called me Aunt Jo. Now her daughter Christy's children call me Aunt Jo. My Catherine always called them Uncle Jack and Aunt Eva.

Eva certainly believed in prayer. She knew how much pain I had to live with from the inoperable nerve damage caused by the bear attack. In 2018, I had a knee replacement that didn't work. It drives me crazy. She wanted me to smoke marijuana. Eva would say, "They say we live in the gateway to the Cumberland Gap, but we really live in the gateway to ignorance." She wanted medical marijuana to be approved. Of course, we were talking about the politicians in our capital, Frankfort.

Eva and I laughed a lot in our life together. But we also had serious conversations about so many beaten-up and battered poor souls in our part of

Kentucky who have spent many years in the coal mines, sawmills, and other places of manual labor. Eva agreed it was terrible to see how strip-mining had destroyed our mountains before there were reclamation laws. There are still lots of old eyesores but no money to fix them. Lots of times, she would call to check on me and would pray for my pain to be taken away. She would sometimes say, "I plead the blood of Jesus on you." Her faith was Pentecostal Holiness, but she loved clothes and jewelry. She would always say, "I love you, and I really mean it. Do you understand how much I really love you?"

Terry and Jill Robinson, who visited us in Zimbabwe and returned to Kentucky for Catherine's wedding.

Doris and her husband Craig, my special California friends for over forty years.

Standing with Terry and Marian in Marian's beautiful living room.

Marian on the back porch during a visit to Kentucky.

With Doris, my friend who I met on the beach when I first came to California.

Uncle Joe at the family celebration of his 90th birthday.

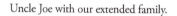

Uncle Joe with our extended family.

Uncle Joe's sister, my Aunt Della who was a lover of gardening.

Uncle Joe with his sister Janie's (my mother's) five children. Left to right: Jim, Pauline, Alvie, Bill, and me.

Pauline and her Husband Ed Hicks

Visiting Graceland after the bear attack.

The meditation garden at Graceland where Elvis is buried.

Darius, the best emotional support dog in the world.

My little lover boy.

Chapter 122

I have a granddaughter. What did I do to get so lucky? But I never forget my Catherine, and without her, there could have been no Grace Ann. If my guardian angels continue to stay around me, then perhaps I can see Grace graduate from high school. That may be a stretch because I am seventy-five now and not in the best of health. I hope I will have time to see her grow into a lovely young woman.

Grace Ann was born in 2017. She is a living, breathing doll baby like her mother at her age, one little girl who is loved by her family on both sides. Matthew's parents, Dr. Bill Randolph and his wife, Karen, have a beautiful farm in Southern Virginia, and Grace loves visiting them just as she does coming to our home in the Kentucky mountains. She puts her beautiful little hands on both sides of her mother's face and kisses her all over, as Catherine and I used to do. Now I watch Catherine and Grace Ann doing our butterfly kisses from long ago. It is a beautiful show of love, and it is special to see history repeating itself.

When Catherine was a baby, I would put her legs around my waist and dance with her. As she got older, I put her down and taught her some moves. We danced to Motown music, and later, she would work out her own moves to Michael Jackson songs. My baby has rhythm. Now Catherine is dancing with Grace Ann. I hope my granddaughter will be as good as her mother. Catherine and I used to go dancing, mostly in Africa at parties at the residence. We used to request a song called "Red Red Wine." I must have heard Neil Diamond's version and I liked it. I could never sing except in a group, and I never learned to paint, but I could dance and always try to make people happy.

I knew I was a good storyteller, and I dreamed I would write a book. I knew if I did, it would be about my life. In thinking about that life, I've been very fortunate to have had the love and support of my family and friends from my country and outside the USA. I'm very honored to feel I made a difference to our embassy families, both Foreign Service personnel and our foreign national community. I gave and received love in return. I've learned so much from traveling to other countries. The poet Maya Angelou said, "It's very important for women to learn from travel."

We don't get to choose the time of our entry or exit from this world, our parents, or what century or country we are born in. At a certain age, we get to make decisions that will direct our lives. I am blessed by being Catherine's mother. My heart tells me I have succeeded in being a very special mother and friend to my daughter. If my guardian angels continue to stay around me, then perhaps I can see Grace graduate from high school. That may be a stretch because I am seventy-five now and not in the best of health. I hope I will have time to see her grow into a lovely young woman.

Chapter 123

In closing, I wish to share some words that have brought me pleasure and calmed my soul. Through the years, I send poems to my special friends. My friend Lillian Bronson, who lived in Laguna Beach, California, shared the following excerpt of a poem with me. It's by Marjorie Bauersfeld from her poem titled "Now Is the Accepted Time":

> With guilt in the past and fear far in the future
> the present is mine
> and I will live in it.
> Whether there comes a second act
> or a good, long rest
> disturbs me not at all,
> either will be welcome.

Bringing Grace Ann home. Prayers do come true.

Matthew and Grace. A father's love!

Grace Ann, ready to explore life

Grace in her Mini cooper heading off on her own path to experiences life's adventures.

Acknowledgements

There are so many people to thank for making my dream of writing a book a reality. I can't list them all, but here are those who were especially helpful to me:

Kyle Fager, President, Your Words, LLC. Kyle was the first to perform an evaluation of my manuscript in its early stages and offered good advice on how to prepare it for publishing.

Tom at Proofreadingpal who not only performed a comprehensive proofreading of the manuscript, but also provided a thorough edit that highlighted subject matter areas that needed more clarity and consistency.

The staff at Friesen Press for helping me understand and guiding me through the daunting publishing process.

My sister Pauline Hicks, brother Alvie Fuson along with nephews Ben and Billy Fuson who at a certain point got excited when they realized this book was really going to be published.

My Uncle Joe and Aunt Della, both deceased, encouraged me for years to write a book. Sadly, they didn't live to see a published copy put into their beautiful hands.

Daughter Catherine who, with Husband Matthew and granddaughter Grace Ann, reminds me of how blessed I am in this world.

My husband George, who excelled as a U.S. Ambassador. Without his computer skills and research abilities, I would have had to hire an assistant.

Last but not least, special mention goes to Darius, my Shih Tzu and emotional support dog, who was at my side in his director chair while the world was sleeping, even if it was three o'clock in the morning. His comforting, reassuring presence and soft touch helped me finish my story.

9 781039 174429